3rd Workshop on Predicting and Improving Text Readability for Target Reader Populations

(PITR 2014)

Held at the 14th Conference of the European Chapter of the Association for Computational Linguistics

Gothenburg, Sweden
27 April 2014

Editors:

S. Williams
A. Nenkova
A. Siddharthan

ISBN: 978-1-63266-407-5

Printed from e-media with permission by:

Curran Associates, Inc.
57 Morehouse Lane
Red Hook, NY 12571

CURRAN ASSOCIATES INC. proceedings.com

Some format issues inherent in the e-media version may also appear in this print version.

Printed by Curran Associates, Inc. (2014)

Association for Computational Linguistics
209 N. Eighth Street
Stroudsburg, Pennsylvania 18360

Phone: 1-570-476-8006
Fax: 1-570-476-0860

acl@aclweb.org

Additional copies of this publication are available from:

Curran Associates, Inc.
57 Morehouse Lane
Red Hook, NY 12571 USA
Phone: 845-758-0400
Fax: 845-758-2634
Email: curran@proceedings.com
Web: www.proceedings.com

EACL 2014

14th Conference of the European Chapter of the Association for Computational Linguistics

Proceedings of the 3rd Workshop on Predicting and Improving Text Readability for Target Reader Populations (PITR)

April 27, 2014
Gothenburg, Sweden

Introduction

Welcome to the Third International Workshop on Predicting and Improving Text Readability for Target Reader Populations (PITR).

The last few years have seen a resurgence of work on text simplification and readability. Examples include learning lexical and syntactic simplification operations from Simple English Wikipedia revision histories, exploring more complex lexico-syntactic simplification operations requiring morphological changes as well as constituent reordering, simplifying mathematical form, applications for target users such as dyslexics, deaf students, second language learners and low literacy adults, and fresh attempts at predicting readability.

The PITR 2014 workshop has been organised to provide a cross-disciplinary forum for discussing key issues related to predicting and improving text readability for target users. It will be held on April 27, 2014 in conjunction with the 14th Conference of the European Association for Computational Linguistics in Gothenburg, Sweden, and is sponsored by the ACL Special Interest Group on Speech and Language Processing for Assistive Technologies (SIG-SLPAT).

These proceedings include fifteen papers that cover various perspectives on the topic: simplification in specific domains such as medicine and patents, simplification for specific languages, tailoring text for specific users (e.g., dyslexia and autism), development of new corpora, automatic system evaluation, analyses of human simplifications, studies of human reading, and predicting the reading level of text in general and for particular genres.

We hope this volume is a valuable addition to the literature, and look forward to an exciting Workshop.

Sandra Williams
Advaith Siddharthan
Ani Nenkova

Organizers:

Sandra Williams, The Open University, UK.
Advaith Siddharthan, University of Aberdeen, UK.
Ani Nenkova, University of Pennsylvania, USA.

Programme Committee:

Stefan Bott, Universitat Pompeu Fabra, Spain
Kevyn Collins-Thompson, University of Michigan, USA
Siobhan Devlin, University of Sunderland, UK
Micha Elsner, Ohio State University, USA
Richard Evans, University of Wolverhampton, UK
Oliver Ferschke, Technische Universität Darmstadt, Germany
Thomas Francois, University of Louvain, Belgium
Caroline Gasperin, SwiftKey, UK
Albert Gatt, University of Malta, Malta
Raquel Hervas, Universidad Complutense de Madrid, Spain
Veronique Hoste, University College Ghent, Belgium
Matt Huenerfauth, The City University of New York (CUNY), USA
David Kauchak, Middlebury College, USA
Annie Louis, University of Edinburgh, UK
Ruslan Mitkov, University of Wolverhampton, UK
Hitoshi Nishikawa, NTT, Japan
Ehud Reiter, University of Aberdeen, UK
Matthew Shardlow, Uni of Manchester, UK
Lucia Specia, University of Sheffield, UK
Ivelina Stoyanova, BAS, Bulgaria
Irina Temnikova, Qatar Computing Research Institute, Qatar
Sowmya Vajjala, Uni Tuebingen, Germany
Ielka van der Sluis, University of Groningen, The Netherlands
Jennifer Williams, MIT, USA
Kristian Woodsend, University of Edinburgh, UK

Table of Contents

Workshop Program

Sunday April 27, 2014

(09:00) Session 1 - Keynote

09:00 Welcome and opening remarks

09:10 Keynote: Ehud Reiter *Choosing Appropriate Words in Generated Texts for Low-Skill Readers*

10:30 Coffee break

(11:00) Session 2 - Papers

11:00 *One Step Closer to Automatic Evaluation of Text Simplification Systems*
Sanja Štajner, Ruslan Mitkov and Horacio Saggion

11:20 *Automatic diagnosis of understanding of medical words*
Natalia Grabar, Thierry Hamon and Dany Amiot

11:40 *Exploring Measures of "Readability" for Spoken Language: Analyzing linguistic features of subtitles to identify age-specific TV programs*
Sowmya Vajjala and Detmar Meurers

12:00 *Keyword Highlighting Improves Comprehension for People with Dyslexia*
Luz Rello, Horacio Saggion and Ricardo Baeza-Yates

12:20 Discussion

12:30 Lunch break

(14:00) Session 3 - Papers

14:00 *An eye-tracking evaluation of some parser complexity metrics*
Matthew J. Green

14:20 *Syntactic Sentence Simplification for French*
Laetitia Brouwers, Delphine Bernhard, Anne-Laure Ligozat and Thomas Francois

14:40 Panel

15:30 Coffee break

(16:00) Session 4 - Posters

Medical text simplification using synonym replacement: Adapting assessment of word difficulty to a compounding language
Emil Abrahamsson, Timothy Forni, Maria Skeppstedt and Maria Kvist

Segmentation of patent claims for improving their readability
Gabriela Ferraro, Hanna Suominen and Jaume Nualart

Improving Readability of Swedish Electronic Health Records through Lexical Simplification: First Results
Gintare Grigonyte, Maria Kvist, Sumithra Velupillai and Mats Wirén

An Open Corpus of Everyday Documents for Simplification Tasks
David Pellow and Maxine Eskenazi

EACL - Expansion of Abbreviations in CLinical text
Lisa Tengstrand, Beáta Megyesi, Aron Henriksson, Martin Duneld and Maria Kvist

A Quantitative Insight into the Impact of Translation on Readability
Alina Maria Ciobanu and Liviu Dinu

Classifying easy-to-read texts without parsing
Johan Falkenjack and Arne Jonsson

An Analysis of Crowdsourced Text Simplifications
Marcelo Amancio and Lucia Specia

An evaluation of syntactic simplification rules for people with autism
Richard Evans, Constantin Orasan and Iustin Dornescu

\+ Guest Poster, a preview of an EACL Main Session Paper: *Assessing the Relative Reading Level of Sentence Pairs for Text Simplification*
Sowmya Vajjala and Detmar Meurers

16:50 Closing Remarks

One Step Closer to Automatic Evaluation of Text Simplification Systems

Sanja Štajner[1] and **Ruslan Mitkov**[1] and **Horacio Saggion**[2]
[1]Research Group in Computational Linguistics, University of Wolverhampton, UK
[2]TALN Research Group, Universitat Pompeu Fabra, Spain
S.Stajner@wlv.ac.uk, R.Mitkov@wlv.ac.uk, horacio.saggion@upf.edu

Abstract

This study explores the possibility of replacing the costly and time-consuming human evaluation of the grammaticality and meaning preservation of the output of text simplification (TS) systems with some automatic measures. The focus is on six widely used machine translation (MT) evaluation metrics and their correlation with human judgements of grammaticality and meaning preservation in text snippets. As the results show a significant correlation between them, we go further and try to classify simplified sentences into: (1) those which are acceptable; (2) those which need minimal post-editing; and (3) those which should be discarded. The preliminary results, reported in this paper, are promising.

1 Introduction

Lexically and syntactically complex sentences can be difficult to understand for non-native speakers (Petersen and Ostendorf, 2007; Aluísio et al., 2008b), and for people with language impairments, e.g. people diagnosed with aphasia (Carroll et al., 1999; Devlin, 1999), autism spectrum disorder (Štajner et al., 2012; Martos et al., 2012), dyslexia (Rello, 2012), congenital deafness (Inui et al., 2003), and intellectual disability (Feng, 2009). At the same time, long and complex sentences are also a stumbling block for many NLP tasks and applications such as parsing, machine translation, information retrieval, and summarisation (Chandrasekar et al., 1996). This justifies the need for Text Simplification (TS) systems which would convert such sentences into their simpler and easier-to-read variants, while at the same time preserving the original meaning.

So far, TS systems have been developed for English (Siddharthan, 2006; Zhu et al., 2010; Woodsend and Lapata, 2011a; Coster and Kauchak, 2011; Wubben et al., 2012), Spanish (Saggion et al., 2011), and Portuguese (Aluísio et al., 2008a), with recent attempts at Basque (Aranzabe et al., 2012), Swedish (Rybing et al., 2010), Dutch (Ruiter et al., 2010), and Italian (Barlacchi and Tonelli, 2013).

Usually, TS systems are either evaluated for: (1) the quality of the generated output, or (2) the effectiveness/usefulness of such simplification on reading speed and comprehension of the target population. For the purpose of this study we focused only on the former. The quality of the output generated by TS systems is commonly evaluated by using a combination of readability metrics (measuring the degree of simplification) and human assessment (measuring the grammaticality and meaning preservation). Despite the noticeable similarity between evaluation of the fluency and adequacy of a machine translation (MT) output, and evaluation of grammaticality and meaning preservation of a TS system output, there have been no works exploring whether any of the MT evaluation metrics are well correlated with the latter, and could thus replace the time-consuming human assessment.

The contributions of the present work are the following:

- It is the first study to explore the possibility of replacing human assessment of the quality of TS system output with automatic evaluation.
- It is the first study to investigate the correlation of human assessment of TS system output with MT evaluation metrics.
- It proposes a decision-making procedure for the classification of simplified sentences into: (1) those which are acceptable; (2) those which need further post-editing; and (3) those which should be discarded.

2 Related Work

The output of the TS system proposed by Siddharthan (2006) was rated for grammaticality and meaning preservation by three human evaluators. Similarly, Drndarevic et al. (2013) evaluated the grammaticality and the meaning preservation of automatically simplified Spanish sentences on a Likert scale with the help of twenty-five human annotators. Additionally, the authors used seven readability metrics to assess the degree of simplification. Woodsend and Lapata (2011b), and Glavaš and Štajner (2013) used human annotators' ratings for evaluating simplification, meaning preservation, and grammaticality, while additionally applying several readability metrics for evaluating complexity reduction in entire texts.

Another set of studies approached TS as an MT task translating from "original" to "simplified" language, e.g. (Specia, 2010; Woodsend and Lapata, 2011a; Zhu et al., 2010). In this case, the quality of the output generated by the system was evaluated using several standard MT evaluation metrics: BLEU (Papineni et al., 2002), NIST (Doddington, 2002), and TERp (Snover et al., 2009).

3 Methodology

All experiments were conducted on a freely available sentence-level dataset[1], fully described in (Glavaš and Štajner, 2013), and the two datasets we derived from it. The original dataset and the instructions for the human assessment are given in the next two subsections. Section 3.3 explains how we derived two additional datasets from the original one, and to what end. Section 3.4 describes the automatic MT evaluation metrics used as features in correlation and classification experiments; Section 3.5 presents the main goals of the study; and Section 3.6 describes the conducted experiments.

3.1 Original dataset

The dataset contains 280 pairs of original sentences and their corresponding simplified versions annotated by humans for grammaticality, meaning preservation, and simplicity of the simplified version. We used all sentence pairs, focusing only on four out of eight available features: (1) the original text, (2) the simplified text, (3) the grammaticality score, and (4) the score for meaning preservation.[2]

Category	weighted κ	Pearson	MAE
Grammaticality	0.68	0.77	0.18
Meaning	0.53	0.67	0.37
Simplicity	0.54	0.60	0.28

Table 1: IAA from (Glavaš and Štajner, 2013)

The simplified versions of original sentences were obtained by using four different simplification methods: baseline, sentence-wise, event-wise, and pronominal anaphora. The baseline retains only the main clause of a sentence, and discards all subordinate clauses, based on the output of the Stanford constituency parser (Klein and Manning, 2003). Sentence-wise simplification eliminates all those tokens in the original sentence that do not belong to any of the extracted factual event mentions, while the event-wise simplification transforms each factual event mention into a separate sentence of the output. The last simplification scheme (pronominal anaphora) additionally employs pronominal anaphora resolution on top of the event-wise simplification scheme.[3]

3.2 Human Assessment

Human assessors were asked to score the given sentence pairs (or text snippets in the case of split sentences) on a 1–3 scale based on three criteria: Grammaticality (1 – ungrammatical, 2 – minor problems with grammaticality, 3 – grammatical), Meaning (1 – meaning is seriously changed or most of the relevant information lost, 2 – some of the relevant information is lost but the meaning of the remaining information is unchanged, 3 – all relevant information is kept without any change in meaning), and Simplicity (1 – a lot of irrelevant information is retained, 2 – some of irrelevant information is retained, 3 – all irrelevant information is eliminated). The inter-annotator agreement (IAA) was calculated using weighted Kappa (*weighted κ*), Pearson's correlation (*Pearson*), and mean average error (*MAE*), and the obtained results are presented in Table 1. A few examples of assigned scores are given in Table 2, where *G*, *M*, and *S* denote human scores for grammaticality, meaning preservation and simplicity respectively.

[1] http://takelab.fer.hr/data/evsimplify/

[2] The other four features contain the pairID, groupID, the method with which the simplification was obtained, and the score for simplicity, which are not relevant here.

[3] For more detailed explanation of simplification schemes and the dataset see (Glavaš and Štajner, 2013).

Ex.	Original	Simplified	G	M	S	SM
(a)	*"It is understood the dead girl had been living at her family home, in a neighbouring housing estate, and was visiting her older sister at the time of the shooting."*	*"The dead girl had been living at her family home, in a neighbouring housing estate and was visiting her older sister."*	3	3	3	S
(b)	*"On Facebook, more than 10,000 people signed up to a page announcing an opposition rally for Saturday."*	*"On Facebook, more than 10,000 people signed to a page announcing an opposition rally for Saturday."*	2	3	3	S
(c)	*"Joel Elliott, also 22, of North Road, Brighton, was charged on May 3 with murder. He appeared at Lewes Crown Court on May 8 but did not enter a plea."*	*"Joel Elliott was charged on May 3 with murder. He appeared at Lewes Crown Court on May 8."*	3	2	3	S
(d)	*"For years the former Bosnia Serb army commander Ratko Mladic had evaded capture and was one of the world's most wanted men, but his time on the run finally ended last year when he was arrested near Belgrade."*	*"For years the former Bosnia Serb army commander Ratko Mladic had evaded but his time the run ended last year he was arrested near Belgrade."*	1	2	3	S
(e)	*"Police have examined the scene at a house at William Court in Bellaghy, near Magherafelt for clues to the incident which has stunned the community."*	*"Police have examined the scene at William Court near Magherafelt. The incident has stunned the community."*	3	1	3	P
(f)	*"Rastan, 25 km (15 miles) north of Homs city, has slipped in and out of government control several times since the uprising against Assad erupted in March 2011."*	*"Rastan has slipped government control several times. The uprising erupted in March 2011."*	2	1	3	P
(g)	*"But opposition parties and international observers said the vote was marred by vote-rigging, including alleged ballot-box stuffing and false voter rolls."*	*"But opposition parties and international observers said ."*	1	1	3	B
(h)	*"Foreign Affairs Secretary Albert del Rosario was seeking a diplomatic solution with Chinese Ambassador Ma Keqing, the TV network said."*	*"Foreign Affairs Secretary Albert del Rosario was seeking a diplomatic solution with Chinese Ambassador Ma Keqing, the TV network said."*	3	3	1	B
(h)	*" On Wednesday, two video journalists working for the state-owned RIA Novosti news agency were briefly detained outside the Election Commission building where Putin was handing in his application to run."*	*"On Wednesday two video journalists were briefly detained outside the Election Commission building. Two video journalists worked for the state-owned RIA Novosti news agency. Putin was handing in his application."*	3	2	2	E

Table 2: Human evaluation examples (*G*, *M*, and *S* correspond to the human scores for grammaticality, meaning preservation and simplicity, and *SM* denotes the simplification method used: *B* – baseline, *S* – sentence-wise, *E* – event-wise, and *P* – pronominal anaphora)

3.3 Derived Datasets

The original dataset (*Original*) contains separate scores for grammaticality (G), meaning preservation (M), and simplicity (S), each of them on a 1–3 scale. From this dataset we derived two additional ones: *Total3* and *Total2*.

The *Total3* dataset contains three marks (*OK* – use as it is, *PE* – post-editing required, and *Dis* – discard) derived from *G* and *M* in the *Original* dataset. Those simplified sentences which scored '3' for both meaning preservation (M) and grammaticality (G) are placed in the *OK* class as they do not need any kind of post-editing. A closer look at the remaining sentences suggests that any simplified sentence which got a score '2' or '3' for meaning preservation (*M*) could be easily post-edited, i.e. it requires minimal changes which are obvious from its comparison to the corresponding original. For instance, in the sentence (b) in Table 2 the only change that needs to be made is adding the word "up" after "signed". Those sentences which scored '2' for meaning need slightly more, albeit simple modification. The simplified text snippet (c) in Table 2 would need "but did not enter a plea" added at the end of the last sentence. The next sentence (d) in the same table needs a few more changes, but still very minor ones: adding the word "capture" after "had evaded", adding the preposition "on" before "the run", and adding "when" after "last year". Therefore, we grouped all those sentences into one class – *PE* (sentences which require a minimal post-editing effort). Those sentences which scored '1' for meaning need to either be left in their original form or simplified from scratch. We thus classify them as *Dis*. This newly created dataset (*Total3*) allows us to investigate whether we could automatically classify simplified sentences into those three categories, taking into account both grammaticality and meaning preservation at the same time.

The *Total2* dataset contains only two marks ('0' and '1') which correspond to the sentences which should be discarded ('0') and those which should be retained ('1'), where '0' corresponds to *Dis* in *Total3*, and '1' corresponds to the union of *OK* and *PE* in *Total3*. The derivation procedure for both datasets is presented in Table 3. We wanted to investigate whether the classification task would be simpler (better performed) if there were only two classes instead of three. In the case that such classification could be performed with satisfactory accuracy, all sentences classified as '0' would be left in their original form or simplified with some different simplification strategy, while those classified as '1' would be sent for a quick human post-editing procedure.

Original		Total3	Total2
G	M		
3	3	OK	1
2	3	PE	1
1	3	PE	1
3	2	PE	1
2	2	PE	1
1	2	PE	1
3	1	Dis	0
2	1	Dis	0
1	1	Dis	0

Table 3: Datasets

Here it is important to mention that we decided not to use human scores for simplicity (S) for several reasons. First, simplicity was defined as the amount of irrelevant information which was eliminated. Therefore, we cannot expect that any of the six MT evaluation metrics would have a significant correlation with this score (except maybe TERp and, in particular, one of its parts – 'number of deletions'. However, none of the two demonstrated any significant correlation with the simplicity score, and those results are thus not reported in this paper). Second, the output sentences with a low simplicity score are not as detrimental for the TS system as those with a low grammaticality or meaning preservation score. The sentences with a low simplicity score would simply not help the target user read faster or understand better, but would not do any harm either. Alternatively, if the target "user" is an MT or information extraction (IE) system, or a parser for example, such sentences would not lower the performance of the system; they would just not improve it. Low scores for G and M, however, would lead to a worse performance for such NLP systems, longer reading time, and a worse or erroneous understanding of the text. Third, the simplicity of the output (or complexity reduction performed by a TS system) could be evaluated separately, in a fully automatic manner – using some readability measures or average sentence length as features (as in (Drndarević et al., 2013; Glavaš and Štajner,

2013) for example).

3.4 Features: MT Evaluation Metrics

In all experiments, we focused on six commonly used MT evaluation metrics. These are cosine similarity (using the bag-of-words representation), METEOR (Denkowski and Lavie, 2011), TERp (Snover et al., 2009), TINE (Rios et al., 2011), and two components of TINE: T-BLEU (which differs from the standard BLEU (Papineni et al., 2002) by using 3-grams, 2-grams, and 1-grams when there are no 4-grams found, where the "original" BLEU would give score '0') and SRL (which is the component of TINE based on semantic role labeling using SENNA[4]). Although these two components contribute equally to TINE (thus being linearly correlated with TINE), we wanted to investigate which one of them contributes more to the correlation of TINE with human judgements. Given their different natures, we expect T-BLEU to contribute more to the correlation of TINE with human judgements of grammaticality, and SRL to contribute more to the correlation of TINE with human judgements of meaning preservation.

As we do not have the reference for the simplified sentence, all metrics are applied in a slightly different way than in MT. Instead of evaluating the translation hypothesis (output of the automatic TS system in our case) with the corresponding reference translation (which would be a 'gold standard' simplified sentence), we apply the metrics to the output of the automatic TS system comparing it with the corresponding original sentence. Given that the simplified sentences in the used dataset are usually shorter than the original ones (due to the elimination of irrelevant content which was the main focus of the TS system proposed by Glavaš and Štajner (2013)), we expect low scores of T-BLEU and METEOR which apply a brevity penalty. However, our dataset does not contain any kind of lexical simplification, but rather copies all relevant information from the original sentence[5]. Therefore, we expect the exact matches of word forms and semantic role labels (which are components of the MT evaluation metrics) to have a good correlation to human judgements of grammaticality and meaning preservation.

[4]http://ml.nec-labs.com/senna/

[5]The exceptions being changes of gerundive forms into past tense, and anaphoric pronoun resolution in some simplification schemes. See Section 3.1 and (Glavaš and Štajner, 2013) for more details.

3.5 Goal

After we obtained the six automatic metrics (cosine, METEOR, TERp, TINE, T-BLEU, and SRL), we performed two sets of experiments, trying to answer two main questions:

1. Are the chosen MT evaluation metrics correlated with the human judgements of grammaticality and meaning preservation of the TS system output?
2. Could we automatically classify the simplified sentences into those which are: (1) correct, (2) require a minimal post-editing, (3) incorrect and need to be discarded?

A positive answer to the first question would mean that there is a possibility of finding an automatic metric (or a combination of several automatic metrics) which could successfully replace the time consuming human evaluation. The search for that "ideal" combination of automatic metrics could be performed by using various classification algorithms and carefully designed features. If we manage to classify simplified sentences into the three aforementioned categories with a satisfying accuracy, the benefits would be two-fold. Firstly, such a classification system could be used for an automatic evaluation of TS systems and an easy comparison of their performances. Secondly, it could be used inside a TS system to mark those sentences of low quality which need to be checked further, or those sentences whose original meaning changed significantly. The latter could then be left in their original form or simplified using some different technique.

3.6 Experiments

The six experiments conducted in this study are presented in Table 4. The first two experiments had the aim of answering the first question (Section 3.5) as to whether the chosen MT metrics correlate with the human judgements of grammaticality (G) and meaning preservation (M) of the TS system output. The results were obtained in terms of Pearson's, Kendall's and Spearman's correlation coefficients. The third and the fourth experiments (Table 4) could be seen as the intermediate experiments exploring the possibility of automatic classification of simplified sentences according to their grammaticality, and meaning preservation. The main experiment was the fifth experiment, trying to answer the second question (Section 3.5)

Exp.	Description
1.	Correlation of the six automatic MT metrics with the human scores for *Grammaticality*
2.	Correlation of the six automatic MT metrics with the human scores for *Meaning* preservation
3.	Classification of the simplified sentences into 3 classes ('1' – *Bad*, '2' – *Medium*, and '3' – *Good*) according to their *Grammaticality*
4.	Classification of the simplified sentences into 3 classes ('1' – *Bad*, '2' – *Medium*, and '3' – *Good*) according to their *Meaning* preservation
5.	Classification of the simplified sentences into 3 classes (*OK, PE, Dis*) according to their *Total3* score
6.	Classification of the simplified sentences into 2 classes ('1' – *Retain*, '0' – *Discard*) according to their *Total2* score

Table 4: Experiments

as to whether we could automatically classify the simplified sentences into those which are: (1) correct (*OK*), (2) require minimal post-editing (*PE*), and (3) incorrect and need to be discarded (*Dis*). The last experiment (Table 4) was conducted with the aim of exploring whether the classification of simplified sentences into only two classes – *Retain* (for further post-editing) and *Discard* – would lead to better results than the classification into three classes (*OK*, *PE*, and *Dis*) in the fifth experiment.

All classification experiments were performed in Weka workbench (Witten and Frank, 2005; Hall et al., 2009), using seven classification algorithms in a 10-fold cross-validation setup:

- NB – NaiveBayes (John and Langley, 1995),
- SMO – Weka implementation of Support Vector Machines (Keerthi et al., 2001) with normalisation (n) or with standardisation (s),
- Logistic (le Cessie and van Houwelingen, 1992),
- Lazy.IBk – K-nearest neighbours (Aha and Kibler, 1991),
- JRip – a propositional rule learner (Cohen, 1995),
- J48 – Weka implementation of C4.5 (Quinlan, 1993).

As a baseline we use the classifier which assigns the most frequent (majority) class to all instances.

4 Results and Discussion

The results of the first two experiments (correlation experiments in Table 4) are presented in Section 4.1, while the results of the other four experiments (classification experiments in Table 4) can be found in Section 4.2. When interpreting the results of all experiments, it is important to keep in mind that human agreements for meaning preservation (M) and grammaticality (G) were acceptable but far from perfect (Section 3.2), and thus it would be unrealistic to expect the correlation between the MT evaluation metrics and human judgements or the agreement of the classification system with human assessments to be higher than the reported IAA agreement.

4.1 Correlation of Automatic Metrics with Human Judgements

The correlations of automatic metrics with human judgements of grammaticality and meaning preservation are given in Tables 5 and 6 respectively. Statistically significant correlations (at a 0.01 level of significance) are presented in bold.

Metric	Pearson	Kendall	Spearman
cosine	0.097	0.092	0.115
METEOR	**0.176**	**0.141**	**0.178**
T-BLEU	**0.226**	**0.185**	**0.234**
SRL	0.097	0.076	0.095
TINE	**0.175**	**0.145**	**0.181**
TERp	**-0.208**	**-0.158**	**-0.198**

Table 5: Correlation between automatic evaluation metrics and human scores for grammaticality

Metric	Pearson	Kendall	Spearman
cosine	**0.293**	**0.262**	**0.334**
METEOR	**0.386**	**0.322**	**0.405**
T-BLEU	**0.442**	**0.382**	**0.475**
SRL	**0.348**	**0.285**	**0.356**
TINE	**0.427**	**0.385**	**0.447**
TERp	**-0.414**	**-0.336**	**-0.416**

Table 6: Correlation between automatic evaluation metrics and human scores for meaning preservation

It can be noted that human perception of grammaticality is positively correlated with three auto-

Algorithm	Grammaticality			Meaning			Total3			Total2		
	P	R	F	P	R	F	P	R	F	P	R	F
NB	0.53	0.46	0.48	0.54	0.54	0.54	0.54	0.53	0.53	0.74	0.69	0.71
SMO(n)	0.39	0.63	0.48	0.52	0.49	0.45	0.43	0.53	0.44	0.55	0.74	0.63
SMO(s)	0.39	0.63	0.48	0.57	0.56	0.55	0.57	0.55	0.51	0.60	0.73	0.63
Logistic	0.45	0.61	0.49	**0.57**	**0.57**	**0.56**	**0.61**	**0.60**	**0.59**	**0.75**	**0.77**	**0.74**
Lazy.IBk	**0.57**	**0.58**	**0.57**	0.50	0.50	0.50	0.54	0.54	0.54	0.73	0.73	0.73
JRip	0.41	0.59	0.48	0.53	0.50	0.48	0.57	0.56	0.55	0.72	0.75	0.73
J48	0.45	0.61	0.49	0.48	0.47	0.47	0.59	0.57	0.54	0.68	0.71	0.69
baseline	0.39	0.63	0.48	0.17	0.41	0.24	0.21	0.46	0.29	0.55	0.74	0.63

Table 7: Classification results (the best performances are shown in bold; baseline uses the majority class)

Actual	Grammaticality			Meaning		
	Good	Med.	Bad	Good	Med.	Bad
Good	127	21	**23**	50	31	**7**
Med.	29	19	10	24	73	16
Bad	**24**	9	10	**9**	31	31

Table 8: Confusion matrices for the best classifications according to *Grammaticality* (Lazy.IBk) and *Meaning* (Logistic). The number of "severe" classification mistakes (classifying *Good* as *Bad* or vice versa) are presented in bold.

matic measures – METEOR, T-BLEU, and TINE, while it is negatively correlated with TERp (TERp measures the number of edits necessary to perform on the simplified sentence to transform it into its original one, i.e. the higher the value of TERp, the less similar the original and its corresponding simplified sentence are. The other five MT metrics measure the similarity between the original and its corresponding simplified version, i.e. the higher their value is, the more similar are the sentences are). All the MT metrics appear to be even better correlated with the human scores for meaning preservation (Table 6), demonstrating six positive and one (TERp) negative statistically significant correlation with *M*. The correlation is the highest for T-BLEU, TINE, and TERp, though closely followed by all others.

4.2 Sentence Classification

The results of the four classification experiments (Section 3.6) are given in Table 7.

At first glance, the performance of the classification algorithms seems similar for the first two tasks (classification of the simplified sentences according to their *Grammaticality* and *Meaning* preservation). However, one needs to take into account that the baseline for the first task was much much higher than for the second task (Table 7). Furthermore, it can be noted that for the first task, recall was significantly higher than precision for most classification algorithms (all except NB and Logistic), while for the second task they were very similar in all cases. More importantly, a closer look at the confusion matrices reveals that most of the incorrectly classified sentences were assigned to the nearest class (*Medium* into *Bad* or *Good*; *Bad* into *Medium*; and *Good* into *Medium*[6]) in the second task, while it was not the case in the first task (Table 8).

Classification performed on the *Total3* dataset outperformed both previous classifications – that based on *Grammaticality* and that based on *Meaning* – on four different algorithms (NB, Logistic, JRip, and J48). Classification conducted on *Total3* using Logistic outperformed all results of classifications on either *Grammaticality* or *Meaning* separately (Table 7). It reached a 0.61, 0.60, and 0.59 score for the weighted precision (P), recall (R), and F-measure (F), respectively, thus outperforming the baseline significantly. More importantly, classification on the *Total3* dataset led to significantly fewer mis-classifications between *Good* and *Bad* (Table 9) than the classification based on *Grammaticality*, and slightly less than

[6] *Bad*, *Medium*, and *Good* correspond to marks '1', '2', and '3' given by human evaluators.

Actual	Total3		
	OK	PE	Dis.
OK	41	32	**4**
PE	17	85	12
Dis.	**6**	31	28

Table 9: Confusion matrix for the best classification according to *Total3* (Logistic). The number of "severe" classification mistakes (classifying *Good* as *Bad* or vice versa) are presented in bold.

Actual	Total2	
	Retain	Discard
Retain	21	**50**
Discard	**12**	189

Table 10: Confusion matrix for the best classification according to *Total2* (Logistic). The number of "severe" classification mistakes (classifying *Retain* as *Discard* or vice versa) are presented in bold.

the classification based only on *Meaning* (Table 8). Therefore, it seems that simplified sentences are better classified into three classes giving a unique score for both grammaticality and preservation of meaning together.

The binary classification experiments based on the *Total2* led to results which significantly outperformed the baseline in terms of precision and F-measure (Table 7). However, they resulted in a great number of sentences which should be retained (*Retain*) being classified into those which should be discarded (*Discard*) and vice versa (Table 10). Therefore, it seems that it would be better to opt for classification into three classes (*Total3*) than for classification into two classes (*Total2*).

Additionally, we used CfsSubsetEval attribute selection algorithm (Hall and Smith, 1998) in order to identify the 'best' subset of features. The 'best' subsets of features for each of the four classification tasks returned by the algorithm are listed in Table 11. However, the classification performances achieved (P, R, and F) when using only the 'best' features did not differ significantly from those when using all initially selected features, and thus are not presented in this paper.

5 Limitations

The used dataset does not contain any kind of lexical simplification (Glavaš and Štajner, 2013).

Classification	'Best' features
Meaning	{TERp, T-BLEU, SRL, TINE}
Grammaticality	{TERp, T-BLEU}
New3	{TERp, T-BLEU, SRL, TINE}
New2	{TERp, T-BLEU, SRL}

Table 11: The 'best' features (CfsSubsetEval)

Therefore, one should consider the limitation of this TS system which performs only syntactic simplification and content reduction. On the other hand, the dataset used contains a significant content reduction in most of the sentences. If the same experiments were conducted on a dataset which performs only syntactic simplification, we would expect much higher correlation of MT evaluation metrics to human judgements, due to the lesser impact of the brevity penalty in that case.

If we were to apply the same MT evaluation metrics to a TS system which additionally performs some kind of lexical simplification (either a simple lexical substitution or paraphrasing), the correlation results for T-BLEU and cosine similarity would be lower (due to the lower number of exact matches), but not for METEOR, TERp and SRL (and thus TINE as well). As a similar problem is also present in the evaluation of MT systems where the obtained output could differ from the reference translation (while still being equally good), METEOR, TERp, and SRL in TINE additionally use inexact matching. The first two use the stem, synonym, and paraphrase matches, while SRL uses ontologies and thesaurus.

6 Conclusions and Future Work

While the results reported are preliminary and their universality needs to be validated on different TS datasets, the experiments and results presented can be regarded as a promising step towards an automatic assessment of grammaticality and meaning preservation for the output of TS systems. In addition and to the best of our knowledge, there are no such datasets publicly available other than the one used. Nevertheless, we hope that these results would initiate an interesting discussion in the TS community and start a new direction of studies towards automatic evaluation of text simplification systems.

Acknowledgements

The research described in this paper was partially funded by the European Commission under the Seventh (FP7-2007-2013) Framework Programme for Research and Technological Development (FP7-ICT-2011.5.5 FIRST 287607).

References

D. Aha and D. Kibler. 1991. Instance-based learning algorithms. *Machine Learning*, 6:37–66.

S. M. Aluísio, L. Specia, T. A. S. Pardo, E. G. Maziero, H. M. Caseli, and R. P. M. Fortes. 2008a. A corpus analysis of simple account texts and the proposal of simplification strategies: first steps towards text simplification systems. In *Proceedings of the 26th annual ACM international conference on Design of communication*, SIGDOC '08, pages 15–22, New York, NY, USA. ACM.

S. M. Aluísio, L. Specia, T. A.S. Pardo, E. G. Maziero, and R. P.M. Fortes. 2008b. Towards brazilian portuguese automatic text simplification systems. In *Proceedings of the eighth ACM symposium on Document engineering*, DocEng '08, pages 240–248, New York, NY, USA. ACM.

M. J. Aranzabe, A. Díaz De Ilarraza, and I. González. 2012. First Approach to Automatic Text Simplification in Basque. In *Proceedings of the first Natural Language Processing for Improving Textual Accessibility Workshop (NLP4ITA)*.

G. Barlacchi and S. Tonelli. 2013. ERNESTA: A sentence simplification tool for childrens stories in italian. In *Computational Linguistics and Intelligent Text Processing*.

J. Carroll, G. Minnen, D. Pearce, Y. Canning, S. Devlin, and J. Tait. 1999. Simplifying text for language-impaired readers. In *Proceedings of the 9th Conference of the European Chapter of the ACL (EACL'99)*, pages 269–270.

R. Chandrasekar, Christine Doran, and B. Srinivas. 1996. Motivations and methods for text simplification. In *In Proceedings of the Sixteenth International Conference on Computational Linguistics (COLING '96*, pages 1041–1044.

W. Cohen. 1995. Fast Effective Rule Induction. In *Proceedings of the Twelfth International Conference on Machine Learning*, pages 115–123.

W. Coster and D. Kauchak. 2011. Learning to Simplify Sentences Using Wikipedia. In *Proceedings of the 49th Annual Meeting of the Association for Computational Linguistics*, pages 1–9.

M. Denkowski and A. Lavie. 2011. Meteor 1.3: Automatic Metric for Reliable Optimization and Evaluation of Machine Translation Systems. In *Proceedings of the EMNLP Workshop on Statistical Machine Translation*.

S. Devlin. 1999. *Simplifying natural language text for aphasic readers*. Ph.D. thesis, University of Sunderland, UK.

G. Doddington. 2002. Automatic evaluation of machine translation quality using n-gram coocurrence statistics. In *Proceedings of the second international conference on Human Language Technology Research*, pages 138–145. Morgan Kaufmann Publishers Inc.

B. Drndarević, S. Štajner, S. Bott, S. Bautista, and H. Saggion. 2013. Automatic Text Simplication in Spanish: A Comparative Evaluation of Complementing Components. In *Proceedings of the 12th International Conference on Intelligent Text Processing and Computational Linguistics. Lecture Notes in Computer Science. Samos, Greece, 24-30 March, 2013.*, pages 488–500.

L. Feng. 2009. Automatic readability assessment for people with intellectual disabilities. In *SIGACCESS Access. Comput.*, number 93, pages 84–91. ACM, New York, NY, USA, jan.

G. Glavaš and S. Štajner. 2013. Event-Centered Simplication of News Stories. In *Proceedings of the Student Workshop held in conjunction with RANLP 2013, Hissar, Bulgaria*, pages 71–78.

M. A. Hall and L. A. Smith. 1998. Practical feature subset selection for machine learning. In C. McDonald, editor, *Computer Science '98 Proceedings of the 21st Australasian Computer Science Conference ACSC'98*, pages 181–191. Berlin: Springer.

M. Hall, E. Frank, G. Holmes, B. Pfahringer, P. Reutemann, and I. H. Witten. 2009. The weka data mining software: an update. *SIGKDD Explor. Newsl.*, 11:10–18, November.

K. Inui, A. Fujita, T. Takahashi, R. Iida, and T. Iwakura. 2003. Text simplification for reading assistance: a project note. In *Proceedings of the second international workshop on Paraphrasing - Volume 16*, PARAPHRASE '03, pages 9–16, Stroudsburg, PA, USA. Association for Computational Linguistics.

G. H. John and P. Langley. 1995. Estimating Continuous Distributions in Bayesian Classifiers. In *Proceedings of the Eleventh Conference on Uncertainty in Artificial Intelligence*, pages 338–345.

S. S. Keerthi, S. K. Shevade, C. Bhattacharyya, and K. R. K. Murthy. 2001. Improvements to Platt's SMO Algorithm for SVM Classifier Design. *Neural Computation*, 13(3):637–649.

D. Klein and C.D. Manning. 2003. Accurate unlexicalized parsing. In *Proceedings of the 41st Annual Meeting on Association for Computational Linguistics*, volume 1, pages 423–430. Association for Computational Linguistics.

S. le Cessie and J.C. van Houwelingen. 1992. Ridge Estimators in Logistic Regression. *Applied Statistics*, 41(1):191–201.

J. Martos, S. Freire, A. González, D. Gil, and M. Sebastian. 2012. D2.1: Functional requirements specifications and user preference survey. Technical report, FIRST technical report.

K. Papineni, S. Roukos, T. Ward, and W. Zhu. 2002. BLEU: a method for automatic evaluation of machine translation. In *Proceedings of ACL*.

S. E. Petersen and M. Ostendorf. 2007. Text Simplification for Language Learners: A Corpus Analysis. In *Proceedings of Workshop on Speech and Language Technology for Education*.

R. Quinlan. 1993. *C4.5: Programs for Machine Learning*. Morgan Kaufmann Publishers, San Mateo, CA.

L. Rello. 2012. Dyswebxia: a model to improve accessibility of the textual web for dyslexic users. In *SIGACCESS Access. Comput.*, number 102, pages 41–44. ACM, New York, NY, USA, January.

M. Rios, W. Aziz, and L. Specia. 2011. TINE: A metric to assess MT adequacy. In *Proceedings of the Sixth Workshop on Statistical Machine Translation (WMT-2011), Edinburgh, UK*.

M. B. Ruiter, T. C. M. Rietveld, Cucchiarini C., Krahmer E. J., and H. Strik. 2010. Human Language Technology and communicative disabilities: Requirements and possibilities for the future. In *Proceedings of the the seventh international conference on Language Resources and Evaluation (LREC)*.

J. Rybing, C. Smithr, and A. Silvervarg. 2010. Towards a Rule Based System for Automatic Simplification of Texts. In *The Third Swedish Language Technology Conference*.

H. Saggion, E. Gómez Martínez, E. Etayo, A. Anula, and L. Bourg. 2011. Text Simplification in Simplext: Making Text More Accessible. *Revista de la Sociedad Española para el Procesamiento del Lenguaje Natural*, 47:341–342.

A. Siddharthan. 2006. Syntactic simplification and text cohesion. *Research on Language & Computation*, 4(1):77–109.

M. Snover, N. Madnani, B. Dorr, and R. Schwartz. 2009. Fluency, Adequacy, or HTER? Exploring Different Human Judgments with a Tunable MT Metric. In *Proceedings of the Fourth Workshop on Statistical Machine Translation at the 12th Meeting of the European Chapter of the Association for Computational Linguistics (EACL-2009), Athens, Greece*.

L. Specia. 2010. Translating from complex to simplified sentences. In *Proceedings of the 9th international conference on Computational Processing of the Portuguese Language*, pages 30–39, Berlin, Heidelberg.

S. Štajner, R. Evans, C. Orasan, and R. Mitkov. 2012. What Can Readability Measures Really Tell Us About Text Complexity? In *Proceedings of the LREC'12 Workshop: Natural Language Processing for Improving Textual Accessibility (NLP4ITA)*, Istanbul, Turkey.

I. H. Witten and E. Frank. 2005. *Data mining: practical machine learning tools and techniques*. Morgan Kaufmann Publishers.

K. Woodsend and M. Lapata. 2011a. Learning to Simplify Sentences with Quasi-Synchronous Grammar and Integer Programming. In *Proceedings of the 2011 Conference on Empirical Methods in Natural Language Processing (EMNLP)*.

K. Woodsend and M. Lapata. 2011b. WikiSimple: Automatic Simplification of Wikipedia Articles. In *Proceedings of the 25th AAI Coference on Artificial Intelligence*.

S. Wubben, A. van den Bosch, and E. Krahmer. 2012. Sentence simplification by monolingual machine translation. In *Proceedings of the 50th Annual Meeting of the Association for Computational Linguistics: Long Papers - Volume 1*, ACL '12, pages 1015–1024, Stroudsburg, PA, USA. Association for Computational Linguistics.

Z. Zhu, D. Berndard, and I. Gurevych. 2010. A Monolingual Tree-based Translation Model for Sentence Simplification. In *Proceedings of the 23rd International Conference on Computational Linguistics (Coling 2010)*, pages 1353–1361.

Automatic diagnosis of understanding of medical words

Natalia Grabar
CNRS UMR 8163 STL
Université Lille 3
59653 Villeneuve d'Ascq, France
natalia.grabar@univ-lille3.fr

Thierry Hamon
LIMSI-CNRS, BP133, Orsay
Université Paris 13
Sorbonne Paris Cité, France
hamon@limsi.fr

Dany Amiot
CNRS UMR 8163 STL
Université Lille 3
59653 Villeneuve d'Ascq, France
dany.amiot@univ-lille3.fr

Abstract

Within the medical field, very specialized terms are commonly used, while their understanding by laymen is not always successful. We propose to study the understandability of medical words by laymen. Three annotators are involved in the creation of the reference data used for training and testing. The features of the words may be linguistic (*i.e.*, number of characters, syllables, number of morphological bases and affixes) and extra-linguistic (*i.e.*, their presence in a reference lexicon, frequency on a search engine). The automatic categorization results show between 0.806 and 0.947 F-measure values. It appears that several features and their combinations are relevant for the analysis of understandability (*i.e.*, syntactic categories, presence in reference lexica, frequency on the general search engine, final substring).

1 Introduction

The medical field has deeply penetrated our daily life, which may be due to personal or family health condition, watching TV and radio broadcasts, reading novels and journals. Nevertheless, the availability of this kind of information does not guarantee its correct understanding, especially by laymen, such as patients. The medical field has indeed a specific terminology (*e.g.*, *abdominoplasty*, *hepatic*, *dermabrasion* or *hepatoduodenostomy*) commonly used by medical professionals. This fact has been highlighted in several studies dedicated for instance to the understanding of pharmaceutical labels (Patel et al., 2002), of information provided by websites (Rudd et al., 1999; Berland et al., 2001; McCray, 2005; Oregon Evidence-based Practice Center, 2008), and more generally the understanding between patients and medical doctors (AMA, 1999; McCray, 2005; Jucks and Bromme, 2007; Tran et al., 2009).

We propose to study the understanding of words used in the medical field, which is the first step towards the simplification of texts. Indeed, before the simplification can be performed, it is necessary to know which textual units may show understanding difficulty and should be simplified. We work with data in French, such as provided by an existing medical terminology. In the remainder, we present first some related work, especially from specialized fields (section 2). We then introduce the linguistic data (section 4) and methodology (section 5) we propose to test. We present and discuss the results (section 6), and conclude with some directions for future work (section 7).

2 Studying the understanding of words

The understanding (of words) may be seen as a scale going from *I can understand* to *I cannot understand*, and containing one or more intermediate positions (*i.e.*, *I am not sure*, *I have seen it before but do not remember the meaning*, *I do not know but can interpret*). Notice that it is also related to the ability to provide correct explanation and use of words. As we explain later, we consider words out of context and use a three-position scale. More generally, understanding is a complex notion closely linked to several other notions studied in different research fields. For instance, lexical complexity is studied in linguistics and gives clues on lexical processes involved, that may impact the word understanding (section 2.1). Work in psycholinguistics is often oriented on study of word opacity and the mental processes involved in their understanding (Jarema et al., 1999; Libben et al., 2003). Readability provides a set of methods to compute and quantify the understandability of words (section 2.3). The specificity of words to specialized areas is another way to capture their understandability (section 2.2). Finally, lexical simplification aims at providing simpler words to be used in a given context (section 2.3).

2.1 Linguistics

In linguistics, the question is closely related to lexical complexity and compoundings. It has been indeed observed that at least five factors, linguistic and extra-linguistic, may be involved in the semantic complexity of the compounds. One factor is related to the knowledge of the components of the complex words. Formal (how the words, such as *aérenchyme*, can be segmented) and semantic (how the words can be understood and used) points of view can be distinguished. A second factor is that complexity is also due to the variety of morphological patterns and relations among the components. For instance, *érythrocyte* (*erythrocyte*) and *ovocyte* (*ovocyte*) instantiate the *[N1N2]* pattern in which *N2* (*cyte*) can be seen as a constant element (Booij, 2010), although the relations between *N1* and *N2* are not of the same type in these two compounds: in *érythrocyte*, *N1 érythr(o)* denotes a property of *N2* (color), while in *ovocyte*, *N1 ovo* (*egg*) corresponds to a specific development stage of female cells. Another factor appears when some components are polysemous, within a given field (*i.e.*, medical field) or across the fields. For instance, *aér(o)* does not always convey the same meaning: in *aérocèle*, *aér-* denotes 'air' (*tumefaction (cèle) formed by an air infiltration*), but not in *aérasthénie*, which refers to an *asthenia (psychic disorder)* observable among jet pilots. Yet another factor may be due to the difference in the order of components: according to whether the compounding is standard (in French, the main semantic element is then on the left, such as in *pneu neige* (*snow tyre*), which is fundamentally a *pneu* (*tyre*)) or neoclassical (in French, the main semantic element is then on the right, such as *érythrocyte*, which is a kind of cyte *cell / corpuscle* with red color). It is indeed complicated for a user without medical training to correctly interpret a word that he does not know and for which he cannot reuse the existing standard compounding patterns. This difficulty is common to all Roman languages (Iacobini, 2003), but not to Germanic languages (Lüdeling et al., 2002). Closely related is the fact that with neoclassical compounds, a given component may change its place according to the global semantics of the compounds, such as *path-* in *pathology, polyneuropathe, cardiopathy*. Finally, the formal similarity between some derivation processes (such as the derivation in *-oide*, like in *lipoid*) and neoclassical compounding (such as *-ase* in *lipase*), which apply completely different interpretation patterns (Iacobini, 1997; Amiot and Dal, 2005), can also make the understanding more difficult.

2.2 Terminology

In the terminology field, the automatic identification of difficulty of terms and words remains implicit, while this notion is fundamental in terminology (Wüster, 1981; Cabré and Estopà, 2002; Cabré, 2000). The specificity of terms to a given field is usually studied. The notion of understandability can be derived from it. Such studies can be used for filtering the terms extracted from specialized corpora (Korkontzelos et al., 2008). The features exploited include for instance the presence and the specificity of pivot words (Drouin and Langlais, 2006), the neighborhood of the term in corpus or the diversity of its components computed with statistical measures such as C-Value or PageRank (Daille, 1995; Frantzi et al., 1997; Maynard and Ananiadou, 2000). Another possibility is to check whether lexical units occur within reference terminologies and, if they do, they are considered to convey specialized meaning (Elhadad and Sutaria, 2007).

2.3 NLP studies

The application of the readability measures is another way to evaluate the complexity of words and terms. Among these measures, it is possible to distinguish classical readability measures and computational readability measures (François, 2011). Classical measures usually rely on number of letters and/or of syllables a word contains and on linear regression models (Flesch, 1948; Gunning, 1973), while computational readability measures may involve vector models and a great variability of features, among which the following have been used to process the biomedical documents and words: combination of classical readability formulas with medical terminologies (Kokkinakis and Toporowska Gronostaj, 2006); n-grams of characters (Poprat et al., 2006), manually (Zheng et al., 2002) or automatically (Borst et al., 2008) defined weight of terms, stylistic (Grabar et al., 2007) or discursive (Goeuriot et al., 2007) features, lexicon (Miller et al., 2007), morphological features (Chmielik and Grabar, 2011), combi-

Categories	A1 (%)	A2 (%)	A3 (%)	Unanimity (%)	Majority (%)
1. I can understand	8,099 (28)	8,625 (29)	7,529 (25)	5,960 (26)	7,655 (27)
2. I am not sure	1,895 (6)	1,062 (4)	1,431 (5)	61 (0.3)	597 (2)
3. I cannot understand	19,647 (66)	19,954 (67)	20,681 (70)	16,904 (73.7)	20,511 (71)
Total annotations	29,641	29,641	29,641	22,925	28,763

Table 1: Number (and percentage) of words assigned to reference categories by three annotators (A1, A2 and A3), and in the derived datasets *unanimity* and *majority*.

nations of different features (Wang, 2006; Zeng-Treiler et al., 2007; Leroy et al., 2008).

Specific task has been dedicated to the lexical simplification within the *SemEval* challenge in 2012[1]. Given a short input text and a target word in English, and given several English substitutes for the target word that fit the context, the goal was to rank these substitutes according to how "simple" they are (Specia et al., 2012). The participants applied rule-based and/or machine learning systems. Combinations of various features have been used: lexicon from spoken corpus and Wikipedia, Google n-grams, WordNet (Sinha, 2012); word length, number of syllables, latent semantic analysis, mutual information and word frequency (Jauhar and Specia, 2012); Wikipedia frequency, word length, n-grams of characters and of words, random indexing and syntactic complexity of documents (Johannsen et al., 2012); n-grams and frequency from Wikipedia, Google n-grams (Ligozat et al., 2012); WordNet and word frequency (Amoia and Romanelli, 2012).

3 Aims of the present study

We propose to investigate how the understandability of French medical words can be diagnosed with NLP methods. We rely on the reference annotations performed by French speakers without medical training, which we associate with patients. The experiments performed rely on machine learning algorithms and a set of 24 features. The medical words studied are provided by an existing medical terminology.

4 Linguistic data and their preparation

The linguistic data are obtained from the medical terminology Snomed International (Côté, 1996). This terminology's aim is to describe the whole medical field. It contains 151,104 medical terms structured into eleven semantic axes such as disorders and abnormalities, procedures, chemical products, living organisms, anatomy, social status, etc. We keep here five axes related to the main medical notions (disorders, abnormalities, procedures, functions, anatomy). The objective is not to consider axes such as chemical products (*trisulfure d'hydrogène* (hydrogen sulfide)) and living organisms (*Sapromyces, Acholeplasma laidlawii*) that group very specific terms hardly known by laymen. The 104,649 selected terms are tokenized and segmented into words (or tokens) to obtain 29,641 unique words: *trisulfure d'hydrogène* gives three words (*trisulfure, de, hydrogène*). This dataset contains compounds (*abdominoplastie* (abdominoplasty), *dermabrasion* (dermabrasion)), constructed (*cardiaque* (cardiac), *acineux* (acinic), *lipoïde* (lipoid)) and simple (*acné* (acne), *fragment* (fragment)) words. These data are annotated by three speakers 25-40 year-old, without medical training, but with linguistic background. We expect the annotators to represent the average knowledge of medical words amongst the population as a whole. The annotators are presented with a list of terms and asked to assign each word to one of the three categories: (1) I can understand the word; (2) I am not sure about the meaning of the word; (3) I cannot understand the word. The assumption is that the words, which are not understandable by the annotators, are also difficult to understand by patients. These manual annotations correspond to the reference data (Table 1).

5 Methodology

The proposed method has two aspects: generation of the features associated to the analyzed words and a machine learning system. The main research question is whether the NLP methods can distinguish between understandable and non-understandable medical words and whether they can diagnose these two categories.

[1] http://www.cs.york.ac.uk/semeval-2012/

5.1 Generation of the features

We exploit 24 linguistic and extra-linguistic features related to general and specialized languages. The features are computed automatically, and can be grouped into ten classes:

Syntactic categories. Syntactic categories and lemmas are computed by TreeTagger (Schmid, 1994) and then checked by Flemm (Namer, 2000). The syntactic categories are assigned to words within the context of their terms. If a given word receives more than one category, the most frequent one is kept as feature. Among the main categories we find for instance nouns, adjectives, proper names, verbs and abbreviations.

Presence of words in reference lexica. We exploit two reference lexica of the French language: TLFi[2] and *lexique.org*[3]. TLFi is a dictionary of the French language covering XIX and XX centuries. It contains almost 100,000 entries. *lexique.org* is a lexicon created for psycholinguistic experiments. It contains over 135,000 entries, among which inflectional forms of verbs, adjectives and nouns. It contains almost 35,000 lemmas.

Frequency of words through a non specialized search engine. For each word, we query the Google search engine in order to know its frequency attested on the web.

Frequency of words in the medical terminology. We also compute the frequency of words in the medical terminology Snomed International.

Number and types of semantic categories associated to words. We exploit the information on the semantic categories of Snomed International.

Length of words in number of their characters and syllables. For each word, we compute the number of its characters and syllables.

Number of bases and affixes. Each lemma is analyzed by the morphological analyzer Dérif (Namer and Zweigenbaum, 2004), adapted to the treatment of medical words. It performs the decomposition of lemmas into bases and affixes known in its database and it provides also semantic explanation of the analyzed lexemes. We exploit the morphological decomposition information (number of affixes and bases).

Initial and final substrings of the words. We compute the initial and final substrings of different length, from three to five characters.

[2]http://www.atilf.fr/

[3]http://www.lexique.org/

Number and percentage of consonants, vowels and other characters. We compute the number and the percentage of consonants, vowels and other characters (*i.e.*, hyphen, apostrophe, comas).

Classical readability scores. We apply two classical readability measures: Flesch (Flesch, 1948) and its variant Flesch-Kincaid (Kincaid et al., 1975). Such measures are typically used for evaluating the difficulty level of a text. They exploit surface characteristics of words (number of characters and/or syllables) and normalize these values with specifically designed coefficients.

5.2 Machine learning system

The machine learning algorithms are used to study whether they can distinguish between words understandable and non-understandable by laymen and to study the importance of various features for the task. The functioning of machine learning algorithms is based on a set of positive and negative examples of the data to be processed, which have to be described with suitable features such as those presented above. The algorithms can then detect the regularities within the training dataset to generate a model, and apply the generated model to process new unseen data. We apply various algorithms available within the WEKA (Witten and Frank, 2005) platform.

The annotations provided by the three annotators constitute our reference data. We use on the whole five reference datasets (Table 1): 3 sets of separate annotations provided by the three annotators (29,641 words each); 1 *unanimity* set, on which all the annotators agree (n=22,925); 1 *majority* set, for which we can compute the majority agreement (n=28,763). By definition, the two last datasets should present a better coherence and less annotation ambiguity because some ambiguities have been resolved by unanimity or by majority vote.

5.3 Evaluation

The inter-annotator agreement is computed with the Cohen's Kappa (Cohen, 1960), applied to pairs of annotators, which values are then leveraged to obtain the unique average value; and Fleiss' Kappa (Fleiss and Cohen, 1973), suitable for processing data provided by more than two annotators. The interpretation of the scores are for instance (Landis and Koch, 1977): substantial agreement between 0.61 and 0.80, almost perfect agreement between 0.81 and 1.00.

With machine learning, we perform a ten-fold cross-validation, which means that the evaluation test is performed ten times on different randomly generated test sets (1/10 of the whole dataset), while the remaining 9/10 of the whole dataset is used for training the algorithm and creating the model. In this way, each word is used during the test step. The success of the applied algorithms is evaluated with three classical measures: $\mathcal{R}$ recall, $\mathcal{P}$ precision and $\mathcal{F}$ F-measure. In the perspective of our work, these measures allow evaluating the suitability of the methodology to the distinction between understandable and non-understandable words and the relevance of the chosen features.

The baseline corresponds to the assignment of words to the biggest category, *e.g.*, *I cannot understand*, which represents 66 to 74%, according to datasets. We can also compute the gain, which is the effective improvement of performance P given the baseline BL (Rittman, 2008): $\frac{P-BL}{1-BL}$.

6 Automatic analysis of understandability of medical words: Results and Discussion

We address the following aspects: annotations (inter-annotator agreement, assignment of words to three categories), quantitative results provided by the machine learning algorithms, impact of the individual features on the distinction between categories, and usefulness of the method.

6.1 Annotations and inter-annotator agreement

The time needed for performing the manual reference annotations depends on annotators and ranges from 3 to 6 weeks. The annotation results presented in Table 1 indicate that the annotators 1 and 2 often provide similar results on their understanding of the medical words, while for the third annotator the task appears to be more difficult as he indicates globally a higher number of non-understandable words. The non-understandable words are the most frequent for all annotators and cover 66 to 70% of the whole dataset. The inter-annotator agreement shows substantial agreement: Fleiss' Kappa 0.735 and Cohen's Kappa 0.736. This is a very good result, especially when working with linguistic data for which the agreement is usually difficult to obtain.

The evolution of annotations per category (Figure 1), such as provided by the annotators, can distinguish easily between the three categories: (1) the most frequently chosen category is *I cannot understand* and it grows rapidly with new words; (2) the next most frequently chosen category is *I can understand*, although it grows more slowly; (3) the third category, which gathers the words on which the annotators show some hesitation, is very small. Given the proximity between the lines in each category, we can conclude that the annotators have similar difficulties in understanding the words from the dataset.

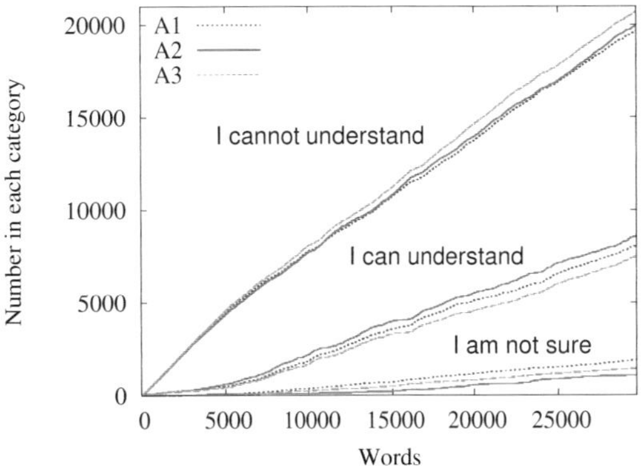

Figure 1: Evolution of the annotations within the reference data.

6.2 Quantitative results obtained with machine learning

	$\mathcal{P}$	$\mathcal{R}$	$\mathcal{F}$
J48	0.876	0.889	0.881
RandomForest	0.880	0.892	0.884
REPTree	0.874	0.890	0.879
DecisionTable	0.872	0.891	0.880
LMT	0.876	0.895	0.884
SMO	0.858	0.876	0.867

Table 2: Performance obtained on the *majority* dataset with various algorithms.

We tested several machine learning algorithms to discover which of them are the most suitable to the task at hand. In Table 2, with results computed on the *majority* dataset, we can observe that the algorithms provide with similar performance (between 0.85 and 0.90 $\mathcal{P}$ and $\mathcal{R}$). In the remaining of the paper, we present results obtained with J48 (Quinlan, 1993). Table 3 shows $\mathcal{P}$, $\mathcal{R}$ and $\mathcal{F}$ values for the five datasets: three annotators, majority and unanimity datasets. We can observe that, among the three annotators, it is easier to reproduce the annotations of the third annotator: we gain then 0.040 with $\mathcal{F}$ comparing to the two other annotators. The results become even better with the majority dataset ($\mathcal{F}$=0.881), and reach $\mathcal{F}$ up to 0.947 on the unanimity dataset. As we expected, these two last datasets present less annotation ambiguity. The best categorization results are observed with *I can understand* and *I cannot understand* categories, while the *I am not sure* category is poorly managed by machine learning algorithms. Because this category is very small, the average performance obtained on all three categories remains high.

	A1	*A2*	*A3*	*Una.*	*Maj.*
$\mathcal{P}$	0.794	0.809	0.834	0.946	0.876
$\mathcal{R}$	0.825	0.826	0.862	0.949	0.889
$\mathcal{F}$	0.806	0.814	0.845	0.947	0.881

Table 3: J48 performance obtained on five datasets (A1, A2, A3, *unanimity* and *majority*).

In Table 4, we indicate the gain obtained by J48 compared to baseline: it ranges from 0.13 to 0.20, which is a good improvement, despite the category *I am not sure* that is difficult to discriminate. We also indicate the accuracy obtained on these datasets.

	A1	*A2*	*A3*	*Una.*	*Maj.*
BL	0.66	0.67	0.70	0.74	0.71
$\mathcal{F}$	0.806	0.814	0.845	0.947	0.881
gain	0.14	0.13	0.14	0.20	0.16
Acc.	0.825	0.826	0.862	0.948	0.889

Table 4: Gain obtained for $\mathcal{F}$ by J48 on five datasets (A1, A2, A3, *unanimity* and *majority*).

6.3 Impact of individual features on understandability of medical words

To observe the impact of individual features, we did several iterations of experiments during which we incrementally increased the set of features: we started with one feature and then, at each iteration, we added one new feature, up to the 24 features available. We tried several random orders. The test presented here is done again on the *majority* dataset. Figures 2 present the results obtained in terms of $\mathcal{P}$, $\mathcal{R}$ and $\mathcal{F}$. Globally, we can observe that some features show positive impact while others show negative or null impact:

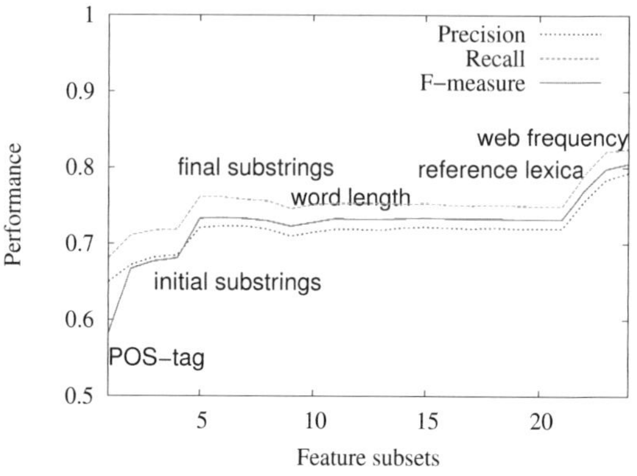

Figure 2: Impact of individual features.

- with the syntactic categories (POS-tags) alone we obtain $\mathcal{P}$ and $\mathcal{R}$ between 0.65 and 0.7. The performance is then close to the baseline performance. Often, proper names and abbreviations are associated with the non-understandable words. There is no difference between TreeTagger alone and the combination of TreeTagger with Flemm;
- the initial and final substrings have positive impact. Among the final substrings, those with three and four characters (ie, *-omie* of *-tomie* (*meaning* cut), *-phie* of *-rraphie* (*meaning* stitch), *-émie* (*meaning* blood)) show positive impact, but substrings with five characters have negative impact and the previously gained improvement is lost. We may conclude that the five-character long final substrings may be too specific;
- the length of words in characters have negative impact on the categorization results. There seems to be no strong link between this feature and the understanding of words: short and long words may be experienced as both understandable or not by annotators;
- the presence of words in the reference lexica (TLFI and *lexique.org*) is beneficial to both precision and recall. We assume these lexica may represent common lexical competence of French speakers. For this reason, words that are present in these lexica, are also easier to understand;
- the frequencies of words computed through a general search engine are beneficial.

Words with higher frequencies are often associated with a better understanding, although the frequency range depends on the words. For instance, *coccyx* (*coccyx*) or *drain* (*drain*) show high frequencies (1,800,000 and 175,000,000, respectively) and they belong indeed to the *I can understand* category. Words like *colique* (*diarrhea*) or *clitoridien* (*clitoral*) show lower frequencies (807,000 and 9,821, respectively), although they belong to the same category. On contrary, other words with quite high frequencies, like *coagulase* (*coagulase*), *clivage* (*cleavage*) or *douve* (*fluke*) (655,000, 1,350,000 and 1,030,000, respectively) are not understood by the annotators.

According to these experiments, our results point out that, among the most efficient features, we can find syntactic categories, presence of words in the reference lexica, frequencies of words on Google and three- and four-character end substring. In comparison to the existing studies, such as those presented during the SemEval challenge (Specia et al., 2012), we propose to exploit a more complete set of features, several of which rely on the NLP methods (*e.g.*, syntactic tagging, morphological analysis). Especially the syntactic tagging appears to be salient for the task. In comparison to work done on general language data (Gala et al., 2013), our experiment shows better results (between 0.825 and 0.948 *accuracy* against 0.62 *accuracy* in the cited work), which indicates that specialized domains have indeed very specific words. Additional tests should be performed to obtain a more detailed impact of the features.

6.4 Usefulness of the method

We applied the proposed method to words from discharge summaries. The documents are preprocessed according to the same protocol and the words are assigned the same features as previously (section 5). The model learned on the *unanimity* set is applied. The results are shown in Figure 3. Among the words categorized as non-understandable (in red and underlined), we find:

- abbreviations (*NIHSS, OAP, NaCl, VNI*);
- technical medical terms (*hypoesthésie* (*hypoesthesia*), *parésie* (*paresia*), *thrombolyse* (*thrombolysis*), *iatrogène* (*iatrogenic*), *oxygénothérapie* (*oxygen therapy*), *désaturation* (*desaturation*));

Histoire de la maladie
Le patient a été hospitalisé le 18 / 7 / 11 à PELLEGRIN pour un AVC ischémique dans le territoire profond de l' artère cérébrale postérieure droite , thrombolysé à H + 3 .

Le patient présente , comme déficit , une hypoesthésie gauche et une parésie gauche (force motrice à 1 / 5 au membre supérieur gauche et 2 / 5 au membre inférieur gauche) , un NIHSS à 8 , une désorientation tempora-spatiale et une vigilance fluctuante . Dans les suites , est survenu un OAP post thrombolyse , probablement iatrogène (scanner injecté et NaCl afin de visualiser la zone de thrombolyse) .

Le patient est donc transféré en réanimation : l' OAP est résolutif sous VNI et oxygénothérapie .

La majoration de l' insuffisance rénale nécessite 2 cures de dialyse . Mr K . est ensuite transféré en post-réanimation devant l' évolution favorable et revient en service de neurologie à Pellegrin pour suite de la prise en charge .

Le 11 / 8 / 2011 , le patient présente une douleur thoracique associée à une désaturation à 83 % , il est donc transféré en Unité de soins intensifs cardiologiques . Une embolie pulmonaire basale droite est mise en évidence par une scintigraphie pulmonaire . Une anticoagulation curative par CALCIPARINE est mise en place .

Figure 3: Detection of non-understandable words within discharge summaries.

- medication names (*CALCIPARINE*);

In the example from Figure 3, three types of errors can be distinguished when common words are categorized as non-understandable:

- inflected forms of words (*suites* (*consequences*), *cardiologiques* (*cardiological*));
- constructed forms of words (*thrombolysé* (*with thrombolysis*));
- hyphenated words (*post-réanimation* (*post emergency medical service*)).

Notice that in other processed documents, other errors occur. For instance, misspelled words and words that miss accented characters (*probleme* instead of *problème* (*problem*), *realise* instead of *réalisé* (*done*), *particularite* instead *particularité* (*particularity*)) are problematic. Another type of errors may occur when technical words (*e.g. prolapsus* (*prolapsus*), *paroxysme* (*paroxysm*), *tricuspide* (*tricuspid*)) are considered as understandable.

Besides, only isolated words are currently processed, which is the limitation of the current method. Still, consideration of complex medical terms, that convey more complex medical notions, should also be done. Such terms may indeed change the understanding of words, as in these examples: *AVC ischémique* (*ischemic CVA (cerebrovascular accident)*), *embolie pulmonaire basale droite* (*right basal pulmonary embolism*), *désaturation à 83 %*

(*desaturation at 83%*), *anticoagulation curative* (*curative anticoagulation*). In the same way, numerical values may also arise misunderstanding of medical information. Processing of these additional aspects (inflected and constructed forms of words, hyphenated or misspelled words, complex terms composed with several words and numerical values) is part of the future work.

6.5 Limitations of the current study

We proposed several experiments for analyzing the understandability of medical words. We tried to analyze these data from different points of view to get a more complete picture. Still, there are some limitations. These are mainly related to the linguistic data and to their preparation.

The whole set of the analyzed words is large: almost 30,000 entries. We assume it is possible that annotations provided may show some intra-annotator inconsistencies due for instance to the tiredness and instability of the annotators (for instance, when a given unknown morphological components is seen again and again, the meaning of this component may be deduced by the annotator). Nevertheless, in our daily life, we are also confronted to the medical language (our personal health or health of family or friend, TV and radio broadcast, various readings of newspapers and novels) and then, it is possible that the new medical notions may be learned during the annotation period of the words, which lasted up to four weeks. Nevertheless, the advantage of the data we have built is that the whole set is completely annotated by each annotator.

When computing the features of the words, we have favored those, which are computed at the word level. In the future work, it may be interesting to take into account features computed at the level of morphological components or of complex terms. The main question will be to decide how such features can be combined all together.

The annotators involved in the study have a training in linguistics, although their relation with the medical field is poor: they have no specific health problems and no expertise in medical terminology. We expect they may represent the average level of patients with moderate health literacy. Nevertheless, the observed results may remain specific to the category of young people with linguistic training. Additional experiments are required to study this aspect better.

7 Conclusion and Future research

We proposed a study of words from the medical field, which are manually annotated as understandable, non-understandable and possibly understandable to laymen. The proposed approach is based on machine learning and a set with 24 features. Among the features, which appear to be salient for the diagnosis of understandable words, we find for instance the presence of words in the reference lexica, their syntactic categories, their final substring, and their frequencies on the web. Several features and their combinations can be distinguished, which shows that the understandability of words is a complex notion, which involves several linguistic and extra-linguistic criteria.

The avenue for future research includes for instance the exploitation of corpora, while currently we use features computed out of context. We assume indeed that corpora may provide additional relevant information (semantic or statistical) for the task aimed in this study. Additional aspects related to the processing of documents (inflected and constructed forms of words, hyphenated or misspelled words, complex terms composed with several words and numerical values) is another perspective. Besides, the classical readability measures exploited have been developed for the processing of English language. Working with French-language data, we should use measures, which are adapted to this language (Kandel and Moles, 1958; Henry, 1975). In addition, we can also explore various perspectives, which appear from the current limitations, such as computing and using features computed at different levels (morphological components, words and complex terms), applying other classical readability measures adapted to the French language, and adding new reference annotations provided by laymen from other social-professional categories.

Acknowledgments

This work is performed under the grant ANR/DGA Tecsan (ANR-11-TECS-012) and the support of MESHS (COMETE project). The authors are thankful to the CHU de Bordeaux for making available the clinical documents.

References

AMA. 1999. Health literacy: report of the council on scientific affairs. Ad hoc committee on health literacy for the council on scientific affairs, American Medical Association. *JAMA*, 281(6):552–7.

D Amiot and G Dal. 2005. Integrating combining forms into a lexeme-based morphology. In *Mediterranean Morphology Meeting (MMM5)*, pages 323–336.

M Amoia and M Romanelli. 2012. Sb: mmsystem - using decompositional semantics for lexical simplification. In **SEM 2012*, pages 482–486, Montréal, Canada, 7-8 June. Association for Computational Linguistics.

GK Berland, MN Elliott, LS Morales, JI Algazy, RL Kravitz, MS Broder, DE Kanouse, JA Munoz, JA Puyol, M Lara, KE Watkins, H Yang, and EA McGlynn. 2001. Health information on the internet. accessibility, quality, and readability in english ans spanish. *JAMA*, 285(20):2612–2621.

Geert Booij. 2010. *Construction Morphology*. Oxford University Press, Oxford.

A Borst, A Gaudinat, C Boyer, and N Grabar. 2008. Lexically based distinction of readability levels of health documents. In *MIE 2008*. Poster.

MT Cabré and R Estopà. 2002. On the units of specialised meaning uses in professional com- munication. In *International Network for Terminology*, pages 217–237.

TM Cabré. 2000. Terminologie et linguistique: la thorie des portes. *Terminologies nouvelles*, 21:10–15.

J Chmielik and N Grabar. 2011. Détection de la spécialisation scientifique et technique des documents biomédicaux grâce aux informations morphologiques. *TAL*, 51(2):151–179.

Jacob Cohen. 1960. A coefficient of agreement for nominal scales. *Educational and Psychological Measurement*, 20(1):37–46.

RA Côté, 1996. *Répertoire d'anatomopathologie de la SNOMED internationale, v3.4*. Université de Sherbrooke, Sherbrooke, Québec.

B Daille. 1995. Repérage et extraction de terminologie par une approche mixte statistique et linguistique. *Traitement Automatique des Langues (T.A.L.)*, 36(1-2):101–118.

P Drouin and P Langlais. 2006. valuation du potentiel terminologique de candidats termes. In *JADT*, pages 379–388.

N Elhadad and K Sutaria. 2007. Mining a lexicon of technical terms and lay equivalents. In *BioNLP*, pages 49–56.

JL Fleiss and J Cohen. 1973. The equivalence of weighted kappa and the intraclass correlation coefficient as measures of reliability. *Educational and Psychological Measurement*, 33:613–619.

R Flesch. 1948. A new readability yardstick. *Journal of Applied Psychology*, 23:221–233.

T François. 2011. *Les apports du traitements automatique du langage la lisibilit du franais langue trangre*. Phd thesis, Universit Catholique de Louvain, Louvain.

KT Frantzi, S Ananiadou, and J Tsujii. 1997. Automatic term recognition using contextual clues. In *MULSAIC IJCAI*, pages 73–79.

N Gala, T François, and C Fairon. 2013. Towards a french lexicon with difficulty measures: NLP helping to bridge the gap between traditional dictionaries and specialized lexicons. In *eLEX-2013*.

L Goeuriot, N Grabar, and B Daille. 2007. Caractérisation des discours scientifique et vulgarisé en français, japonais et russe. In *TALN*, pages 93–102.

N Grabar, S Krivine, and MC Jaulent. 2007. Classification of health webpages as expert and non expert with a reduced set of cross-language features. In *AMIA*, pages 284–288.

R Gunning. 1973. *The art of clear writing*. McGraw Hill, New York, NY.

G Henry. 1975. *Comment mesurer la lisibilit*. Labor, Bruxelles.

C Iacobini. 1997. Distinguishing derivational prefixes from initial combining forms. In *First mediterranean conference of morphology*, Mytilene, Island of Lesbos, Greece, septembre.

C Iacobini, 2003. *Composizione con elementi neoclassici*, pages 69–96.

Gonia Jarema, Cline Busson, Rossitza Nikolova, Kyrana Tsapkini, and Gary Libben. 1999. Processing compounds: A cross-linguistic study. *Brain and Language*, 68(1-2):362–369.

SK Jauhar and L Specia. 2012. Uow-shef: Simplex – lexical simplicity ranking based on contextual and psycholinguistic features. In **SEM 2012*, pages 477–481, Montréal, Canada, 7-8 June. Association for Computational Linguistics.

A Johannsen, H Martínez, S Klerke, and A Søgaard. 2012. Emnlp@cph: Is frequency all there is to simplicity? In **SEM 2012*, pages 408–412, Montréal, Canada, 7-8 June. Association for Computational Linguistics.

R Jucks and R Bromme. 2007. Choice of words in doctor-patient communication: an analysis of health-related internet sites. *Health Commun*, 21(3):267–77.

L Kandel and A Moles. 1958. Application de lindice de flesch la langue franaise. *Cahiers tudes de Radio-Tlvision*, 19:253–274.

JP Kincaid, RP Jr Fishburne, RL Rogers, and BS Chissom. 1975. Derivation of new readability formulas (automated readability index, fog count and flesch reading ease formula) for navy enlisted personnel. Technical report, Naval Technical Training, U. S. Naval Air Station, Memphis, TN.

D Kokkinakis and M Toporowska Gronostaj. 2006. Comparing lay and professional language in cardiovascular disorders corpora. In Australia Pham T., James Cook University, editor, *WSEAS Transactions on BIOLOGY and BIOMEDICINE*, pages 429–437.

I Korkontzelos, IP Klapaftis, and S Manandhar. 2008. Reviewing and evaluating automatic term recognition techniques. In *GoTAL*, pages 248–259.

JR Landis and GG Koch. 1977. The measurement of observer agreement for categorical data. *Biometrics*, 33:159–174.

G Leroy, S Helmreich, J Cowie, T Miller, and W Zheng. 2008. Evaluating online health information: Beyond readability formulas. In *AMIA 2008*, pages 394–8.

Gary Libben, Martha Gibson, Yeo Bom Yoon, and Dominiek Sandra. 2003. Compound fracture: The role of semantic transparency and morphological headedness. *Brain and Language*, 84(1):50–64.

AL Ligozat, C Grouin, A Garcia-Fernandez, and D Bernhard. 2012. Annlor: A naïve notation-system for lexical outputs ranking. In **SEM 2012*, pages 487–492.

A Lüdeling, T Schmidt, and S Kiokpasoglou. 2002. Neoclassical word formation in german. *Yearbook of Morphology*, pages 253–283.

D Maynard and S Ananiadou. 2000. Identifying terms by their family and friends. In *Proceedings of COLING 2000*, pages 530–536, Saarbrucken, Germany.

A McCray. 2005. Promoting health literacy. *J of Am Med Infor Ass*, 12:152–163.

T Miller, G Leroy, S Chatterjee, J Fan, and B Thoms. 2007. A classifier to evaluate language specificity of medical documents. In *HICSS*, pages 134–140.

Fiammetta Namer and Pierre Zweigenbaum. 2004. Acquiring meaning for French medical terminology: contribution of morphosemantics. In *Annual Symposium of the American Medical Informatics Association (AMIA)*, San-Francisco.

F Namer. 2000. FLEMM : un analyseur flexionnel du français à base de règles. *Traitement automatique des langues (TAL)*, 41(2):523–547.

Oregon Evidence-based Practice Center. 2008. Barriers and drivers of health information technology use for the elderly, chronically ill, and underserved. Technical report, Agency for healthcare research and quality.

V Patel, T Branch, and J Arocha. 2002. Errors in interpreting quantities as procedures : The case of pharmaceutical labels. *International journal of medical informatics*, 65(3):193–211.

M Poprat, K Markó, and U Hahn. 2006. A language classifier that automatically divides medical documents for experts and health care consumers. In *MIE 2006 - Proceedings of the XX International Congress of the European Federation for Medical Informatics*, pages 503–508, Maastricht.

JR Quinlan. 1993. *C4.5 Programs for Machine Learning*. Morgan Kaufmann, San Mateo, CA.

R Rittman. 2008. *Automatic discrimination of genres*. VDM, Saarbrucken, Germany.

R Rudd, B Moeykens, and T Colton, 1999. *Annual Review of Adult Learning and Literacy*, page ch 5.

H Schmid. 1994. Probabilistic part-of-speech tagging using decision trees. In *Proceedings of the International Conference on New Methods in Language Processing*, pages 44–49, Manchester, UK.

R Sinha. 2012. Unt-simprank: Systems for lexical simplification ranking. In **SEM 2012*, pages 493–496, Montréal, Canada, 7-8 June. Association for Computational Linguistics.

L Specia, SK Jauhar, and R Mihalcea. 2012. Semeval-2012 task 1: English lexical simplification. In **SEM 2012*, pages 347–355.

TM Tran, H Chekroud, P Thiery, and A Julienne. 2009. Internet et soins : un tiers invisible dans la relation médecine/patient ? *Ethica Clinica*, 53:34–43.

Y Wang. 2006. Automatic recognition of text difficulty from consumers health information. In IEEE, editor, *Computer-Based Medical Systems*, pages 131–136.

I.H. Witten and E. Frank. 2005. *Data mining: Practical machine learning tools and techniques*. Morgan Kaufmann, San Francisco.

Eugen Wüster. 1981. L'tude scientifique gnrale de la terminologie, zone frontalire entre la linguistique, la logique, l'ontologie, l'informatique et les sciences des choses. In G. Rondeau et H. Felber, editor, *Textes choisis de terminologie*, volume I. Fondements thoriques de la terminologie, pages 55–114. GISTERM, Universit de Laval, Qubec. sous la direction de V.I. Siforov.

Q Zeng-Treiler, H Kim, S Goryachev, A Keselman, L Slaugther, and CA Smith. 2007. Text characteristics of clinical reports and their implications for the readability of personal health records. In *MEDINFO*, pages 1117–1121, Brisbane, Australia.

W Zheng, E Milios, and C Watters. 2002. Filtering for medical news items using a machine learning approach. In *AMIA*, pages 949–53.

Exploring Measures of "Readability" for Spoken Language: Analyzing linguistic features of subtitles to identify age-specific TV programs

Sowmya Vajjala and **Detmar Meurers**
LEAD Graduate School, Department of Linguistics
University of Tübingen
{sowmya,dm}@sfs.uni-tuebingen.de

Abstract

We investigate whether measures of readability can be used to identify age-specific TV programs. Based on a corpus of BBC TV subtitles, we employ a range of linguistic readability features motivated by Second Language Acquisition and Psycholinguistics research.

Our hypothesis that such readability features can successfully distinguish between spoken language targeting different age groups is fully confirmed. The classifiers we trained on the basis of these readability features achieve a classification accuracy of 95.9%. Investigating several feature subsets, we show that the authentic material targeting specific age groups exhibits a broad range of linguistics and psycholinguistic characteristics that are indicative of the complexity of the language used.

1 Introduction

Reading, listening, and watching television programs are all ways to obtain information partly encoded in language. Just like books are written for different target groups, current TV programs target particular audiences, which differ in their interests and ability to understand language. For books and text in general, a wide range of readability measures have been developed to determine for which audience the information encoded in the language used is accessible. Different audiences are commonly distinguished in terms of the age or school level targeted by a given text.

While for TV programs the nature of the interaction between the audio-visual presentation and the language used is a relevant factor, in this paper we want to explore whether the language by itself is equally characteristic of the particular age groups targeted by a given TV program. We thus focused on the language content of the program as encoded in TV subtitles and explored the role of text complexity in predicting the intended age group of the different programs.

The paper is organized as follows. Section 2 introduces the corpus we used, and section 3 the readability features employed and their motivation. Section 4 discusses the experimental setup, the experiments we conducted and their results. Section 5 puts our research into the context of related work, before section 6 concludes and provides pointers to future research directions.

2 Corpus

The BBC started subtitling all the scheduled programs on its main channels in 2008, implementing UK regulations designed to help the hearing impaired. Van Heuven et al. (2014) constructed a corpus of subtitles from the programs run by nine TV channels of the BBC, collected over a period of three years, January 2010 to December 2012. They used this corpus to compile an English word frequencies database SUBTLEX-UK[1], as a part of the British Lexicon Project (Keuleers et al., 2012). The subtitles of four channels (CBeebies, CBBC, BBC News and BBC Parliament) were annotated with the channel names.

While CBeebies targets children aged under 6 years, CBBC telecasts programs for children 6–12 years old. The other two channels (News, Parliament) are not assigned to a specific age-group, but it seems safe to assume that they target a broader, adult audience. In sum, we used the BBC subtitle corpus with a three-way categorization: CBeebies, CBBC, Adults.

Table 1 shows the basic statistics for the overall corpus. For our machine learning experiments, we use a balanced subcorpus with 3776 instances for each class. As shown in the table, the programs for

[1] `http://crr.ugent.be/archives/1423`

Program Category	Age group	# texts	avg. tokens per text	avg. sentence length (in words)
CBEEBIES	< 6 years	4846	1144	4.9
CBBC	6–12 years	4840	2710	6.7
Adults (News + Parliament)	> 12 years	3776	4182	12.9

Table 1: BBC Subtitles Corpus Description

the older age-groups tend to be longer (i.e., more words per text) and have longer sentences. While text length and sentence length seem to constitute informative features for predicting the age-group, we hypothesized that other linguistic properties of the language used may be at least as informative as those superficial (and easily manipulated) properties. Hence, we explored a broad linguistic feature set encoding various aspects of complexity.

3 Features

The feature set we experimented with consists of 152 lexical and syntactic features that are primarily derived from the research on text complexity in Second Language Acquisition (SLA) and Psycholinguistics. There are four types of features:

Lexical richness features (LEX): This group consists of various part-of-speech (POS) tag densities, lexical richness features from SLA research, and the average number of senses per word.

Concretely, the POS tag features are: the proportion of words belonging to different parts of speech (nouns, proper nouns, pronouns, determiners, adjectives, verbs, adverbs, conjunctions, interjections, and prepositions) and different verb forms (VBG, VBD, VBN, VBP in the Penn Treebank tagset; Santorini 1990) per document.

The SLA-based lexical richness features we used are: type-token ratio and corrected type-token ratio, lexical density, ratio of nouns, verbs, adjectives and adverbs to the number of lexical words in a document, as described in Lu (2012).

The POS information required to extract these features was obtained using Stanford Tagger (Toutanova et al., 2003). The average number of senses for a non-function word was obtained by using the MIT WordNet API[2] (Finlayson, 2014).

Syntactic complexity features (SYNTAX): This group of features encodes the syntactic complexity of a text derived from the constituent structure of the sentences. Some of these features are derived from SLA research (Lu, 2010), specifically: mean lengths of production units (sentence, clause, t-unit), sentence complexity ratio (# clauses/sentence), subordination in a sentence (# clauses per t-unit, # complex t-units per t-unit, # dependent clauses per clause and t-unit), co-ordination in a sentence (# co-ordinate phrases per clause and t-unit, # t-units/sentence), and specific syntactic structures (# complex nominals per clause and t-unit, # VP per t-unit). Other syntactic complexity features we made use of are the number of NPs, VPs, PPs, and SBARs per sentence and their average length (in terms of # words), the average parse tree height and the average number of constituents per sub-tree.

All of these features were extracted using the Berkeley Parser (Petrov and Klein, 2007) and the Tregex pattern matcher (Levy and Andrew, 2006).

While the selection of features for these two classes is based on Vajjala and Meurers (2012), for the following two sets of features, we explored further information available through psycholinguistic resources.

Psycholinguistic features (PSYCH): This group of features includes an encoding of the average Age-of-acquisition (AoA) of words according to different norms as provided by Kuperman et al. (2012), including their own AoA rating obtained through crowd sourcing. It also includes measures of word familiarity, concreteness, imageability, meaningfulness and AoA as assigned in the MRC Psycholinguistic database[3] (Wilson, 1988). For each feature, the value per text we computed is the average of the values for all the words in the text that had an entry in the database.

While these measures were not developed with readability analysis in mind, we came across one paper using such features as measures of word difficulty in an approach to lexical simplification (Jauhar and Specia, 2012).

[2] http://projects.csail.mit.edu/jwi

[3] http://www.psych.rl.ac.uk/

Celex features (CELEX): The Celex lexical database (Baayen et al., 1995) for English consists of annotations for the morphological, syntactic, orthographic and phonological properties for more than 50k words and lemmas. We included all the morphological and syntactic properties that were encoded using character or numeric codes in our feature set. We did not use frequency information from this database.

In all, this feature set consists of 35 morphological and 49 syntactic properties per lemma. The set includes: proportion of morphologically complex words, attributive nouns, predicative adjectives, etc. in the text. A detailed description of all the properties of the words and lemmas in this database can be found in the Celex English Linguistic Guide[4].

For both the PSYCH and CELEX features, we encode the average value for a given text. Words which were not included in the respective databases were ignored for this computation. On average, around 40% of the words from texts for covered by CELEX, 75% by Kuperman et al. (2012) and 77% by the MRC database.

We do not use any features encoding the occurrence or frequency of specific words or n-grams in a document.

4 Experiments and Results

4.1 Experimental Setup

We used the WEKA toolkit (Hall et al., 2009) to perform our classification experiments and evaluated the classification accuracy using 10-fold cross validation. As classification algorithm, we used the Sequential Minimal Optimization (SMO) implementation in WEKA, which marginally outperformed (1–1.5%) some other classification algorithms (J48 Decision tree, Logistic Regression and Random Forest) we tried in initial experiments.

4.2 Classification accuracy with various feature groups

We discussed in the context of Table 1 that sentence length may be a good surface indicator of the age-group. So, we first constructed a classification model with only one feature. This yielded a classification accuracy of 71.4%, which we consider as our baseline (instead of a basic random baseline of 33%).

[4]http://catalog.ldc.upenn.edu/docs/LDC96L14/eug_a4.pdf

We then constructed a model with all the features we introduced in section 3. This model achieves a classification accuracy of 95.9%, which is a 23.7% improvement over the sentence length baseline in terms of classification accuracy.

In order to understand what features contribute the most to classification accuracy, we applied feature selection on the entire set, using two algorithms available in WEKA, which differ in the way they select feature subsets:

- *InfoGainAttributeEval* evaluates the features individually based on their Information Gain (IG) with respect to the class.
- *CfsSubsetEval* (Hall, 1999) chooses a feature subset considering the correlations between features in addition to their predictive power.

Both feature selection algorithms use methods that are independent of the classification algorithm as such to select the feature subsets.

Information Gain-based feature selection results in a ranked list of features, which are independent of each other. The Top-10 features according to this algorithm are listed in Table 2.

Feature	**Group**
avg. AoA (Kuperman et al., 2012)	PSYCH
avg. # PPs in a sentence	SYNTAX
avg. # instances where the lemma has stem and affix	CELEX
– avg. parse tree height	SYNTAX
– avg. # NPs in a sentence	SYNTAX
avg. # instances of affix substitution	CELEX
– avg. # prep. in a sentence	LEX
avg. # instances where a lemma is not a count noun	CELEX
avg. # clauses per sentence	SYNTAX
– sentence length	SYNTAX

Table 2: Ranked list of Top-10 features using IG

As is clear from their description, all Top-10 features encode different linguistic aspects of a text. While there are more syntactic features followed by Celex features in these Top-10 features, the most predictive feature is a psycholinguistic feature encoding the average age of acquisition of words. A classifier using only the Top-10 IG features achieves an accuracy of 84.5%.

Applying CfsSubsetEval to these Top-10 features set selects the six features not prefixed by a hyphen in the table, indicating that these features do not correlate with each other (much). A classifier using only this subset of 6 features achieves an accuracy of 84.1%.

We also explored the use of CfsSubsetEval feature selection on the entire feature set instead of using only the Top 10 features. From the total of 152 features, CfsSubsetEval selected a set of 41 features. Building a classification model with only these features resulted in a classification accuracy of 93.9% which is only 2% less than the model including all the features.

Table 3 shows the specific feature subset selected by the CfsSubsetEval method, including

preposition phrases
t-units
co-ordinate phrases per t-unit
lexical words in total words
interjections
conjunctive phrases
word senses
verbs
verbs, past participle (VBN)
proper nouns
plural nouns
avg. corrected type-token ratio
avg. AoA acc. to ratings of Kuperman et al. (2012)
avg. AoA acc. to ratings of Cortese and Khanna (2008)
avg. word imageability rating (MRC)
avg. AoA according to MRC
morph. complex words (e.g., *sandbank*)
morph. conversion (e.g., *abandon*)
morph. irrelevant (e.g., *meow*)
morph. obscure (e.g., *dedicate*)
morph. may include root (e.g., *imprimatur*)
foreign words (e.g., *eureka*)
words with multiple analyses (e.g., *treasurer*)
noun verb affix compounds (e.g., *stockholder*)
lemmas with stem and affix (e.g., *abundant=abound+ant*)
flectional forms (e.g., *bagpipes*)
clipping allomorphy (e.g., *phone* vs. *telephone*)
deriv. allomorphy (e.g., *clarify–clarification*)
flectional allomorphy (e.g., verb *bear* $\mapsto$ adjective *born*)
conversion allomorphy (e.g., *halve–half*)
lemmas with affix substitution (e.g., *active=action+ive*)
words with reversion (e.g., *downpour*)
uncountable nouns
collective, countable nouns
collective, uncountable nouns
post positive nouns.
verb, expression (e.g., *bell the cat*)
adverb, expression (e.g., *run amok*)
reflexive pronouns
wh pronouns
determinative pronouns

Table 3: CfsSubsetEval feature subset

some examples illustrating the morphological features. The method does not provide a ranked list, so the features here simply appear in the order in which they are included in the feature vector.
All of these features except for the psycholinguistic features encode the number of occurrences averaged across the text (e.g., average number of prepositions/sentence in a text) unless explicitly stated otherwise. The psycholinguistic features encode the average ratings of words for a given property (e.g., average AoA of words in a text).

Table 4 summarizes the classification accuracies with the different feature subsets seen so far, with the feature count shown in parentheses.

Feature Subset (#)	Accuracy	SD
All Features (152)	95.9%	0.37
Cfs on all features (41)	93.9%	0.59
Top-10 IG features (10)	84.5%	0.70
Cfs on IG (6)	84.1%	0.55

Table 4: Accuracy with various feature subsets

We performed statistical significance tests between the feature subsets using the Paired T-tester (corrected), provided with WEKA and all the differences in accuracy were found to be statistically significant at $p < 0.001$. We also provide the Standard Deviation (SD) of the test set accuracy in the 10 folds of CV per dataset, to make it possible to compare these experiments with future research on this dataset in terms of statistical significance.

Table 5 presents the classification accuracies of individual features from the Top-10 features list (introduced in Table 2).

Feature	Accuracy
AoA_Kup_Lem	82.4%
# pp	74.0%
# stem & affix	77.7%
avg. parse tree height	73.4%
# np	73.0%
# substitution	74.3%
# prep	72.0%
# uncountable nouns	68.3%
# clauses	72.5%
sentence length	71.4%

Table 5: Accuracies of Top-10 individual features

The table shows that all but one of the features individually achieves a classification accuracy above 70%. The first feature (AoA_Kup_Lem) alone resulted in an accuracy of 82.4%, which is quite close to the accuracy obtained by all the Top-10 features together (84.5%).

To obtain a fuller picture of the impact of different feature groups, we also performed ablation tests removing some groups of features at a time. Table 6 shows the results of these tests along with the SD of the 10 fold CV. All the results that are statistically different at $p < 0.001$ from the model with all features (95.9% accuracy, 0.37 SD) are indicated with a *.

Features	**Acc.**	**SD**
All − AoA_Kup_Lem	95.9%	0.37
All − All AoA Features	95.6%	0.58
All − PSYCH	95.8%	0.31
All − CELEX	94.7%*	0.51
All − CELEX − PSYCH	93.6%*	0.66
All − CELEX − PSYCH − LEX (= SYNTAX only)	77.5%*	0.99
LEX	93.1%*	0.70
CELEX	90.0%*	0.79
PSYCH	84.5%*	1.12

Table 6: Ablation test accuracies

Interestingly, removing the most predictive individual feature (AoA_Kup_Lem) from the feature set did not change the overall classification accuracy at all. Removing all of the AoA features or all of the psycholinguistic features also resulted in only a very small drop. The combination of the linguistic features, covering lexical and syntactic characteristics as well as the morphological, syntactic, orthographic, and phonological properties from Celex, thus seem to be equally characteristic of the texts targeting different age-groups as the psycholinguistic properties, even though the features are quite different in nature.

In terms of separate groups of features, syntactic features alone performed the worst (77.5%) and lexical richness features the best (93.1%).

To investigate which classes were mixed up by the classifier, consider Table 7 showing the confusion matrix for the model with all features on a 10-fold CV experiment.

We find that CBeebies is more often confused with the CBBC program for older children (156+214) and very rarely with the program for adults (1+2). The older children programs (CBBC) are more commonly confused with programs for adults (36+58) compared to CBeebies (1+2), which is expected given that the CBBC audience is closer in age to adults than the CBeebies audience.

classified as →	**CBeebies**	**CBBC**	**Adults**
CBeebies (0–6)	3619	156	1
CBBC (6–12)	214	3526	36
Adults (12+)	2	58	3716

Table 7: Confusion Matrix

Summing up, we can conclude from these experiments that the classification of transcripts into age groups can be informed by a wide range of linguistics and psycholinguistic features. While for some practical tasks a few features may be enough to obtain a classification of sufficient accuracy, the more general take-home message is that authentic texts targeting specific age groups exhibit a broad range of linguistics characteristics that are indicative of the complexity of the language used.

4.3 Effect of text size and training data size

When we first introduced the properties of the corpus in Table 1, it appeared that sentence length and the overall text length could be important predictors of the target age-groups. However, the list of Top-10 features based on information gain was dominated by more linguistically oriented syntactic and psycholinguistic features.

Sentence length was only the tenth best feature by information gain and did not figure at all in the 43 features chosen by the CfsSubsetEval method selecting features that are highly correlated with the class prediction while having low correlation between themselves. As mentioned above, sentence length as an individual feature only achieved a classification accuracy of 71.4%.

The text length is not a part of any feature set we used, but considering the global corpus properties we wanted to verify how well it would perform and thus trained a model with only text length (#sentences per text) as a feature. This achieved a classification accuracy of only 56.7%.

The corpus consists of transcripts of whole TV programs and hence an individual transcript text typically is longer than the texts commonly used in readability classification experiments. This raises the question whether the high classification accuracies we obtained are the consequences of the larger text size.

As a second issue, the training size available for the 10-fold cross-validation experiments is comparatively large, given the 3776 text per level available in the overall corpus. We thus also wanted to study the impact of the training size on the classification accuracy achieved.

Pulling these threads together, we compared the classification accuracy against text length and training set size to better understand their impact. For this, we trained models with different text sizes (by considering the first 25%, 50%, 75% or 100% of the sentences from each text) and with different training set sizes (from 10% to 100%).

Figure 1 presents the resulting classification accuracy in relation to training set size for the different text sizes. All models were trained with the full feature set (152 features), using 10-fold cross-validation as before.

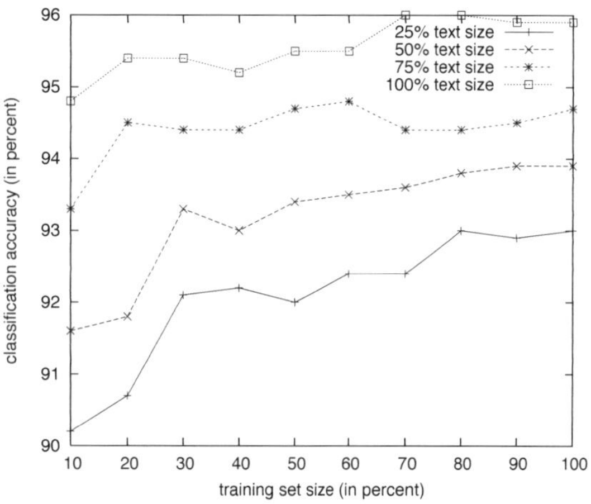

Figure 1: Classification accuracy for different text sizes and training set sizes

As expected, both the training set size and the text size affect the classification accuracy. However, the classification accuracy even for the smallest text and training set size is always above 90%, which means that the unusually large text and training size is not the main factor behind the very high accuracy rates.

In all four cases of text size, there was a small effect of training set size on the classification accuracy. But the effect reduced as the text size increased. At 25% text size, for example, the classification accuracy ranged 90–93% (mean 92.1%, SD 0.9) as the training set size increased from 10% to 100%. However, at 100% text size, the range was only 94.8–96% (mean 95.6%, SD 0.4).

Comparing the results in terms of text size alone, larger text size resulted in better classification accuracy in all cases, irrespective of the training set size. A longer text will simply provide more information for the various linguistic features, enabling the model to deliver better judgments about the text. However, despite the text length being reduced to one fourth of its size, the models built with our feature set always collect enough information to ensure a classification accuracy of at least 90%.

In the above experiments, we varied the text size from 10% to 100%. But since these are percentages, texts from CBBC and Adults on average still are longer than CBEEBIES texts. While this reflects the fact that TV transcripts in real life are of different length, we also wanted to see what happens when we eliminate such length differences.

We thus trained classification models fixing the length of all documents to a concrete absolute length, starting from 100 words (rounded off to the nearest sentence boundary) increasing the text size until we achieve the best overall performance. Figure 2 displays the classification accuracy we obtained for the different (maximum) text sizes, for all features and feature subsets.

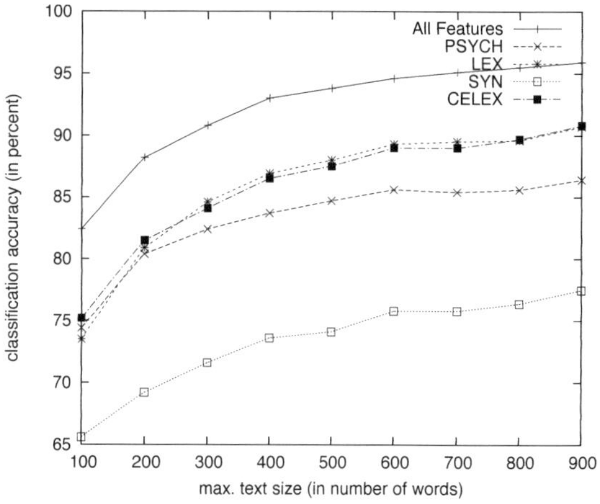

Figure 2: Classification accuracy for different absolute text sizes (in words)

The plot shows that the classification accuracy already reaches 80% accuracy for short texts, 100 words in length, for the model with all features. It rises to above 90% for texts which are 300 words long and reaches the best overall accuracy of almost 96% for texts which are 900 words in length. All the feature subsets too follow the same trend, with varying degrees of accuracy that is always lower than the model with all features.

While in this paper, we focus on documents, the issue whether the data can be reduced further to perform readability at the sentence level is discussed in Vajjala and Meurers (2014a).

5 Related Work

Analyzing the complexity of written texts and choosing suitable texts for various target groups including children is widely studied in computational linguistics. Some of the popular approaches include the use of language models and machine learning approaches (e.g., Collins-Thompson and Callan, 2005; Feng, 2010). Web-based tools such as REAP[5] and TextEvaluator[6] are some examples of real-life applications for selecting English texts by grade level.

In terms of analyzing spoken language, research in language assessment has analyzed spoken transcripts in terms of syntactic complexity (Chen and Zechner, 2011) and other textual characteristics (Crossley and McNamara, 2013).

In the domain of readability assessment, the Common Core Standards (`http://www.corestandards.org`) guideline texts were used as a standard test set in the recent past (Nelson et al., 2012; Flor et al., 2013). This test set contains some transcribed speech. However, to the best of our knowledge, the process of selecting suitable TV programs for children as explored in this paper has not been considered as a case of readability assessment of spoken language before.

Subtitle corpora have been created and used in computational linguistics for various purposes. Some of them include video classification (Katsiouli et al., 2007), machine translation (Petukhova et al., 2012), and simplification for deaf people (Daelemans et al., 2004). But, we are not aware of any such subtitle research studying the problem of automatically identifying TV programs for various age-groups.

This paper thus can be seen as connecting several threads of research, from the analysis of text complexity and readability, via the research on measuring SLA proficiency that many of the linguistic features we used stem from, to the computational analysis of speech as encoded in subtitles. The range of linguistic characteristics which turn out to be relevant and the very high precision with which the age-group classification can be performed, even when restricting the input to artificially shortened transcripts, confirm the usefulness of connecting these research threads.

[5] `http://reap.cs.cmu.edu`

[6] `https://texteval-pilot.ets.org/TextEvaluator`

6 Conclusions

In this paper, we described a classification approach identifying TV programs for different age-groups based on a range of linguistically-motivated features derived from research on text readability, proficiency in SLA, and psycholinguistic research. Using a collection of subtitle documents classified into three groups based on the targeted age-group, we explored different classification models with our feature set.

The experiments showed that our linguistically motivated features perform very well, achieving a classification accuracy of 95.9% (section 4.2). Apart from the entire feature set, we also experimented with small groups of features by applying feature selection algorithms. As it turns out, the single most predictive feature was the age-of-acquisition feature of Kuperman et al. (2012), with an accuracy of 82.4%. Yet when this feature is removed from the overall feature set, the classification accuracy is not reduced, highlighting that such age-group classification is informed by a range of different characteristics, not just a single, dominating one. Authentic texts targeting specific age groups exhibit a broad range of linguistics and psycholinguistic characteristics that are indicative of the complexity of the language used.

While an information gain-based feature subset consisting of 10 features resulted in an accuracy of 84.5%, a feature set chosen using the CfsSubsetEval method in WEKA gave an accuracy of 93.9%. Any of the feature groups we tested exceeded the random baseline (33%) and a baseline using the popular sentence length feature (71.4%) by a large margin. Individual feature groups also performed well at over 90% accurately in most of the cases. The analysis thus supports multiple, equally valid perspectives on a given text, each view encoding a different linguistic aspect.

Apart from the features explored, we also studied the effect of the training set size and the length of the text considered for feature extraction on classification accuracy (Section 4.3). The size of training set mattered more when the text size was smaller. Text size, which did not work well as an individual feature, clearly influences classification accuracy by providing more information for model building and testing.

In terms of the practical relevance of the results, one question that needs some attention is how well the features and trained models generalize across different type of TV programs or languages. While we have not yet investigated this for TV subtitles, in experiments investigating the cross-corpus performance of a model using the same feature set, we found that the approach performs well for a range of corpora composed of reading materials for language learners (Vajjala and Meurers, 2014b). The very high classification accuracies of the experiments we presented in the current paper thus seem to support the assumption that the approach can be useful in practice for automatically identifying TV programs for viewers of different age groups.

Regarding the three class distinctions and the classifier setup we used in this paper, the approach can also be generalized to other scales and a regression setup (Vajjala and Meurers, 2013).

6.1 Outlook

The current work focused mostly on modeling and studying different feature groups in terms of their classification accuracy. Performing error analysis and looking at the texts where the approach failed may yield further insights into the problem. Some aspects of the text that we did not consider include discourse coherence or topic effects. Studying these two aspects can provide more insights into the nature of the language used in TV programs directed at viewers of different ages. A cross-genre evaluation between written and spoken language complexity across age-groups could also be insightful.

On the technical side, it would also be useful to explore the possibility of using a parser tuned to spoken language, to check if this helps improve the classification accuracy of syntactic features.

While in this paper we focused on English, a related readability model also performed well for German (Hancke et al., 2012) so that we expect the general approach to be applicable to other languages, subject to the availability of the relevant resources and tools.

Acknowledgements

We would like to thank Marc Brysbaert and his colleagues for making their excellent resources available to the research community. We also thank the anonymous reviewers for their useful feedback. This research was funded by LEAD Graduate School (GSC 1028, `http://purl.org/lead`), a project of the Excellence Initiative of the German federal and state governments.

References

Harald R. Baayen, Richard Piepenbrock, and Leon Gulikers. 1995. The CELEX lexical database. `http://catalog.ldc.upenn.edu/LDC96L14`.

Maio Chen and Klaus Zechner. 2011. Computing and evaluating syntactic complexity features for automated scoring of spontaneous non-native speech. In *Proceedings of the 49th Annual Meeting of the Association for Computational Linguistics (ACL)*, pages 722–731, Portland, Oregon, June.

Kevyn Collins-Thompson and Jamie Callan. 2005. Predicting reading difficulty with statistical language models. *Journal of the American Society for Information Science and Technology*, 56(13):1448–1462.

Michael J. Cortese and Maya M. Khanna. 2008. Age of acquisition ratings for 3,000 monosyllabic words. *Behavior Research Methods*, 43:791–794.

Scott Crossley and Danielle McNamara. 2013. Applications of text analysis tools for spoken response grading. *Language Learning & Technology*, 17:171–192.

Walter Daelemans, Anja Hoethker, and Erik F. Tjong Kim Sang. 2004. Automatic sentence simplification for subtitling in Dutch and English. In *Fourth International Conference on Language Resources And Evaluation (LREC)*, pages 1045–1048.

Lijun Feng. 2010. *Automatic Readability Assessment*. Ph.D. thesis, City University of New York (CUNY).

Mark Alan Finlayson. 2014. Java libraries for accessing the princeton wordnet: Comparison and evaluation. In *Proceedings of the 7th Global Wordnet Conference*, pages 78–85.

Michael Flor, Beata Beigman Klebanov, and Kathleen M. Sheehan. 2013. Lexical tightness and text complexity. In *Proceedings of the Second Workshop on Natural Language Processing for Improving Textual Accessibility (PITR) held at ACL*, pages 29–38, Sofia, Bulgaria. ACL.

Mark Hall, Eibe Frank, Geoffrey Holmes, Bernhard Pfahringer, Peter Reutemann, and Ian H. Witten. 2009. The weka data mining software: An update. *The SIGKDD Explorations*, 11:10–18.

Mark A. Hall. 1999. *Correlation-based Feature Selection for Machine Learning*. Ph.D. thesis, The University of Waikato, Hamilton, NewZealand.

Julia Hancke, Detmar Meurers, and Sowmya Vajjala. 2012. Readability classification for german using lexical, syntactic, and morphological features. In *Proceedings of the 24th International Conference on Computational Linguistics (COLING): Technical Papers*, pages 1063–1080, Mumbai, India.

Sujay Kumar Jauhar and Lucia Specia. 2012. Uowshef: Simplex – lexical simplicity ranking based on contextual and psycholinguistic features. In *In proceedings of the First Joint Conference on Lexical and Computational Semantics (SEM)*.

Polyxeni Katsiouli, Vassileios Tsetsos, and Stathes Hadjiefthymiades. 2007. Semantic video classification based on subtitles and domain terminologies. In *Proceedings of the 1st International Workshop on Knowledge Acquisition from Multimedia Content (KAMC)*.

Emmanuel Keuleers, Paula Lacey, Kathleen Rastle, and Marc Brysbaert. 2012. The british lexicon project: Lexical decision data for 28,730 monosyllabic and disyllabic english words. *Behavior Research Methods*, 44:287–304.

Victor Kuperman, Hans Stadthagen-Gonzalez, and Marc Brysbaert. 2012. Age-of-acquisition ratings for 30,000 english words. *Behavior Research Methods*, 44(4):978–990.

Roger Levy and Galen Andrew. 2006. Tregex and tsurgeon: tools for querying and manipulating tree data structures. In *5th International Conference on Language Resources and Evaluation*, pages 2231–2234, Genoa, Italy. European Language Resources Association (ELRA).

Xiaofei Lu. 2010. Automatic analysis of syntactic complexity in second language writing. *International Journal of Corpus Linguistics*, 15(4):474–496.

Xiaofei Lu. 2012. The relationship of lexical richness to the quality of ESL learners' oral narratives. *The Modern Languages Journal*, pages 190–208.

Jessica Nelson, Charles Perfetti, David Liben, and Meredith Liben. 2012. Measures of text difficulty: Testing their predictive value for grade levels and student performance. Technical report, The Council of Chief State School Officers.

Slav Petrov and Dan Klein. 2007. Improved inference for unlexicalized parsing. In *Human Language Technologies 2007: The Conference of the North American Chapter of the Association for Computational Linguistics; Proceedings of the Main Conference*, pages 404–411, Rochester, New York, April.

Volha Petukhova, Rodrigo Agerri, Mark Fishel, Yota Georgakopoulou, Sergio Penkale, Arantza del Pozo, Mirjam Sepesy Maucec, Martin Volk, and Andy Way. 2012. Sumat: Data collection and parallel corpus compilation for machine translation of subtitles. In *Proceedings of the Eighth International Conference on Language Resources and Evaluation (LREC-2012)*, pages 21–28, Istanbul, Turkey. European Language Resources Association (ELRA).

Beatrice Santorini. 1990. Part-of-speech tagging guidelines for the Penn Treebank, 3rd revision, 2nd printing. Technical report, Department of Computer Science, University of Pennsylvania.

Kristina Toutanova, Dan Klein, Christopher D. Manning, and Yoram Singer. 2003. Feature-rich partofspeech tagging with a cyclic dependency network. In *HLT-NAACL*, pages 252–259, Edmonton, Canada.

Sowmya Vajjala and Detmar Meurers. 2012. On improving the accuracy of readability classification using insights from second language acquisition. In *In Proceedings of the 7th Workshop on Innovative Use of NLP for Building Educational Applications (BEA) at NAACL-HLT*, pages 163—-173, Montréal, Canada. ACL.

Sowmya Vajjala and Detmar Meurers. 2013. On the applicability of readability models to web texts. In *Proceedings of the Second Workshop on Natural Language Processing for Improving Textual Accessibility (PITR) held at ACL*, pages 59—-68, Sofia, Bulgaria. ACL.

Sowmya Vajjala and Detmar Meurers. 2014a. Assessing the relative reading level of sentence pairs for text simplification. In *Proceedings of the 14th Conference of the European Chapter of the Association for Computational Linguistics (EACL)*. ACL.

Sowmya Vajjala and Detmar Meurers. 2014b. Readability assessment for text simplification: From analyzing documents to identifying sentential simplifications. *International Journal of Applied Linguistics, Special Issue on Current Research in Readability and Text Simplification, edited by Thomas François and Delphine Bernhard.*

Walter J.B. Van Heuven, Pawel Mandera, Emmanuel Keuleers, and Marc Brysbaert. 2014. Subtlex-UK: A new and improved word frequency database for British English. *The Quarterly Journal of Experimental Psychology*, pages 1–15.

Michael D. Wilson. 1988. The mrc psycholinguistic database: Machine readable dictionary, version 2. *Behavioural Research Methods, Instruments and Computers*, 20(1):6–11.

Keyword Highlighting Improves Comprehension for People with Dyslexia

Luz Rello
NLP & Web Research Groups
Universitat Pompeu Fabra
Barcelona, Spain
luzrello@acm.org

Horacio Saggion
NLP Research Group
Universitat Pompeu Fabra
Barcelona, Spain
horacio.saggion@upf.edu

Ricardo Baeza-Yates
Yahoo Labs Barcelona &
Web Research Group, UPF
Barcelona, Spain
rbaeza@acm.org

Abstract

The use of certain font types and sizes improve the reading performance of people with dyslexia. However, the impact of combining such features with the semantics of the text has not yet been studied. In this eye-tracking study with 62 people (31 with dyslexia), we explore whether highlighting the main ideas of the text in boldface has an impact on readability and comprehensibility. We found that highlighting keywords improved the comprehension of participants with dyslexia. To the best of our knowledge, this is the first result of this kind for people with dyslexia.

1 Introduction

Dyslexia is a neurological reading disability which is characterized by difficulties with accurate and/or fluent word recognition as well as by poor spelling and decoding abilities. These difficulties typically result from a deficit in the phonological component of language that is often unrelated to other cognitive disabilities. Secondary consequences include problems in reading comprehension and reduced reading experience that can impede vocabulary growth and background knowledge (International Dyslexia Association, 2011).

From 10 to 17.5% of the population in the U.S.A. (Interagency Commission on Learning Disabilities, 1987) and from 8.6 to 11% of the Spanish speaking population (Carrillo et al., 2011; Jiménez et al., 2009) have dyslexia. Even if dyslexia is also popularly identified with brilliant famous people, the most frequent way to detect a child with dyslexia is by low-performance in school (Carrillo et al., 2011). In Spain, it is estimated that four out of six cases of school failure are related to dyslexia.[1] The prevalence of dyslexia and its impact in school failure are the main motivations of our work.

Previous eye-tracking studies with people with dyslexia have shown that their reading performance can improve when the presentation of the text contains certain font types (Rello and Baeza-Yates, 2013) or font sizes (O'Brien et al., 2005; Dickinson et al., 2002; Rello et al., 2013c).

Keywords – or key-phrases[2]– are words that capture the main ideas of a text. Highlighting keywords in the text is a well known strategy to support reading tasks (Weinstein and Mayer, 1986). In fact, highlighting keywords is recommended to students with dyslexia (Hargreaves, 2007), as well as to teachers for making texts more accessible for this target group (Peer and Reid, 2001).

Here, we present the first study which explores the modification of the text presentation in relationship with its semantics, by highlighting keywords. We measure the impact of highlighting the text on the reading performance (readability and comprehensibility) of people with dyslexia using eye-tracking. Our hypotheses are:

- **H1:** *The presence of highlighted keywords in the text increases readability for people with dyslexia.*
- **H2:** *The presence of highlighted keywords in the text increases comprehensibility for people with dyslexia.*

Next section reviews related work, while Section 3 explains the experimental methodology. Section 4 presents the results, which are discussed in Section 5. In Section 6 we draw the conclusions and we mention future lines of research.

[1]The percentage of school failure is calculated by the number or students who drop school before finishing secondary education (high school). While the average of school failure in the European Union is around 15%, Spain has around 25-30% of school failure, 31% in 2010 (Enguita et al., 2010).

[2]We use "keywords", meaning also "key-phrase", to refer to both single words or phrases that are highlighted.

2 Related Work

Related work to ours can be found in: (1) natural language processing (NLP) literature about key-phrase and keyword extraction (Section 2.1), and (2) accessibility literature about dyslexia and keywords (Section 2.2).

2.1 Key-phrase and Keyword Extraction

There is a vast amount of NLP literature on key-phrase extraction (Kim et al., 2010; Witten et al., 1999; Frank et al., 1999).

The semantic data provided by key-phrase extraction can be used as metadata for refining NLP applications, such as summarization (D'Avanzo and Magnini, 2005; Lawrie et al., 2001), text ranking (Mihalcea and Tarau, 2004), indexing (Medelyan and Witten, 2006), query expansion (Song et al., 2006), or document management and topic search (Gutwin et al., 1999).

The closest work to ours is (Turney, 1999) because they highlight key-phrases in the text to facilitate its skimming. They compare the highlighting outputs of two different systems, *Search 97* and *GenEx*, using six corpora belonging to different genre.

2.2 Accessibility

In accessibility and education literature, highlighting keywords is a broadly recommended learning strategy (Weinstein and Mayer, 1986). Regarding students with dyslexia, teachers are encouraged to highlight keywords to make texts more accessible (Peer and Reid, 2001; Hargreaves, 2007). These recommendations are based on qualitative analysis and direct observations with students.

In the applications for people with dyslexia highlighting is used not for keywords or main ideas but to help users for tracking their position when reading such as in *ScreenRuler* (ClaroSoftware, 2012). Sometimes highlighting is used simultaneously with text-to-speech technology (Kanvinde et al., 2012; ClaroSoftware, 2012). In the *SeeWord* tool for *MS Word* (Dickinson et al., 2002; Gregor et al., 2003), highlighting is used on the letters where people with dyslexia normally make mistakes in order to attract the user's attention.

Previous studies similar to ours have used eye-tracking to show how people with dyslexia can read significantly faster as using certain font types (Rello and Baeza-Yates, 2013) or font sizes (O'Brien et al., 2005; Dickinson et al., 2002; Rello et al., 2013c).

2.3 What is Missing?

First, we did not find any study that measured objectively the impact of highlighting keywords in a text on the readability and comprehensibility for people with dyslexia. Second, to the best of our knowledge, there are no studies in assistive technology that uses an NLP based engine to highlight keywords for people with dyslexia. In this work we address the first issue, taking the second one into consideration. Hence, we emulated in the experiment the output that a potential NLP tool would give for highlighting the main ideas in the text.

3 Methodology

To study the effect of keywords on readability and comprehensibility of texts on the screen, we conducted an experiment where 62 participants (31 with dyslexia) had to read two texts on a screen, where one of them had the main ideas highlighted using boldface. Readability and comprehensibility were measured via eye-tracking and comprehension tests, respectively. The participants' preferences were gathered via a subjective ratings questionnaire.

3.1 Design

In the experiment there was one condition, *Keywords*, with two levels: [+keywords] denotes the condition where main ideas of the text were highlighted in boldface and [−keywords] denotes the condition where the presentation of the text was not modified.

The experiments followed a within-subjects design, so every participant contributed to each of the levels of the condition. The order of the conditions was counter-balanced to cancel out sequence effects.

When measuring the reading performance of people with dyslexia we need to separate *readability*[3] from *comprehensibility*[4] because they are not necessarily related. In the case of dyslexia, texts that might seen not readable for the general population, such as texts with errors, can be better understood by people with dyslexia, and *vice versa*,

[3]The ease with which a text can be read.

[4]The ease with which a text can be understood.

people with dyslexia find difficulties with standard texts (Rello and Baeza-Yates, 2012).

To measure *readability* we consider two dependent variables derived from the eye-tracking data: *Reading Time* and *Fixation Duration*. To measure *comprehensibility* we used a comprehension score as dependent variable.

- *Fixation Duration.* When reading a text, the eye does not move contiguously over the text, but alternates saccades and visual fixations, that is, jumps in short steps and rests on parts of the text. *Fixation duration* denotes how long the eye rests on a single place of the text. Fixation duration has been shown to be a valid indicator of readability. According to (Rayner and Duffy, 1986; Hyönä and Olson, 1995), shorter fixations are associated with better readability, while longer fixations can indicate that the processing load is greater. On the other hand, it is not directly proportional to reading time as some people may fixate more often in or near the same piece of text (re-reading). Hence, we used fixation duration average as an objective approximation of readability.

- *Reading Time.* The total time it takes a participant to completely read one text. Shorter reading durations are preferred to longer ones, since faster reading is related to more readable texts (Williams et al., 2003). Therefore, we use *Reading Time*, that is, the time it takes a participant to completely read one text, as a measure of readability, in addition to *Fixation Duration*.

- *Comprehension Score.* To measure text comprehensibility we used inferential items, that is, questions that require a deep understanding of the content of the text. We used multiple-choice questions with three possible choices, one correct, and two wrong. We compute the text comprehension score as the number of correct answers divided by the total number of questions.

- *Subjective Ratings.* In addition, we asked the participants to rate on a five-point Likert scale their personal preferences and perception about how helpful the highlighted keywords were.

3.2 Participants

We had 62 native Spanish speakers, 31 with a confirmed diagnosis of dyslexia.[5] The ages of the participants with dyslexia ranged from 13 to 37, with a mean age of 21.09 years (s = 8.18). The ages of the control group ranged from 13 to 40, with a mean age of 23.03 years (s = 7.10).

Regarding the group with dyslexia, three of them were also diagnosed with attention deficit disorder. Fifteen people were studying or already finished university degrees, fourteen were attending school or high school, and two had no higher education. All participants were frequent readers and the level of education was similar for the control group.

3.3 Materials

In this section we describe how we designed the texts and keywords that were used as study material, as well as the comprehension and subjective ratings questionnaires.

Base Texts. We picked two similar texts from the Spanish corpus Simplext (Bott and Saggion, 2012). To meet the comparability requirements among the texts belonging to the same experiment, we adapted the texts maintaining as much as possible the original text. We matched the readability of the texts by making sure that the parameters commonly used to compute readability (Drndarevic and Saggion, 2012), had the same or similar values. Both texts:

(a) are written in the same genre (news);

(b) are about similar topics (culture);

(c) have the same number of words (158 words):

(d) have a similar word length average (4.83 and 5.61 letters);

(e) are accessible news, readable for the general public so they contained no rare or technical words, which present an extra difficulty for people with dyslexia (Rello et al., 2013a).

(f) have the same number of proper names (one per text);

[5]All of them presented official clinical results to prove that dyslexia was diagnosed in an authorized center or hospital. The Catalonian protocol of dyslexia diagnosis (Speech Therapy Association of Catalonia, 2011) does not consider different kinds of dyslexia.

The Museo Picasso Málaga includes **new works of the artist** in its permanent collection

The Andalusian Minister of Culture, Paulino Plata, presented a **new reorganization of the permanent collection of the Picasso Museum** that, coinciding with the birth anniversary of the painter, incorporates a **wide selection of works by Pablo Picasso** provided by the Almine and Bernard Ruiz-Picasso Foundation for Art. Paintings, sculptures and ceramics from different periods and styles compose this **set of 43 pieces** given for 15 years by the mentioned foundation. The incorporation of these creations assumes, according to the Andalusian Council, a **valuable contribution to the permanent collection of the Museum Picasso Málaga**. In this way, a visitor can now contemplate **paintings and sculptures** that, for the first time, are exposed in the gallery.

Figure 1: Example slide used in the experiment.

(g) have the same number of sentences (five per text) and similar sentence complexity (three sentences per text contain relative clauses);

(h) one text has two numerical expressions (Rello et al., 2013b) and the other has two foreign words (Cuetos and Valle, 1988), both being elements of similar difficulty; and

(i) have the same number of highlighted key-phrases.

An example of a text used (translation from Spanish[6]) is given in Figure 1.

Keywords. For creating the keywords we highlighted using boldface the words which contained the main semantic meaning (focus) of the sentence. This focus normally corresponds with the direct object and contains the new and most relevant information of the sentence (Sperber and Wilson, 1986). We only focused on the main sentences; subordinate or relative clauses were dismissed. For the syntactic analysis of the sentences we used Connexor's Machinese Syntax (Connexor Oy, 2006), a statistical syntactic parser that employes a functional dependency grammar (Tapanainen and Järvinen, 1997). We took direct objects parsed by Connexor without correcting the output.

Comprehension Questionnaires. For each text we manually create three inferential items. The order of the correct answer was counterbalanced and all questions have similar difficulty. An example question is given in Figure 2.

Subjective Questionnaire. The participants rated how much did the keywords helped their reading,

El texto habla de: *'The text is about:'*

- Sobre la obra del pintor y escultor Picasso. *'The work of the painter and sculptor Picasso.'*
- Sobre la Fundación Almine y Bernard Ruiz-Picasso para el Arte. *'The Almine and Bernard Ruiz-Picasso Foundation for Arts.'*
- Sobre incorporación de nuevas obras en el museo Picasso de Málaga. *'About incorporation of new works in the Picasso Museum of Malaga.'*

Figure 2: Comprehension questionnaire item.

their ease to remember the text, and to which extent would they like to find keywords in texts.

Text Presentation. The presentation of the text has an effect on reading speed of people with dyslexia (Kurniawan and Conroy, 2006; Gregor and Newell, 2000). Therefore, we used a text layout that follows the recommendations of previous research. As font type, we chose *Arial, sans serif*, as recommended in (Rello and Baeza-Yates, 2013). The text was left-justified, as recommended by the British Association of Dyslexia (British Dyslexia Association, 2012). Each line did not exceeded 62 characters/column, the font size was 20 point, and the colors used were black font with creme background,[7] as recommended in (Rello et al., 2012).

3.4 Equipment

The eye-tracker used was the Tobii T50 that has a 17-inch TFT monitor with a resolution of 1024×768 pixels. It was calibrated for each participant and the light focus was always in the same position. The time measurements of the eye-tracker have a precision of 0.02 seconds. The dis-

[6] www.luzrello.com/picasso

[7] The CYMK are creme (FAFAC8) and black (000000). Color difference: 700. Brightness difference: 244.

tance between the participant and the eye-tracker was constant (approximately 60 cm. or 24 in.) and controlled by using a fixed chair.

3.5 Procedure

The sessions were conducted at Universitat Pompeu Fabra in a quiet room and lasted from 20 to 30 minutes. First, we began with a questionnaire to collect demographic information. Then, we conducted the experiment using eye-tracking. The participants were asked to read the texts in silence and to complete the comprehension tests after each text read. Finally, we carried out the subjective ratings questionnaire.

4 Results

None of the datasets were normally distributed (Shapiro-Wilk test) and neither of them had an homogeneous variance (Levene test). Hence, to study the effect of *Keywords* on readability and comprehensibility we used the Wilcoxon non-parametric test for repeated measures.

4.1 Differences between Groups

We found a significant difference between the groups regarding *Reading Time* ($W = 2578.5, p < 0.001$), *Fixation Duration* ($W = 2953, p < 0.001$) and *Comprehension Score* ($W = 1544, p = 0.040$).

Participants with dyslexia had lower comprehension scores and longer reading times and fixations than participants from the control group (see Table 1).

4.2 Readability

We did not find a significant effect of *Keywords* on *Reading Time* for the participants with dyslexia ($W = 210$, $p = 0.688$) and for the participants without dyslexia ($W = 702.5, p = 0.351$).

Similarly, there were found no significant effects of *Keywords* on *Fixation Duration* for the participants with dyslexia ($W = 259.5, p = 0.688$) or without dyslexia ($W = 862, p = 0.552$).

4.3 Comprehension

For the participants with dyslexia, we found a significant effect on the *Comprehension Score* ($W = 178.5, p = 0.022$). Text with highlighted keywords led to significantly higher comprehension scores in this target group.

For the control group we did not find an effect on the *Comprehension Score* ($W = 740, p = 0.155$).

4.4 Subjective Ratings

The debate of what analyses are admissible for Likert scales – parametric or non-parametric tests– is pretty contentious (Carifio and Perla, 2008). A Shapiro-Wilk test showed that the datasets were not normally distributed. Hence, we also used the Wilcoxon non-parametric test.

- *Readability.* We found no significant differences between the groups regarding how much highlighting keywords helped them reading the text ($W = 504.5, p = 0.316$).

  Both groups found that keywords can slightly help their reading ($\tilde{x} = 3$, $\bar{x} = 3.0, s = 1.155$)[8] for the participants with dyslexia, and ($\tilde{x} = 3$, $\bar{x} = 2.8, s = 0.966$) for the control group.

- *Memorability.* We found no significant differences between the groups regarding if highlighting keywords help to memorize the text ($W = 484, p = 0.493$).

  Both agree that keywords help them to remember the text moderately ($\tilde{x} = 4$, $\bar{x} = 3.636, s = 1.002$) for the participants with dyslexia and ($\tilde{x} = 4$, $\bar{x} = 3.450, s = 1.085$) for the control group.

- *Preferences.* Also, no differences between groups were found regarding their preferences in finding highlighted keywords in the texts ($W = 463, p = 0.727$).

  Participants with dyslexia would like to find texts including highlighted keywords ($\tilde{x} = 4$, $\bar{x} = 3.636, s = 1.136$), as well as in the control group ($\tilde{x} = 4, \bar{x} = 3.600, s = 1.057$).

5 Discussion

Regarding the differences between the groups, our results are consistent with other eye-tracking studies to diagnose dyslexia that found statistical differences (Eden et al., 1994).

[8]We use $\tilde{x}$ for the median, and s for the standard deviation.

Dependent Variable ($\mu \pm s$)	[+Keywords]	[−Keywords]
	Group with Dyslexia	
Reading Time (s)	59.98 ± 25.32	53.71 ± 18.42
Fixation Duration (s)	0.22 ± 0.06	0.23 ± 0.060
Comprehension Score (%)	100 ± 0	77.27 ± 42.89
	Control Group	
Reading Time (s)	36.31 ± 15.17	33.81 ± 12.82
Fixation Duration (s)	0.18 ± 0.04	0.19 ± 0.04
Comprehension Score (%)	100 ± 0	94.87 ± 22.35

Table 1: Results of the *Keywords* experiment.

5.1 Hypothesis 1

Shorter reading times and fixation durations are associated with better readability (Just and Carpenter, 1980). Since *Keywords* had no significant effect on readability, we cannot confirm **H.1**: *The presence of highlighted keywords in the text increases readability for people with dyslexia.*

One possible reason for this is that text presentation might only have an impact on readability when the whole text is modified, not only portions of it. Most probably, if one text was presented all in boldface or italics and the other one in roman, significant differences could have been found as in (Rello and Baeza-Yates, 2013) where the effect of different font styles was evaluated. Another explanation could be that the text might look different to what the participants were used to see and participants might need some time to get used to highlighted keywords in the text before testing readability effects.

From the content point of view, the fact that the readability did not change as expected, since the content of the text is not modified in any of the conditions.

5.2 Hypothesis 2

Because participants with dyslexia had a significantly increase in text comprehension with texts having highlighted keywords, our findings support **H.2**: *The presence of highlighted keywords in the text increases comprehensibility for people with dyslexia.*

This improvement might be due to the possibility that keywords might help to remember the text better. This is consistent with the pedagogic literature that recommends this strategy for learning and retaining text content (Weinstein and Mayer, 1986).

5.3 Subjective Perception of Keywords

The fact that using keywords for learning is a shared strategy for both groups (Weinstein and Mayer, 1986), may explain that no significant differences between groups were found regarding their preference and perception of keywords on readability and memorability. Also, highlighted keywords in bold are found in general school books, not only in materials for people with dyslexia, so both groups were familiar with the conditions.

5.4 Limitations

This study has at least two limitations. First, the study was performed with a manually annotated dataset. These annotations were based on the output of the Connexor parser. We have not found any evaluation of Connexor's accuracy when parsing syntactic constituents. Nevertheless, it has been observed that the accuracy for direct objects in Spanish achieves results that varies from 85.7% to 93.1%, depending on the test set (Padró et al., 2013). Second, the participants read only two texts because we did not wanted to fatigue participants with dyslexia. Now that we have observed that they could have read more texts, we will carry out further studies with more texts that will incorporate automatic keyword extraction.

6 Conclusions and Future Work

Our main conclusion is that highlighted keywords in the text increases the comprehension by people with dyslexia. For the control group no effects were found. Our results support previous educational recommendations by adding the analysis of the impact of highlighting keywords using objective measures.

These results can have impact on systems that rely on text as the main information medium. By applying keyword extraction automatically and highlighting them, digital texts could become easier to understand by people with dyslexia.

Future work include the integration of automatic keyword extraction and its evaluation using a larger number of texts. Also, different strategies to select keywords will be explored and the comprehension questionnaires will be enriched combining inferential and literal questions. Future work also includes testing memorability using objective measures in addition to the subjective responses of the participants.

Acknowledgements

We are grateful to the three anonymous reviewers for their comments and suggestions. We acknowledge the support from grant TIN2012-38584-C06-03 (SKATER-UPF-TALN) from Ministerio de Economía y Competitividad, Secretaría de Estado de Investigación, Desarrollo e Innovación, Spain.

References

S. Bott and H. Saggion. 2012. Text simplification tools for Spanish. In *Proc. LREC'12*, Istanbul, Turkey, May. ELRA.

British Dyslexia Association. 2012. Dyslexia style guide, January. `www.bdadyslexia.org.uk/`.

J. Carifio and R. Perla. 2008. Resolving the 50-year debate around using and misusing Likert scales. *Medical education*, 42(12):1150–1152.

M. S. Carrillo, J. Alegría, P. Miranda, and N. Sánchez Pérez. 2011. Evaluación de la dislexia en la escuela primaria: Prevalencia en español (Evaluation of dyslexia in primary school: The prevalence in Spanish). *Escritos de Psicología (Psychology Writings)*, 4(2):35–44.

ClaroSoftware. 2012. Screenruler. `www.clarosoftware.com/index.php?cPath=348`.

Connexor Oy, 2006. *Machinese language model*. Connexor Oy, Helsinki, Finland.

F. Cuetos and F. Valle. 1988. Modelos de lectura y dislexias (Reading models and dyslexias). *Infancia y Aprendizaje (Infancy and Learning)*, 44:3–19.

E. D'Avanzo and B.Magnini. 2005. A keyphrase-based approach to summarization: the lake system at duc-2005. In *Proceedings of DUC*.

A. Dickinson, P. Gregor, and A.F. Newell. 2002. Ongoing investigation of the ways in which some of the problems encountered by some dyslexics can be alleviated using computer techniques. In *Proc. ASSETS'02*, pages 97–103, Edinburgh, Scotland.

B. Drndarevic and H. Saggion. 2012. Towards automatic lexical simplification in Spanish: an empirical study. In *Proc. NAACL HLT'12 Workshop PITR'12*, Montreal, Canada.

G.F. Eden, J.F. Stein, H.M. Wood, and F.B. Wood. 1994. Differences in eye movements and reading problems in dyslexic and normal children. *Vision Research*, 34(10):1345–1358.

M. Fernández Enguita, L. Mena Martínez, and J. Riviere Gómez. 2010. *Fracaso y abandono escolar en España (School Failure in Spain)*. Obra Social, Fundación la Caixa.

E. Frank, G.W. Paynter, I.H. Witten, C. Gutwin, and C. Nevill-Manning. 1999. Domain-specific keyphrase extraction. In *Proc. Sixteenth International Joint Conference on Artificial Intelligence (IJCAI 1999)*. Morgan Kaufmann Publishers Inc., San Francisco, CA, USA.

P. Gregor and A. F. Newell. 2000. An empirical investigation of ways in which some of the problems encountered by some dyslexics may be alleviated using computer techniques. In *Proc. ASSETS'00*, ASSETS 2000, pages 85–91, New York, NY, USA. ACM Press.

P. Gregor, A. Dickinson, A. Macaffer, and P. Andreasen. 2003. Seeword: a personal word processing environment for dyslexic computer users. *British Journal of Educational Technology*, 34(3):341–355.

C. Gutwin, G. Paynter, I. Witten, C. Nevill-Manning, and E. Frank. 1999. Improving browsing in digital libraries with keyphrase indexes. *Decision Support Systems*, 27(1):81–104.

S. Hargreaves. 2007. *Study skills for dyslexic students*. Sage.

J. Hyönä and R.K. Olson. 1995. Eye fixation patterns among dyslexic and normal readers: Effects of word length and word frequency. *Journal of Experimental Psychology: Learning, Memory, and Cognition*, 21(6):1430.

Interagency Commission on Learning Disabilities. 1987. *Learning Disabilities: A Report to the U.S. Congress*. Government Printing Office, Washington DC, U.S.

International Dyslexia Association. 2011. Definition of dyslexia: `interdys.org/DyslexiaDefinition.htm`. Based in the initial definition of the Research Committee of the Orton Dyslexia Society, former name of the IDA, done in 1994.

J. E. Jiménez, R. Guzmán, C. Rodríguez, and C. Artiles. 2009. Prevalencia de las dificultades específicas de aprendizaje: La dislexia en español (the prevalence of specific learning difficulties: Dyslexia in Spanish). *Anales de Psicología (Annals of Psychology)*, 25(1):78–85.

M.A. Just and P.A. Carpenter. 1980. A theory of reading: From eye fixations to comprehension. *Psychological review*, 87:329–354.

G. Kanvinde, L. Rello, and R. Baeza-Yates. 2012. IDEAL: a dyslexic-friendly e-book reader (poster). In *Proc. ASSETS'12*, pages 205–206, Boulder, USA, October.

S.N. Kim, O. Medelyan, M.Y. Kan, and T. Baldwin. 2010. Semeval-2010 task 5: Automatic keyphrase extraction from scientific articles. In *Proceedings of the 5th International Workshop on Semantic Evaluation*, pages 21–26. Association for Computational Linguistics.

S. Kurniawan and G. Conroy. 2006. Comparing comprehension speed and accuracy of online information in students with and without dyslexia. *Advances in Universal Web Design and Evaluation: Research, Trends and Opportunities, Idea Group Publishing, Hershey, PA*, pages 257–70.

D. Lawrie, W.B. Croft, and A. Rosenberg. 2001. Finding topic words for hierarchical summarization. In *Proceedings of the 24th annual international ACM SIGIR conference on Research and development in information retrieval*, pages 349–357. ACM Press.

O. Medelyan and I.H. Witten. 2006. Thesaurus based automatic keyphrase indexing. In *Proceedings of the 6th ACM/IEEE-CS joint conference on Digital libraries*, pages 296–297. ACM Press.

Rada M. and P. Tarau. 2004. Textrank: Bringing order into texts. In *Proceedings of EMNLP*, volume 4. Barcelona, Spain.

B.A. O'Brien, J.S. Mansfield, and G.E. Legge. 2005. The effect of print size on reading speed in dyslexia. *Journal of Research in Reading*, 28(3):332–349.

M. Padró, M. Ballesteros, H. Martínez, and B. Bohnet. 2013. Finding dependency parsing limits over a large spanish corpus. In *Proceedings of 5th International Joint Conference on Natural Language Processing*, Nagoya, Japan, October.

L. Peer and G. Reid. 2001. *Dyslexia: Successful inclusion in the secondary school*. Routledge.

K. Rayner and S.A. Duffy. 1986. Lexical complexity and fixation times in reading: Effects of word frequency, verb complexity, and lexical ambiguity. *Memory & Cognition*, 14(3):191–201.

L. Rello and R. Baeza-Yates. 2012. Lexical quality as a proxy for web text understandability (poster). In *Proc. WWW '12*, pages 591–592, Lyon, France.

L. Rello and R. Baeza-Yates. 2013. Good fonts for dyslexia. In *Proc. ASSETS'13*, Bellevue, Washington, USA. ACM Press.

L. Rello, G. Kanvinde, and R. Baeza-Yates. 2012. Layout guidelines for web text and a web service to improve accessibility for dyslexics. In *Proc. W4A '12*, Lyon, France. ACM Press.

L. Rello, R. Baeza-Yates, L. Dempere, and H. Saggion. 2013a. Frequent words improve readability and short words improve understandability for people with dyslexia. In *Proc. INTERACT '13*, Cape Town, South Africa.

L. Rello, S. Bautista, R. Baeza-Yates, P. Gervás, R. Hervás, and H. Saggion. 2013b. One half or 50%? An eye-tracking study of number representation readability. In *Proc. INTERACT '13*, Cape Town, South Africa.

L. Rello, M. Pielot, M. C. Marcos, and R. Carlini. 2013c. Size matters (spacing not): 18 points for a dyslexic-friendly Wikipedia. In *Proc. W4A '13*, Rio de Janeiro, Brazil.

M. Song, I. Y. Song, R. B. Allen, and Z. Obradovic. 2006. Keyphrase extraction-based query expansion in digital libraries. In *Proceedings of the 6th ACM/IEEE-CS joint conference on Digital libraries*, pages 202–209. ACM Press.

Speech Therapy Association of Catalonia. 2011. *PRODISCAT: Protocol de detecció i actuació en la dislèxia. Àmbit Educativo (Protocol for detection and management of dyslexia. Educational scope.)*. Education Department of Catalonia.

D. Sperber and D. Wilson. 1986. *Relevance: Communication and cognition*, volume 142. Harvard University Press Cambridge, MA.

P. Tapanainen and T. Järvinen. 1997. A non-projective dependency parser. In *Proceedings of the 5th Conference on Applied Natural Language Processing (ANLP-97)*, pages 64–71.

P. Turney. 1999. Learning to extract keyphrases from text. In *National Research Council, Institute for Information Technology, Technical Report ERB-1057*.

C.E. Weinstein and R.E. Mayer. 1986. The teaching of learning strategies. *Handbook of research on teaching*, 3:315–327.

S. Williams, E. Reiter, and L. Osman. 2003. Experiments with discourse-level choices and readability. In *Proc. ENLG '03)*, Budapest, Hungary.

I.H. Witten, G.W. Paynter, E. Frank, C. Gutwin, and D.G. Nevill-Manning. 1999. Kea: Practical automatic keyphrase extraction. In *Proceedings of the fourth ACM conference on Digital libraries*, pages 254–255. ACM Press.

An eye-tracking evaluation of some parser complexity metrics

Matthew J. Green
University of Aberdeen, UK
mjgreen@abdn.ac.uk

Abstract

Information theoretic measures of incremental parser load were generated from a phrase structure parser and a dependency parser and then compared with incremental eye movement metrics collected for the same temporarily syntactically ambiguous sentences, focussing on the disambiguating word. The findings show that the *surprisal* and *entropy reduction* metrics computed over a phrase structure grammar make good candidates for predictors of text readability for human comprehenders. This leads to a suggestion for the use of such metrics in Natural Language Generation (NLG).

1 Introduction

This work aims to predict automatically how difficult a generated sentence will be for a person to read. Temporarily syntactically ambiguous sentences were presented along with pre-disambiguated controls to people to read while their eye movements were recorded. The same materials were given as input to two NLP parsers, trained on portions of the Wall Street Journal part of the Penn Treebank, that generate incremental word by word metrics of parser load. The metrics of parser load were compared against a standard measure of human sentence processing load *regression path duration*.

The purpose of the present article is to demonstrate that the parser metrics can predict human difficulty for a certain syntactically-ambiguous sentence type (described in the next section). The article also proposes that, if future work shows that the parser metrics here also predict sentence processing difficulty more broadly, then this method would be a useful way for NLG systems to decide on a particular output from among several possible outputs that express the same information.

2 Complement ambiguity

The sentences used in this article were representative of *complement ambiguity*. Sentences like these are syntactically ambiguous until a disambiguating word, which resolves the ambiguity either to *no complement*, *direct object complement*, or *sentential complement*. This section gives the linguistic aspects of this ambiguity type with examples. Material in parentheses indicates how the unambiguous controls were constructed: by means of punctuation indicating the clause boundary in (1); and by means of an overt complementiser establishing the sentential complement in (2). Phrase marker diagrams are given for the examples in Figures (1) and (2).

(1) After the cadet saluted(,) the captain walked to the gates of the enclosure. SENTENCE TYPE 1

(2) The cadet noticed (that) the captain walked to the gates of the enclosure. SENTENCE TYPE 2

Sentential complement ambiguities exploit the properties of 'complement' verbs like *noticed* that can be followed either by a complement clause or by a direct object, or by no complement. When such verbs are followed by complements and an overt complementiser like *that* is used, no temporary syntactic ambiguity is present: however, when the complementiser is omitted, which may be done without violating the grammar, temporary syntactic ambiguity arises with respect to the first few words of the complement. These words may be taken as a direct object instead, and then when the complement verb appears, disambiguation ensues as the words that were taken to be part of a direct object of the verb are revealed necessarily to be part of a complement. Another possibility afforded by the multiple subcategorisation frame of words like *noticed* is that the words immediately following could properly be the start of a main clause where the clause containing *noticed* is properly a subordinate clause. Such cases are sometimes referred to as reduced complements. In these cases only the presence of a main verb resolves the temporary syntactic ambiguity, and when it appears, some major restructuring is involved. Complement ambiguities of both kinds have been used to investigate the parsing of ambiguous clauses (Holmes et al., 1987; Rayner and Frazier, 1987; Sturt et al., 1999; Ferreira and Henderson, 1991; Clifton Jr, 1993; Pickering and Traxler, 1998; Trueswell et al., 1993).

Evidence from studies with human readers support the notion that there is a processing difficulty differential across the two forms such that disambiguation in sentence type (1) is harder than in sentence type (2). This has been shown using grammaticality judgements (Ferreira and Henderson, 1991), self-paced reading times (Sturt et al., 1999), and eye-tracking (Green, 2014).

The current article presents an eye-tracking evaluation of the parser predictions for complement ambiguity, and discusses applications of syntactic complexity metrics for evaluating test readability.

3 Parser metrics

This section gives details of the *surprisal*, *entropy reduction*, and *retrieval time* metrics, and how they are computed.

3.1 Surprisal

Surprisal was computed over a phase structure parser, and over a dependency parser.

Surprisal is computed using two other quantities. These quantities are: (1) the probability of a derivation: a derivation is a set of weighted rule productions that result in the current partial string of input words, such that a sentence fragment with two alternative parses is represented as two derivations; (2) prefix probability: this is the probability of the parse of the fragment seen so far, which is composed of the sum of the probabilities of the two derivations if the fragment is syntactically ambiguous with two alternatives.

Let G be a probabilistic context free grammar (PCFG). Let d be a derivation composed of a sequence of applications of grammar rules. Let i index these applications so that d_i is the ith application in d, and let j be the total number of applications in the derivation. Then the probability p of a derivation d given a grammar G and the current sentence fragment $w_{1...k}$ is given by the product of the probability of each rule applied in the derivation, thus:

$$\mathrm{p}(d, G, w_{1...k}) = \prod_{i=1}^{j} \mathrm{p}(d_i, G, w_{1...k})$$

Let $\mathcal{D}$ represent the set of all derivations d that are present for the current sentence fragment – when there are two alternative parses available for the sentence fragment seen so far, $\mathcal{D}$ has two elements. Let w be the set of words in the sentence fragment seen so far. Let w_k be the word that the parser encountered most recently at the current state. Let w_{k+1} be the first word of the rest of the sentence. As the parser transitions from its state at w_k to its state at w_{k+1} we can derive a *prefix probability* pp at w_{k+1} that represents the sum probability of the derivations of the string $w_{1...k+1}$. So the prefix probability of word w_{k+1} with respect to a probabilistic context free grammar (PCFG) denoted G is given by the sum of the probability of all derivations of the string $w_{1...k+1}$ that the grammar generates.

$$\mathrm{pp}(w_{k+1}, G, w_{1...k}) = \sum_{d \in \mathcal{D}} \mathrm{p}(d, G, w_{1...k})$$

The conditional probability cp of the next word w_{k+1} is the ratio of the prefix probability of the next word w_{k+1} to the prefix probability of the current word w_k.

$$\mathrm{cp}(w_{k+1}, G, w_{1...k}) = \frac{\mathrm{pp}(w_{k+1}, G, w_{1...k})}{\mathrm{pp}(w_k, G, w_{1...k-1})}$$

The surprisal sp, measured in *bits* of information, associated with the next word w_{k+1} is the negative log of the conditional probability of the next word w_{k+1}

$$\mathrm{sp}(w_{k+1}, G, w_{1...k}) = -\log(\mathrm{cp}(w_{k+1}, G, w_{1...k}))$$

The TDPARSE top-down incremental parser provided by Roark (2013) and described in Roark (2001) and Roark (2004) computes surprisal over a phrase structural grammar, incrementally for each word in a sentence. It is a parallel parser that maintains potentially very many parses at each state. For details of how the beam width varies across a sentence, see Roark (2001).

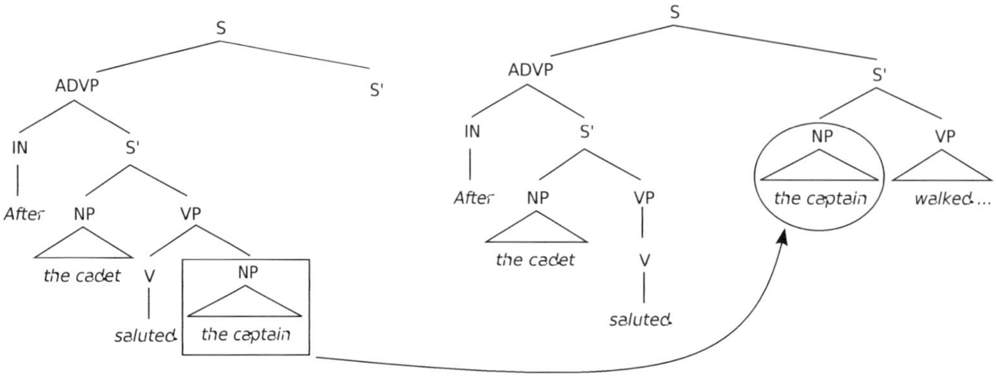

Figure 1: Phrase markers showing disambiguation in sentence type 1. The left phrasemarker shows the initial misattachment. The right phrasemarker shows how the same initially misattached NP is attached in the ultimately correct analysis.

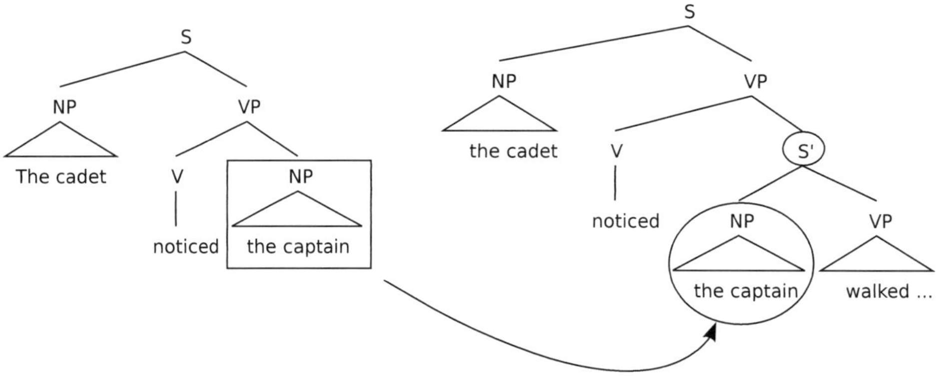

Figure 2: Phrase markers showing disambiguation in sentence type 2. The left phrasemarker shows the initial misattachment. The right phrasemarker shows how the same initially misattached NP is attached in the ultimately correct analysis.

The HUMDEP parser provided by Boston (2013) and described in Boston and Hale (2007) and Boston (2012) computes surprisal over a dependency grammar transition system , incrementally for each word in a sentence. It is a k-best parser. Here the value of k was set to 3, in line with previous use of the parser to model human disambiguation performance for garden-path sentences in Boston and Hale (2007).

Hypothesis 1 Hale (2001), and also Levy (2008), gave the hypothesis that surprisal is linearly related to the human effort of processing a particular word in a sentence fragment. This hypothesis casts disambiguation as the work incurred by disconfirming all parses of the fragment that are inconsistent with the fragment including the disambiguating word.

3.2 Entropy reduction

Entropy reduction was computed over the output of the phrase structure parser TDPARSE. In general, the entropy (Shannon, 1948), denoted H, of a random variable is the uncertainty associated with that variable. Specifically, for a discrete random variable X with outcomes $x_1, x_2, \ldots$ with probabilities $p_1, p_2, \ldots$

$$\mathrm{H}(X) = -\sum_{x \in X} p_x \log_2 p_x$$

Putting this in sentence processing terms, let D be a set of derivations for a sentence fragment W and let X be the extended sentence fragment that results from adding a new word to the fragment.

$$H(\mathcal{G}, D, W) = -\sum prp(\mathcal{G}, X) log(prp(\mathcal{G}, X))$$

The quantity *entropy reduction* is defined with a lower bound of zero so that this quantity is never negative:

$$\text{ER} = max(0, \text{H}(\mathcal{D}|w_{1...k}) - \text{H}(\mathcal{D}|w_{1...k+1}))$$

Hypothesis 2 Hale (2004) and Hale (2006) gave the *entropy reduction hypothesis* that the human effort of processing a particular word in a sentence fragment is the reduction in entropy from its value given the fragment to its value given the fragment including the disambiguating word.

3.3 Retrieval time

Parsing in retrieval theory (Lewis and Vasishth, 2005) is accomplished by condition-action pairs generated with reference to a phrase structure grammar. A series of memory buffers stores elements in short-term and long-term buffers. Parallel associative retrieval (McElree et al., 2003), fluctuation of activation of elements already in a memory buffer, and retrieval interference as a function of similarity are combined to predict the amount of time that it takes to read a word (Vasishth et al., 2008).

A word's activation is based on two quantities: the baseline activation of the word, which is taken to decay given the passage of time; and the amount of similarity based interference with other words that have been parsed. The baseline activation B for a word i is given here, taken from Lewis and Vasishth (2005), and Patil et al. (2009), where t_r is the time since the rth retrieval of the word, the summation is over all n retrievals, and d is a decay factor set to 0.5 as in other ACT-R models (Anderson, 2005).

$$B_i = \ln\left(\sum_{r=1}^{n} t_r - d\right)$$

The equation tracks the log odds that a word will need to be retrieved, given its past usage history. It yields not a smoothly decaying activation from initial encoding to the current time, but a "series of spikes corresponding to the retrieval events" (Lewis and Vasishth, 2005).

The overall activation A for word i is given here

$$A_i = B_i + \sum_j W_j S_{ji}$$

from Lewis and Vasishth (2005). In this equation, B_i is the fluctuating baseline level of activation for word i which is subject to time-based decay. In the model, a *goal buffer* contains retrieval cues for integrating the current word. Overall activation A for word i is found by adding to the baseline activation for word i an associative activation boost received from retrieval cues in the goal buffer that are associated with i. The variable j indexes those retrieval cues in the goal buffer. W_js are weights on the retrieval cues in the goal buffer. The weight on a retrieval cue represents the proportion of the total activation available for the whole goal buffer that is assigned to the particular retrieval cue j in the goal buffer. S_{ji}s are the strengths of association from each retrieval cue j of the goal buffer to word i. This equation is effectively adding to the baseline activation an activation boost received from retrieval cues in the goal buffer.

The amount of similarity based interference is estimated by the weighted strengths of association between the word to be retrieved and retrieval cues from other words already parsed and with a trace in memory. In the following equation, word i is the current word, and retrieval cue j is from a word that is similar to word i, with reference to its part of speech tag, so that nouns interfere with other nouns but not with verbs. If retrieval cue j is similar to word i then the amount by which retrieval cue j interferes with word i varies according to how many words have already been associated with retrieval cue j. The array of words that is associated with retrieval cue j is considered to form a fan so that fan_j gives the number of words in the fan for cue j. The constant S refers to the maximum associative strength of 1.5 (Lewis and Vasishth, 2005).

$$S_{ji} = S - \ln(fan_j)$$

This equation is effectively reducing the maximum associative strength S by the log of the "fan" of cue j, that is, the number of items associated with j.

The mapping from activation level to retrieval time is given next. F is a scaling constant set to 0.14 in Lewis and Vasishth (2005). A_i is the word's activation and e is Euler's constant. T_i is retrieval time for word i:

$$T_i = Fe^{A_i}$$

The retrieval time measure comes from Lewis and Vasishth (2005) where a theory of sentence processing is expressed as set of processes corresponding with skilled retrievals of linguistic components from memory. However in that paper it is computed over a phrase structure grammar. Boston provides a method to compute retrieval time over a dependency grammar in the HUMDEP3.0 parser and Boston's method (Boston, 2013) is used here.

Hypothesis 3 Retrieval time is related to human sentence processing difficulty.

4 Eye movement metrics

This section gives the metrics used to index human sentence processing load at disambiguation. Rayner et al. (2012, p. 93) set out the most common eye tracking measures. These include the following measures: First Fixation Duration (FFD); First Pass Reading Time (FPRT); Regression Path Duration (RPD). These are defined next. First fixation duration (FFD) is the mean duration of the first fixation on a word regardless of other possible fixations on the word. It has traditionally been treated as a measure of early processing. First fixation duration is interpreted to index lexical access. First pass reading time (FPRT): also known as gaze duration, is the sum of the durations of all fixations on the word that occur before leaving the word in any direction. This still captures the early processing (FFD is a subset of FPRT) but FPRT also includes any refixations that there might be on the word before a regression is launched from it. First pass reading time is often interpreted to index lexical integration into the phrase marker. Regression path duration (RPD) includes FPRT but adds to it the durations of fixations on preceding words that the eyes regress to before leaving the word to the right to take in new material, as well as any refixations on the launch word that occur before new material is taken in. In this way RPD is sensitive to integration difficulties that yield regressive eye movements but it also includes early processing. Regression path duration is often interpreted to index incremental syntactic integration of the new word into the sentence's representation including any semantic problems that arise from this.

Since RPD is the measure most sensitive to syntactic disambiguation, it is used in this article as a measure that is representative of human parsing load at disambiguation.

5 Method

This section tells how the eye tracking experiment was carried out.

Participants were forty native speakers of British English who were students of Psychology at the University of Exeter and who participated for course credit. All had normal or corrected-t-normal vision, were naive as to the purpose of the experiment, aged between eighteen and thirty-four.

Apparatus used was an SR Research EyeLink II head-mounted eyetracker. This recorded participants' eye movements with a sampling rate of 500 Hz while they read sentences displayed on a 19 inch Iiyama Vision Master Pro monitor at 1024 x 768 resolution at a refresh rate of 60 Hz. Viewing was binocular but only the right eye was recorded. Participants sat in a dimly lit room in front of the computer at a viewing distance of approximately 75 cm the average viewing distance was approximately 75 cm. At this viewing distance, and assuming that 1 character had 2 mm width on screen, a single character subtended 0.153 degrees of visual angle, and approximately 6.5 characters subtended 1 degree of visual angle. The font used was Courier New 12 point. All sentences in this experiment were displayed on a single line with a maximum length of 100 characters. A 9 point calibration procedure was used, on which participants were required to achieve a score of 'good'. Each trial started with a drift correction routine where the participant was required to fixate a target that appeared in the same location as the first character of the sentence would subsequently occupy, and then required to press a button on the gamepad while fixating this point to start the trial.

Participants were instructed to read silently for comprehension at a comfortable speed. The practice trials and experimental trials were implemented as separate consecutive blocks. The experimental trials were randomised by Experiment Builder each time the experiment was run, i.e., in a different order for each participant, with the constraint that a maximum of two trials of a given type could appear in a continuous sequence. There were four practice sentences, followed by a drift correction routine preceding the experimental block containing 96 sentences, comprising 24 in experimental conditions (6 in each of 4 conditions); 24 foils (sentences that contained complement ambiguities that resolved to NP) and 48 fillers (sentences that did not contain complement ambiguity). Participants were rotated over one of four lists, implementing a Latin square design. 32 of the trials (including 8 of the experimental conditions) were followed immediately by a comprehension question. This was a simple question about the sentence immediately preceding that required the participant to make a yes or no response using the appropriate trigger button on the gamepad. The whole procedure took about 20 to 40 minutes, depending on the participant.

6 Results

This section shows how the comparisons were made between patterns of differential processing load at disambiguation in the parser metrics and the human metrics. Per-condition means of all metrics at the disambiguating word are given in Figure 3.

6.1 Regression path duration (RPD)

A linear mixed effects model (Bates et al., 2013) was constructed for regression path duration at the disambiguating word i.e., *walked* in the example sentences. RPD was modeled as a function of word length, word (unigram) frequency (Brants and Franz, 2006), ambiguity, and sentence type (type 1 is exemplified in sentence 1 and type 2 is exemplified in sentence 2), and the ambiguity x sentence type interaction; with random slopes for the ambiguity x sentence type interaction over both participant ID and over item ID. Word length and word frequency both exerted non-significant influences. There was a significant effect of ambiguity with the ambiguous conditions leading to 146 ms more RPD than the disambiguated conditions ($\beta = 135.15$, $SE = 37.60$, $t = 3.56$). There was a significant disadvantage for type 1 sentences of 79 ms as a main effect ($\beta = -68.59$, $SE = 30.66$, $t = -2.27$). There was significant interaction effect such that the effect of ambiguity in type 1 sentences was greater than the effect of ambiguity for type 2 sentences ($\beta = -64.28$, $SE = 31.33$, $t = -2.05$).

6.2 Phrase structure surprisal

Phrase structure surprisal predicted that the ambiguous cases would be harder then the unambiguous cases; and that the disadvantage of sentence type 1 in the ambiguous cases would turn around into a disadvantage of sentence type 2 in the unambiguous conditions. Individual terms for ambiguity and sentence type were included at each level of item. Effects of ambiguity, sentence type and the ambiguity x sentence type interaction were all significant in the model, and the shapes of these effects were broadly in line with the human data ($\beta = 0.65$, $SE = 0.05$, $t = 12.32$, $\beta = -0.11$, $SE = 0.03$, $t = -3.25$, and $\beta = -0.35$, $SE = 0.01$, $t = -62.35$ respectively).

6.3 Phrase structure entropy reduction

The directions of the entropy reduction hypothesis predictions were the same as for phrase structure surprisal, although there was a relatively greater difficulty with the type 2 cases versus surprisal. Effects of ambiguity, sentence type and the ambiguity x sentence type interaction were all significant in the model ($\beta = 0.32$, $SE = 0.02$, $t = 14.04$, $\beta = -0.03$, $SE = 0.02$, $t = -2.05$, and $\beta = -0.17$, $SE = 0.002$, $t = -55.79$ respectively). The shapes of these effects were broadly in line with the human data.

6.4 Dependency surprisal

The mean values of dependency surprisal at the disambiguating word show that ambiguous sentence types 1 and 2 are predicted to be equal. For the unambiguous cases, type 1 is predicted to be more difficult than type 2. Ambiguity did not exert a significant effect on dependency surprisal ($\beta = 0.0002$, $SE = 0.01$, $t = 0.01$). The effect of sentence type was significant, with type 1 causing more dependency surprisal than type 2 ($\beta = -0.09$, $SE = 0.01$, $t = -6.26$). The ambiguity x sentence type interaction was significant in the model ($\beta = 0.09$, $SE = 0.002$, $t = 39.67$) but the shape of the interaction did not match the shape of the human data: instead the model predicted a large effect of sentence type in the unambiguous conditions and a small effect of sentence type in the unambiguous control sentences.

6.5 Dependency retrieval time

The mean values for retrieval predicted that both of the ambiguous sentence types and unambiguous type 1 sentences should be equally difficult, with unambiguous type 1 predicted to cause the most difficulty. Main effects of ambiguity and sentence type were significant in the model ($\beta = -17.7$, $SE = 0.60$, $t = -29.72$ and $\beta = 17.7$, $SE = 0.6$, $t = 29.72$ respectively). There was a significant ambiguity x sentence type interaction ($\beta = -17.7$, $SE = 0.09$, $t = -191.25$). Comparing these prediction with the human data, the predictions are not in line with human performance at all.

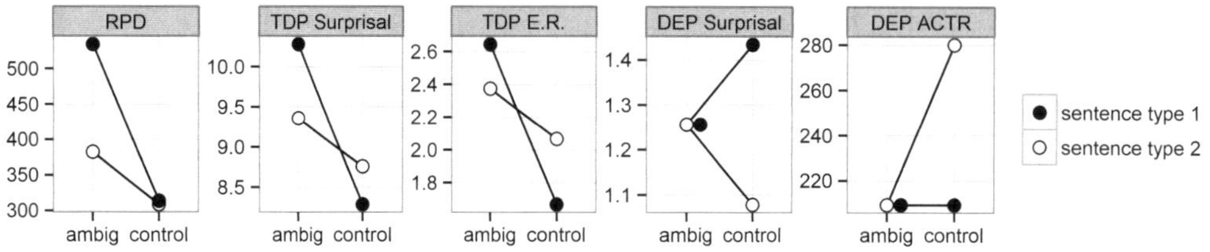

Figure 3: Per-condition means for each metric for the disambiguating word. RPD is the human eye movement measure *regression path duration*, see section 6.1. TDP Surprisal is surprisal computed over a phrase structure grammar, see section 6.2. TDP E.R. is entropy reduction computed over a phrase structure grammar, see section 6.3. DEP Surprisal is surprisal computed over a dependency grammar, section 6.4; DEP ATCR is retrieval time computed over a dependency grammar, section 6.5.

7 Conclusions

This section lays out the the conclusions that can be drawn from this work, paying attention to the question whether an information theoretic measure can be used in the NLG process as a proxy for human reading difficulty, as part of an effort to generate more readable texts.

For the metrics computed over a phrase structure grammar (phrase structure surprisal and phase structure entropy reduction), the comparison with human eye tracking metrics is relatively close. This suggests that phrase structure surprisal and phase structure entropy reduction are tracking human reading difficulty at disambiguation well. Phrase structure surprisal and phase structure entropy reduction are good predictors of the sort of human parsing difficulty that is measured by regression path duration, for these sentence types.

Dependency surprisal computed over a dependency grammar using a k-best parser with k=3 produces the wrong predictions for the complement ambiguity sentence types in this article. There is some scope for improving the predictions of this parser, as follows. Firstly setting k=3 may be restricting the beam width too much such that the ultimately-correct analysis is pruned too early. If so, simulations with increased values of k might be worth exploring. Secondly, one of the sentence types in this article relies on disambiguation by punctuation. Punctuation is well-handled in phrase structural grammars because it serves as a clause boundary marker, and phrase structure grammars natively express sentences as phrase combinations, whereas dependency grammars can only treat punctuation as a terminal in its own right. This might turn out to lead to an unfair comparison between dependency parser performance and phrase structure performance for the sentence types examined here. There is a clear case for examining dependency parsing for disambiguation types that use the sequence of words to effect disambiguation. Future work in this direction could take advantage of previous work with different ambiguities covered in e.g., Boston and Hale (2007) and Boston (2012), and extending it from using self-paced reading times to include eye-tracking metrics.

Dependency retrieval time did not show the interaction evident in the eye movement and phase grammar parser data. This suggests either that the Lewis and Vasishth (2005) model does not cover very well the sentence types used in this experiment, or that whatever coverage the Lewis and Vasishth (2005) model does have of the human data is obscured in the transformation from phrase structure grammar to dependency grammar versions of retrieval.

Previous work aimed at broad-coverage parsing evaluated against human eye movement corpora (Demberg and Keller, 2008; Boston et al., 2011) indicates that, in those corpus-derived linguistic environments, phrase structure surprisal and phase structure entropy reduction account for different components of variance in eye movement patterns. If future work continues to find that surprisal and entropy reduction predict human difficulty in psycholinguistic eye movement lab-based investigations (and the present paper shows how that can be done for one ambiguity type), then it will be reasonable to propose that a good model of sentence processing should use both surprisal and entropy reduction to predict (human) reading difficulty. Such a model would need to consider carefully the nature of the relationship between these different types of parser complexity. A starting point could be the observation that surprisal is essentially backwards-looking (seeks to disconfirm past analyses) whereas entropy reduction is essentially forward-looking (seeks to establish the uncertainty that remains at the current word with respect to how the rest of the sentence might pan out).

For NLG, the importance of this proposal is that such a model could be used to answer, algorithmically, questions that have previously only been satisfactorily answered in the laboratory. For example, in NLG the question often arises "For this proposition P, which we want the generator to put in a surface form SF for some given natural language L, which of the many possible SFs that express P in L should we produce?". So far this question has only been satisfactorily addressed by laboratory studies, which are few in number, expensive to run, and hard to generalise from.

When such generators are faced with this question, a better way forward would be to generate (some finite subset of) all possible SFs that express P in L, and then use surprisal and entropy reduction metrics as thresholds for pruning and ranking the SFs. This would lead the generator to produce only SFs that avoid syntactic complexity for the benefit of human readers. Different thresholds could produce texts tailor-made for groups with different reading abilities, or texts aimed to meet other constraints on acceptable human difficulty, e.g., texts for beginners learning a given natural language for the first time, or texts with different forms aimed at novices and experts.

Reiter and Belz (2009) discuss and evaluate some metrics for automatic evaluation of NLG in the context of generating weather forecasts. However these are designed to fit human measures at the whole-document level of NLG, different from the sentence-level incremental predictions generated and evaluated here. Also the evaluations discussed by those authors are done by fitting measures from offline human ratings of text readability, again different from the fine-grained detail of online human processing provided by the eye-tracking experiment here.

It seems clear that a combination of document-level and sentence-level predictors of human difficulty with generated text would be better than either alone for guiding NLG systems. It is conceivable that surprisal and entropy reduction might become useful automatic metrics for sentence-level evaluation of NLG texts, in the same way that BLEU (Papineni et al., 2002) and similar metrics serve in Machine Translation, but incrementally, and at a finer-grained and level.

References

J.R. Anderson. 2005. Human symbol manipulation within an integrated cognitive architecture. *Cognitive science*, 29(3):313–341.

Douglas Bates, Martin Maechler, Ben Bolker, and Steven Walker. 2013. lme4: Linear mixed-effects models using Eigen and S4. R package version 1.0-5.

M.F. Boston and J. Hale. 2007. Garden-pathing in a statistical dependency parser. In *Proceedings of the Midwest Computational Linguistics Colloquium.*

M.F. Boston, John T. Hale, Shravan Vasishth, and Reinhold Kliegl. 2011. Parallel processing and sentence comprehension difficulty. *Language and Cognitive Processes*, 26(3):301–349.

M.F. Boston. 2012. *A Computational Model of Cognitive Constraints in Syntactic Locality*. Ph.D. thesis, Cornell University, January.

M.F. Boston. 2013. Humdep3.0. An incremental dependency parser developed for human sentence processing modeling. `http://conf.ling.cornell.edu/Marisa`.

Thorsten Brants and Alex Franz. 2006. Web 1T 5-gram Version. computed from Google, published by Linguistic Data Consortium.

C. Clifton Jr. 1993. Thematic roles in sentence parsing. *Canadian Journal of Experimental Psychology*, 47(2):222–46.

V. Demberg and F. Keller. 2008. Data from eye-tracking corpora as evidence for theories of syntactic processing complexity. *Cognition*, 109(2):193–210.

F. Ferreira and J.M. Henderson. 1991. Recovery from misanalyses of garden-path sentences. *Journal of Memory and Language*, 30(6):725–745.

M.J. Green. 2014. *On Repairing Sentences: An Experimental and Computational Analysis of Recovery from Unexpected Syntactic Disambiguation in Sentence Parsing*. Ph.D. thesis, Psychology, Exeter.

J. Hale. 2001. A Probabilistic Earley Parser as a Psycholinguistic Model. In *Proceedings Of The Second Meeting Of The North American Chapter Of The Association For Computational Linguistics*, pages 1–8, Morristown, NJ, USA. Association for Computational Linguistics.

J. Hale. 2004. The information-processing difficulty of incremental parsing. In F. Keller, S. Clark, M Crocker, and M. Steedman, editors, *ACL Workshop Incremental Parsing: Bringing Engineering and Cognition Together*, pages 58–65. Association for Computational Linguistics.

J. Hale. 2006. Uncertainty about the rest of the sentence. *Cognitive Science*, 30(4):643–672.

V.M. Holmes, A. Kennedy, and W.S. Murray. 1987. Syntactic structure and the garden path. *The Quarterly Journal of Experimental Psychology Section A: Human Experimental Psychology*, 39(2):2 – 277.

R. Levy. 2008. Expectation-Based Syntactic Comprehension. *Cognition*, 106(3):1126–1177.

R.L. Lewis and S. Vasishth. 2005. An activation-based model of sentence processing as skilled memory retrieval. *Cognitive Science*, 29:1–45.

B. McElree, S. Foraker, and L. Dyer. 2003. Memory structures that subserve sentence comprehension. *Journal of Memory and Language*, 48(1):67–91.

Kishore Papineni, Salim Roukos, Todd Ward, and Wei-Jing Zhu. 2002. BLEU: a method for automatic evaluation of machine translation. In *Proceedings of the 40th annual meeting on association for computational linguistics*, pages 311–318. Association for Computational Linguistics.

Umesh Patil, Shravan Vasishth, and Reinhold Kliegl. 2009. Compound effect of probabilistic disambiguation and memory retrievals on sentence processing: Evidence from an eyetracking corpus. In *Proceedings of 9th International Conference on Cognitive Modeling*, Manchester.

M.J. Pickering and M.J. Traxler. 1998. Plausibility and recovery from garden paths: An eye-tracking study. *Journal of Experimental Psychology: Learning, Memory, and Cognition*, 24(4):940–961.

K. Rayner and L. Frazier. 1987. Parsing temporarily ambiguous complements. *The Quarterly Journal of Experimental Psychology Section A: Human Experimental Psychology*, 39(4):657 – 673.

K. Rayner, A. Pollatsek, J. Ashby, and C. Clifton Jr. 2012. *Psychology of Reading*. Psychology Press, 2nd edition.

Ehud Reiter and Anja Belz. 2009. An investigation into the validity of some metrics for automatically evaluating natural language generation systems. *Computational Linguistics*, 35(4):529–558.

Brian Roark. 2001. Probabilistic top-down parsing and language modeling. *Computational linguistics*, 27(2):249–276.

Brian Roark. 2004. Robust garden path parsing. *Natural language engineering*, 10(1):1–24.

B. Roark. 2013. tdparse. An incremental top down parser. `http://code.google.com/p/incremental-top-down-parser/`.

Claude Shannon. 1948. A mathematical theory of communication. *Bell Systems Technical Journal*, 27:379—423.

P. Sturt, M.J. Pickering, and M.W. Crocker. 1999. Structural Change and Reanalysis Difficulty in Language Comprehension. *Journal of Memory and Language*, 40:136–150.

J C Trueswell, M K Tanenhaus, and C Kello. 1993. Verb-specific constraints in sentence processing: separating effects of lexical preference from garden-paths. *J Exp Psychol Learn Mem Cogn*, 19(3):528–53.

S. Vasishth, S. Brüssow, R.L. Lewis, and H. Drenhaus. 2008. Processing polarity: How the ungrammatical intrudes on the grammatical. *Cognitive Science*, 32(4):685–712.

Syntactic Sentence Simplification for French

Laetitia Brouwers
Aspirante FNRS
CENTAL, IL&C
UCLouvain
Belgium

Delphine Bernhard
LiLPa
Université de Strasbourg
France

Anne-Laure Ligozat
LIMSI-CNRS
ENSIIE
France

Thomas François
CENTAL, IL&C
UCLouvain
Belgium

Abstract

This paper presents a method for the syntactic simplification of French texts. Syntactic simplification aims at making texts easier to understand by simplifying complex syntactic structures that hinder reading. Our approach is based on the study of two parallel corpora (encyclopaedia articles and tales). It aims to identify the linguistic phenomena involved in the manual simplification of French texts and organise them within a typology. We then propose a syntactic simplification system that relies on this typology to generate simplified sentences. The module starts by generating all possible variants before selecting the best subset. The evaluation shows that about 80% of the simplified sentences produced by our system are accurate.

1 Introduction

In most of our daily activities, the ability to read quickly and effectively is an undeniable asset, even often a prerequisite (Willms, 2003). However, a sizeable part of the population is not able to deal adequately with the texts they face. For instance, Richard et al. (1993) reported that, in 92 applications for an unemployment allowance filled by people with a low level of education, about half of the required information was missing (some of which was crucial for the processing of the application), mainly because of comprehension issues.

These comprehension issues are often related to the complexity of texts, particularly at the lexical and syntactic levels. These two factors are known to be important causes of reading difficulties (Chall and Dale, 1995), especially for young children, learners of a foreign language or people with language impairments or intellectual disabilities.

In this context, automatic text simplification (ATS) appears as a means to help various people access more easily the contents of the written documents. ATS is an application domain of Natural Language Processing (NLP) aiming at making texts more accessible for readers, while ensuring the integrity of their contents and structure. Among the investigations in this regard are those of Caroll et al. (1999), Inui et al. (2003) and, more recently, of Rello et al. (2013), who developed tools to produce more accessible texts for people with language disabilities such as aphasia, deafness or dyslexia. In the FIRST project, Barbu et al. (2013) and Evans and Orăsan (2013) implemented a simplification system for patients with autism, who may also struggle to understand difficult texts.

However, reading assistance is not only intended for readers with disabilities, but also for those who learn a new language (as first or second language). De Belder and Moens (2010) focused on ATS for native English schoolchildren, while Siddharthan (2006), Petersen and Ostendorf (2007) and Medero and Ostendorf (2011) focused on learners of a second language. Williams and Reiter (2008), Aluisio et al. (2008) and Gasperin et al. (2009) addressed ATS for illiterate adults. Most of these studies are dealing with the English language, with the exception of some work in Japanese (Inui et al., 2003), Spanish (Saggion et al., 2011; Bott et al., 2012), Portuguese (Aluísio et al., 2008) and French (Seretan, 2012).

ATS was also used as a preprocessing step to increase the effectiveness of subsequent NLP operations on texts. Chandrasekar et al. (1996) first considered that long and complex sentences were an obstacle for automatic parsing or machine translation and they showed that a prior simplification may result in a better automatic analysis of sentences. More recently, Heilman and Smith (2010) showed that adding ATS in the context of automatic question generation yields better results. Similarly, Lin and Wilbur (2007) and Jonnalagadda et al. (2009) optimized information extraction from biomedical texts using ATS as a preprocessing step.

In these studies, the simplifications carried out are generally based on a set of manually defined transformation rules. However, ATS may also be solved with methods from machine translation and machine learning. This lead some researchers (Zhu et al., 2010; Specia, 2010; Woodsend and Lapata, 2011) to train statistical models from comparable corpora of original and simplified texts. The data used in these studies are often based on the English Wikipedia (for original texts) and the Simple English Wikipedia, a simplified version for children and non-native speakers that currently comprises more than 100,000 articles. Similar resources exist for French, such as Vikidia and Wikimini, but texts are far less numerous in these as in their English counterpart. Moreover, the original and simplified versions of an article are not strictly parallel, which further complicates machine learning. This is why, so far, there was no attempt to adapt this machine learning methodology to French. The only previous work on French, to our knowledge, is that of Seretan (2012), which analysed a corpus of newspapers to semi-automatically detect complex structures that has to be simplified. However, her system of rules has not been implemented and evaluated.

In this paper, we aim to further investigate the issue of syntactic simplification for French. We assume a midway point between the two main tendencies in the field. We use parallel corpora similar to those used in machine learning approaches and analyse it to manually define a set of simplification rules. We have also implemented the syntactic part of our typology through a simplification system. It is based on the technique of overgeneration, which consists in generating all possible simplified variants of a sentence, and then on the selection of the best subset of variants for a given text with the optimization technique known as integer linear programming (ILP). ILP allows us to specify a set of constraints that regulate the selection of the output by the syntactic simplification system. This method has already been applied to ATS in English by Belder and Moens (2010) and Woodsend and Lapata (2011).

To conclude, the contributions of this paper are: (1) a first corpus-based study of simplification processes in French that relies on a corpus of parallel sentences, (2) the organization of this study's results in what might be the first typology of simplification for French based on a corpus analysis of original and simplified texts; (3) two new criteria to select the best subset of simplified sentences among the set of variants, namely the spelling list of Catach (1985) and the use of keywords, and finally (4) a syntactic simplification system for French, a language with little resources as regards text simplification.

In the next sections, we first present the corpora building process (Section 2.1) and describe a general typology of simplification derived from our corpora (Section 2.2). Then, we present the system based on the syntactic part of the typology, which operates in two steps: overgeneration of all possible simplified sentences (Section 2.3.1) and selection of the best subset of candidates using readability criteria (Section 2.3.2) and ILP. Finally, we evaluate the quality of the syntactically simplified sentences as regards grammaticality, before performing some error analysis (Section 3).

2 Methodology

2.1 Corpus Description

We based our typology of simplification rules on the analysis of two corpora. More specifically, since our aim is to identify and classify the various strategies used to transform a complex sentence into a more simple one, the corpora had to include parallel sentences. The reason why we analysed two corpora is to determine whether different genres of texts lead to different simplification strategies. In this study, we focused on the analysis of informative and narrative texts. The informative corpus comprises encyclopaedia articles from Wikipedia [1] and Vikidia [2]. For the narrative texts, we used three classic tales by Perrault, Maupassant and Daudet and their simplified versions for learners of French as a foreign language.

To collect the first of our parallel corpora, we used the MediaWiki API to retrieve Wikipedia and Vikidia articles with the same title. The

[1] http://fr.wikipedia.org

[2] This site is intended for young people from eight to thirteen years and gathers more accessible articles than Wikipedia, both in terms of language and content. It is available at the address http://fr.vikidia.org

WikiExtractor [3] was then applied to the articles to discard the wiki syntax and only keep the raw texts. This corpus comprises 13,638 texts (7,460 from Vikidia and only 6,178 from Wikipedia, since some Vikidia articles had no counterpart in Wikipedia).

These articles were subsequently processed to identify parallel sentences (Wikipedia sentence with a simplified equivalent in Vikidia). The alignment has been made partly manually and partly automatically with the monolingual alignment algorithm described in Nelken and Shieber (2006), which relies on a cosine similarity between sentence vectors weighted with the *tf-idf*. This program outputs alignments between sentences, along with a confidence score. Among these files, twenty articles or excerpts from Wikipedia were selected along with their equivalent in Vikidia. This amounts to 72 sentences for the former and 80 sentences for the latter.

The second corpus is composed of 16 narrative texts, and more specifically tales, by Perrault, Maupassant, and Daudet. We used tales since their simplified version was closer to the original than those of longer novels, which made the sentence alignment simpler. The simplified versions of these tales were found in two collections intended to learners of French as a foreign language (FFL): "Hachette - Lire en français facile" and "De Boeck - Lire et s'entrainer". Their level of difficulty ranges from A1 (Daudet) to B1 (Maupassant) on the CEFR scale (Council of Europe, 2001), with Perrault being A2. The texts were digitized by OCR processing and manually aligned, by two annotators, with an adjudication phase for the disagreement cases. In this corpus, we analysed 83 original sentences and their corresponding 98 simplified versions, which gives us a size roughly similar to the Wikipedia-Vikidia corpus.

The two corpora created are relevant for a manual analysis, as done in the next section, but they are too small for automatic processing. We plan to implement a method to align automatically the narrative texts in the near future and thus be able to collect a larger corpus.

2.2 Simplification Typology

The observations carried out on these two corpora have made it possible to establish a typology organised according to three main linguistic levels of transformation: lexical, discursive and syntactic, which can be further divided into subcategories. It is worth mentioning that in previous work, simplification is commonly regarded as pertaining to two categories of phenomena: lexical and syntactic (Carroll et al., 1999; Inui et al., 2003; De Belder and Moens, 2010). Little attention has been paid to discourse in the area of automatic simplification (Siddharthan, 2006).

The typology is summarized in Table 1. As regards the lexicon, the phenomena we observed involve four types of substitution. First, difficult terms can be replaced by a synonym or an hypernym perceived as simpler. Second, some anaphoric expressions, considered simpler or more explicit, are preferred to their counterparts in the original texts. For example, in our three tales, simplified nominal anaphora are regularly used instead of pronominal anaphora. Third, rather than using synonymy, the authors of the simplified texts sometimes replace difficult words with a definition or an explanatory paraphrase. Finally, in the particular case where the original texts contain concepts in a foreign language, these non-French terms are translated.

At the discourse level, the authors of simple texts pay particular attention to the organization of the information which has to be clear and concise. To this end, clauses may be interchanged to ensure a better presentation of the information. In addition, information of secondary importance can be removed while explanations or examples are added for clarity. These two phenomena can appear to be contradictory (deletion and addition), but they actually operate in a common goal: make the main information more comprehensible. Particular attention is also placed on the coherence and cohesion of the text: Authors tend to explain the pronouns and explicit the relations between sentences. The last observed strategy is that impersonal structures are often personalized.

Finally, at the syntactic level, five types of changes are observed: tense modification, deletion, modification, splitting and grouping. The last two types can be considered together since they are two opposite phenomena.

- First, the tenses used in the simplified versions are more common and less literary than those used in the original texts. Thus, the present and present perfect are preferred to the simple past, imperfect and past perfect.

[3] http://medialab.di.unipi.it/wiki/Wikipedia_Extractor

Lexicon	Discourse	Syntax
Translation	Reorganisation	Tense
Anaphoric synonyms	Addition	Modification
Definition and paraphrase	Deletion	Grouping
Synonym or hypernym	Coherence and cohesion	Deletion
	Personalisation	Splitting

Table 1: Typology of simplifications

- Secondary or redundant information, that is generally considered removable at the syntactic level, is not included in the simplified texts. Adverbial clauses, some adverbs and adjectives and subordinate clauses, among others, are omitted.
- When some complex structures are not deleted, then they are often moved or modified for better clarity. Such structures include negative sentences, impersonal structures, indirect speech and subordinate clauses.
- The authors sometimes choose to divide long sentences or conversely merge several sentences into one. The grouping of elements is much less frequent than the division of sentences. To split a sentence, the authors generally transform a secondary clause–be it relative, coordinate, subordinate, participial or adjectival–into an independent clause.

This classification can be compared with that of Medero et al. (2011) who propose three categories – division, deletion and extension – or that of Zhu et al. (2010), which includes division, deletion, reorganization, and substitution.

Among those transformations, some are hardly implementable. This is the case when a change requires the use of semantics. For example, noun modifiers may sometimes be removed, but in other cases, they are necessary. However, there are often neither typographical nor grammatical marked differences between the two cases.

Another issue is that other syntactic changes should be accompanied by lexical transformations, which are difficult to generalize. For example, transforming a negative sentence into its affirmative equivalent requires to find a verb whose affirmative form includes the meaning of the negative construction to replace.

There are also changes that are very particular and require a manual rather than an automatic processing of the text, in the sense that each case is different (even if part of a more global rule). In addition, they usually involve discourse or lexical information and not just syntactic one.

Finally, the syntactic changes impacting other parts of the text or concerning elements that depend on another structure require more comprehensive changes to the text. Therefore, they are also difficult to handle automatically. Thus, to change the tense of a verb in a sentence, we must ensure that the sequence of tenses agree in the entire text.

2.3 The Sentence Simplification System

We used this typology to implement a system of syntactic simplification for French sentences. The simplification is performed as a two-step process. First, for each sentence of the text, we generate the set of all possible simplifications (overgeneration step), and then, we select the best subset of simplified sentences using several criteria.

2.3.1 Generation of the Simplified Sentences

The sentence overgeneration module is based on a set of rules (19 rules), which rely both on morphosyntactic features of words and on syntactic relationships within sentences. To obtain this information, the texts from our corpus are analyzed by MELT [4] (Denis and Sagot, 2009) and Bonsai [5] (Candito et al., 2010) during a preprocessing phase. As a result, texts are represented as syntax trees that include the information necessary to apply our simplification rules. After preprocessing, the set of simplification rules is applied recursively, one sentence at a time, until there is no further structure to simplify. All simplified sentences produced by a given rule are saved and gathered in a set of variants.

The rules for syntactic simplification included in our program are of three kinds: deletion rules (12 rules), modification rules (3 rules) and splitting rules (4 rules). With regards to our typology, it can be noted that two types of rules have not been implemented: aggregation rules and tense simplification rules. The merging strategies (in which several sentences are aggregated into one) were

[4] https://gforge.inria.fr/projects/lingwb

[5] http://alpage.inria.fr/statgram/frdep/fr_stat_dep_parsing.html

not observed consistently in the corpus. Moreover, aggregation rules could have come into conflict with the deletion rules, since they have opposite goals. Concerning tense aspects, some of them are indeed more likely to be used than others in Vikidia. However, this strategy has not been implemented, since it implies global changes to the text. For instance, when a simple past is replaced by a present form, we must also adapt the verbs in the surrounding context in accordance with tense agreement. This requires to consider the whole text, or at least the paragraph that contains the modified verbal form, and be able to automatically model tense agreement. Otherwise, we may alter the coherence of the text and decrease its readability.

This leaves us with 19 simplification rules.[6] To apply them, the candidate structures for simplification first need to be detected using regular expressions, via `Tregex` [7](Levy and Andrew, 2006) that allows the retrieval of elements and relationships in a parse tree. In a second step, syntactic trees in which a structure requires simplification are modified according a set of operations implemented through `Tsurgeon`.

The operations to perform depend on the type of rules:

1. For the deletion cases, simply deleting all the elements involved is sufficient (via the `delete` operation in Tsurgeon). The elements affected by the deletion rules are adverbial clauses, clauses between brackets, some of the subordinate clauses, clauses between commas or introduced by words such as "comme" (*as*), "voire" (*even*), "soit" (*either*), or similar terms, some adverbs and agent prepositional phrases.
2. For the modification rules, several operations need to be combined: some terms are dropped (via `Tsurgeon delete`), others are moved (operation `Tsurgeon move`) and specific labels are added to the text to signal a possible later processing. These labels are useful for rules implying a modification of tense or mode aspects for a verb. In such cases, tags are added around the verb to indicate that it needs to be modified. The modification is performed later, using the conjugation system `Verbiste`.[8] For instance, to change a passive into an active structure, not only the voice must be changed, but sometimes also the person, so that the verb agrees well with the agent that has become the new subject. As regards modification rules, three changes were implemented: moving adverbial clauses at the beginning of the sentence, transforming passive structures into active forms, and transforming a cleft to a non-cleft.
3. For the splitting rules, we followed a two-step process. The subordinate clause is first deleted, while the main clause is saved as a new sentence. Resuming from the original sentence, the main clause is, in turn, removed to keep only the subordinate clause, which must then be transformed into an independent clause. In general, the verbal form of the subordinate clause needs to be altered in order to operate as a main verb. Moreover, the pronoun governing the subordinated clause must be substituted with its antecedent and the subject must be added when missing. In the case of a relative clause, the relative pronoun thus needs to be substituted by its antecedent, but it is also important to consider the function of the pronoun to find out where to insert this antecedent. Our splitting rules apply when a sentence includes either relative or participle clauses, or clauses introduced by a colon or a coordinating conjunction.

All these simplification rules are applied recursively to a sentence until all possible alternatives have been generated. Therefore, it is common to have more than one simplified variant for a given sentence. In this case, the next step consists in selecting the most suitable variant to substitute the original one. The selection process is described in the next section.

2.3.2 Selection of the Best Simplifications

Given a set of candidate simplified sentences for a text, our goal is to select the best subset of simplified sentences, that is to say the subset that maximizes some measure of readability. More precisely, text readability is measured through different criteria, which are optimized with an Integer Linear Programming (ILP) approach (Gillick and Favre, 2009). These criteria are rather simple in

[6] These 19 rules are available at `http://cental.fltr.ucl.ac.be/team/lbrouwers/rules.pdf`

[7] `http://nlp.stanford.edu/software/tregex.shtml`

[8] This software is available at the address `http://sarrazip.com/dev/verbiste.html` under GNU general public license and was developed by Pierre Sarrazin.

this approach. They are used to ensure that not only the syntactic difficulty, but also the lexical complexity decrease, since syntactic transformations may cause lexical or discursive alterations in the text.

We considered four criteria to select the most suitable sentences among the simplified set: sentence length (in words) (h_w), mean word length (in characters) in the sentence (h_s), familiarity of the vocabulary (h_a), and presence of some keywords (h_c). While the first two criteria are pretty obvious as regards implementation, we measured word familiarity based on Catach's list (1985).[9] It contains about 3,000 of the most frequent words in French, whose spelling should be taught in priority to schoolchildren. The keywords were in this study simply defined as any term occurring more than once in the text.

These four criteria were combined using integer linear programming as follows: [10]

$$\begin{array}{ll} \text{Maximize :} & h_w + h_s + h_a + h_c \\ \text{Where :} & h_w = \text{wps} \times \sum_i s_i - \sum_i l_i^w s_i \\ & h_s = \text{cpw} \times \sum_i l_i^w s_i - \sum_i l_i^c s_i \\ & h_a = \text{aps} \times \sum_i s_i - \sum_i l_i^a s_i \\ & h_c = \sum_j w_j c_j \\ \text{Subject to:} & \sum_{i \in g_k} s_i = 1 \; \forall g_k \\ & s_i \text{occ}_{ij} \leq c_j \; \forall i, j \\ & \sum_i s_i \text{occ}_{ij} \geq c_j \; \forall j \end{array} \quad (1)$$

The above variables are defined as follows:

- wps: desired (mean) number of words per sentence
- cpw: desired (mean) number of characters per word
- aps: desired (mean) number of words absent from Catach's list for a sentence
- s_i: binary variable indicating whether the sentence i should be kept or not, with i varying from 1 to the total number of simplified sentences
- c_j: binary variable indicating whether keyword j is in the simplification or not, with j varying from 1 to the total number of keywords
- l_i^w: length of sentence i in words
- l_i^c: number of characters in sentence i
- l_i^a: number of words absent from Catach's list in sentence i
- w_j: number of occurrences of keyword j
- g_k: set of simplified sentences obtained from the same original sentence k
- occ_{ij}: binary variable indicating the presence of term j in sentence i

wps, cpw and aps are constant parameters whose values have been set respectively to 10, 5 and 2 for this study. 5 for cpw corresponds to the value computed on the Vikidia corpus, while for wps and aps, lower values than observed were used to force simplification (respectively 10 instead of 17 and 2 instead of 31).

However, these parameters may vary depending on the context of use and the target population, as they determine the level of difficulty of the simplified sentences obtained.

The constraints specify that (i) for each original sentence, at most one simplification set should be chosen, (ii) selecting a sentence means selecting all the terms it contains and (iii) selecting a keyword is only possible if it is present in at least one selected sentence.

We illustrate this process with the Wikipedia article entitled *Abel*. This article contains 25 sentences, from which 67 simplified sentences have been generated. For the original sentence (1a) for example, 5 variants were generated and simplification (2) was selected by ILP.

(1a) Original sentence[11] : *Caïn, l'aîné, cultive la terre et Abel (étymologie : de l'hébreu ≪ souffle ≫, ≪ vapeur ≫, ≪ existence précaire ≫) garde le troupeau.*

(1b) Possible simplifications :
Simplification 1 : *Caïn, l'aîné, cultive la terre et Abel garde le troupeau.*
Simplification 2 : *Caïn, l'aîné, cultive la terre. Abel garde le troupeau.*
Simplification 3 : *Caïn, l'aîné, cultive la terre.*
Simplification 4 : *Abel garde le troupeau.*
(...)

(1c) Selected simplification (2) : *Caïn, l'aîné, cultive la terre. Abel garde le troupeau.*

3 Evaluation

Syntactic simplification involves substantial changes within the sentence both in terms of contents and form. It is therefore important to check that the application of a rule does not cause errors that would make the sentences produced unintelligible or ungrammatical. A manual evaluation of our system's efficiency to generate correct simplified sentences was carried out on our two corpora. In each of them, we selected a set of texts that had not been previously used for

[9] This list is available at the site http://www.ia93.ac-creteil.fr/spip/spip.php?article2900.

[10] We used an ILP module based on glpk that is available at the address http://www.gnu.org/software/glpk/

[11] *Caïn, the eldest brother, farms the land and Abel (etymology : from Hebrew ≪ breath ≫, ≪ steam ≫, ≪ fragile existence ≫) looks after the flock.*

	Sentence length	Word length	Word familiarity	Keywords
Expected values	10	5	2	/
Original	19	6.1	11	5
Simplification 1	11	4.3	5	5
Simplification 2	**5**	**4.6**	**2**	**5**
Simplification 3	6	4.5	3	3
Simplification 4	4	4.7	2	2
Simplification 5	9	6.3	5	5
Simplification 6	12	7.3	8	2

Table 2: Values of the criteria in IPL for example (1).

the typological analysis, that is to say 9 articles from Wikipedia (202 sentences) and two tales from Perrault (176 sentences). In this evaluation, all simplified sentences are considered, not only those selected by ILP. The results are displayed in Table 3 and discussed in Section 3.1. Two types of errors can be detected: those resulting from morpho-syntactic preprocessing, and particularly the syntactic parser, and the simplification errors *per se*, that we discuss in larger details in Section 3.2.

3.1 Quantitative Evaluation

Out of the 202 sentences selected in the informative corpus for evaluation, 113 (56%) have undergone one or more simplifications, which gives us 333 simplified variants. Our manual error analysis revealed that 71 sentences (21%) contain some errors, among which we can distinguish those due to the preprocessing from those actually due to the simplification system itself. It is worth mentioning that the first category amounts to 89% of the errors, while the simplification rule are only responsible for 11% of those. We further refined the analysis of the system's errors distinguishing syntactic from semantic errors.

The scores obtained on the narrative corpus are slightly less good: out of the 369 simplified variants produced from the 154 original sentences, 77 (20.9%) contain errors. This value is very similar to the percentage for the informative corpus. However, only 50.7% of these errors are due to the preprocessing, while the remaining 49.3% come from our rules. It means that our rules yield about 10.3% incorrect simplified variants compared to 2.7% for the informative corpus. Nevertheless, these errors are caused mostly by 2 or 3 rules: the deletion of subordinate clauses, of infinitives or of clauses coordinated with a colon. This loss in efficiency can be partly explained by the greater presence of indirect speech in the tales that include more non-removable subordinate clauses, difficult to distinguish from removable clauses.

Globally, our results appear to be in line with those of similar systems developed for English.[12] Yet, few studies have a methodology and evaluation close enough to ours to allow comparison of the results. Siddharthan (2006) assessed his system output using three judges who found that about 80% of the simplified sentences were grammatical, while 87% preserved the original meaning. These results are very similar to our findings that mixed the syntactic and discourse dimensions. Drndarević et al. (2013) also presented the output of their system to human judges who estimated that 60% of the sentences were grammatical and that 70% preserved the initial meaning. These scores appear lower than ours, but Drndarević et al. also used lexical rules, which means that their error rate includes both grammatical and lexical errors.

3.2 Error Analysis

As regards syntax, the structure of a sentence can be modified so that it becomes grammatically incorrect. Three simplification rules are concerned. Deletion rules may cause this kind of problem, because they involve removing a part of the sentence, considered as secondary. However, sometimes the deleted element is essential, as in the case of the removal of the referent of a pronoun. This type of problem arises both with the deletion of a subordinate clause or that of an infinitive clause. Deletion rules are also subject to a different kind of errors. During the reconstruction of the sentence resulting from the subordinate clause, some constituents, such as the subject, may not be properly identified and will be misplaced in the new sentence.

At the semantic level, the information conveyed by the original sentence may be modified or even removed. When an agent or an infinitive clause

[12] We do not discuss French here, since no simplification system were found for French, as explained previously.

Wikipedia-Vikidia corpus				
nb. sent.	% correct	% preproc. errors	% simplification errors	
333	262 (78.7 %)	63 (18.9%)	8 (2.4 %)	
			syntax: 6 (1.8%)	semantics: 2 (0.6%)
Narrative corpus				
nb. sent.	**% correct**	**% preproc. errors**	**% simplification errors**	
369	292 (79.1 %)	39 (10.6%)	38 (10.3 %)	
			syntax: 20 (5.4%)	semantics: 18 (4.9%)

Table 3: Performance of the simplification system on both corpora

are suppressed, the meaning of the sentence may be disrupted or some of the content lost. For instance, in the following sentence – extracted from the Wikipedia article *abbé* (abbot) – the infinitive clause explaining the term is dropped:

(2a) *C'est aussi depuis le XVIIIe siècle le terme en usage pour désigner un clerc séculier ayant au moins reçu la tonsure.*[13]
(2b) *C'est aussi depuis le XVIIIe siècle le terme en usage.*

To fix the errors identified above, our rules should be refined and developed, with the addition of better tools for sentence regeneration as well as some exclusion criteria for the incorrect sentences within the ILP module, as discussed in the next section.

4 Perspectives and Conclusions

This article describes an automatic syntactic simplification system for French intended for children and language learners. It is based on a set of rules defined after a corpus study, which also led to the development of a typology of simplifications in French. It would be easy to extend our typology to other target users based on other appropriate corpora, such as people with language disorders.

Our approach also uses the technique of overgeneration, which makes it possible to retain the best set of simplifications based on readability criteria. Note that among those employed, some had not been considered previously and produce interesting results. Finally, we showed that the performance of our system is good (about 80 % of the generated sentences are correct) and in line with previous studies.

The evaluation showed that the rules implemented are more suitable for expository texts, probably because they are more explicit, as style there is of a minor importance. In addition, the system set up was first tested on and therefore adapted to Wikipedia. It was only subsequently applied to narratives, that revealed new challenges, especially concerning the deletion rules. The information provided in secondary clauses or complements indeed seems most essential to understanding the story, especially when it comes to direct or indirect speech. In order to comprehend the differences in terms of efficiency and rules to be applied between genres, it would be necessary to extend our study to other texts collected in the corpora.

We envision multiple perspectives to improve our system. First, syntactic simplification could be supplemented by lexical simplification, as is done in some studies for English (Woodsend and Lapata, 2011). Moreover, our error analysis has highlighted the need to add or repeat words when a sentence is split. It would therefore be useful to use a tool that manages references in order to improve the quality of simplified text. In addition, the sentence selection module could include additional selection criteria, based on the work done in readability of French (François and Fairon, 2012). A final perspective of improvement would be to make the rule system adapt to the target audience and the genre of the texts. This would require assessing the relevance of various transformations and selection criteria of the best simplifications. This perspective would also require assessing the effectiveness of the rules by means of comprehension tests both on the original and simplified sentences, which we plan to do.

[13] *It is also the term in use since the 18th to refer to a secular cleric who, at least, received the tonsure.*

References

S. Aluísio, L. Specia, T. Pardo, E. Maziero, and R. Fortes. 2008. Towards brazilian portuguese automatic text simplification systems. In *Proceedings of the eighth ACM symposium on Document engineering*, pages 240–248.

E. Barbu, P. de Las Lagunillas, M. Martın-Valdivia, and L. Urena-López. 2013. Open book: a tool for helping asd users' semantic comprehension. *NLP4ITA 2013*, pages 11–19.

S. Bott, L. Rello, B. Drndarevic, and H. Saggion. 2012. Can Spanish Be Simpler? LexSiS: Lexical Simplification for Spanish. In *Proceedings of COLING 2012*, pages 357–374.

M. Candito, B. Crabbé, and P. Denis. 2010. Statistical french dependency parsing: treebank conversion and first results. In *Proceedings of the Seventh International Conference on Language Resources and Evaluation (LREC 2010)*, pages 1840–1847.

J. Carroll, G. Minnen, D. Pearce, Y. Canning, S. Devlin, and J. Tait. 1999. Simplifying Text for Language-Impaired Readers. In *Proceedings of EACL*, pages 269–270.

N. Catach. 1985. *Les listes orthographiques de base du français*. Nathan, Paris.

J.S. Chall and E. Dale. 1995. *Readability Revisited: The New Dale-Chall Readability Formula*. Brookline Books, Cambridge.

R. Chandrasekar, C. Doran, and B. Srinivas. 1996. Motivations and methods for text simplification. In *Proceedings of the 16th conference on Computational linguistics*, pages 1041–1044.

Council of Europe. 2001. *Common European Framework of Reference for Languages: Learning, Teaching, Assessment*. Press Syndicate of the University of Cambridge.

J. De Belder and M.-F. Moens. 2010. Text Simplification for Children. In *Proceedings of the Workshop on Accessible Search Systems*.

P. Denis and B. Sagot. 2009. Coupling an annotated corpus and a morphosyntactic lexicon for state-of-the-art pos tagging with less human effort. In *Proceedings of PACLIC*.

B. Drndarević, S. Štajner, S. Bott, S. Bautista, and H. Saggion. 2013. Automatic text simplification in spanish: a comparative evaluation of complementing modules. In *Computational Linguistics and Intelligent Text Processing*, pages 488–500.

R. Evans and C. Orăsan. 2013. Annotating signs of syntactic complexity to support sentence simplification. In *Text, Speech, and Dialogue*, pages 92–104.

T. François and C. Fairon. 2012. An "AI readability" formula for French as a foreign language. In *Proceedings of EMNLP 2012*, pages 466–477.

C. Gasperin, E. Maziero, L. Specia, T. Pardo, and S. Aluisio. 2009. Natural language processing for social inclusion: a text simplification architecture for different literacy levels. *Proceedings of SEMISH-XXXVI Seminário Integrado de Software e Hardware*, pages 387–401.

D. Gillick and B. Favre. 2009. A scalable global model for summarization. In *Proceedings of the Workshop on Integer Linear Programming for Natural Language Processing*, pages 10–18.

M. Heilman and N. A. Smith. 2010. Extracting Simplified Statements for Factual Question Generation. In *Proceedings of the 3rd Workshop on Question Generation*.

K. Inui, A. Fujita, T. Takahashi, R. Iida, and T. Iwakura. 2003. Text simplification for reading assistance: a project note. In *Proceedings of the second international workshop on Paraphrasing*, pages 9–16.

S. Jonnalagadda, L. Tari, J. Hakenberg, C. Baral, and G. Gonzalez. 2009. Towards Effective Sentence Simplification for Automatic Processing of Biomedical Text. In *Proceedings of NAACL-HLT 2009*.

R. Levy and G. Andrew. 2006. Tregex and tsurgeon: tools for querying and manipulating tree data structures. In *Proceedings of LREC*, pages 2231–2234.

L. Lin and W. J. Wilbur. 2007. Syntactic sentence compression in the biomedical domain: facilitating access to related articles. *Information Retrieval*, 10(4):393–414, October.

J. Medero and M. Ostendorf. 2011. Identifying Targets for Syntactic Simplification. In *Proceedings of the SLaTE 2011 workshop*.

R. Nelken and S.M. Shieber. 2006. Towards robust context-sensitive sentence alignment for monolingual corpora. In *Proceedings of EACL*, pages 161–168.

S. E. Petersen and M. Ostendorf. 2007. Text Simplification for Language Learners: A Corpus Analysis. In *Proceedings of SLaTE2007*, pages 69–72.

L. Rello, C. Bayarri, A. Gòrriz, R. Baeza-Yates, S. Gupta, G. Kanvinde, H. Saggion, S. Bott, R. Carlini, and V. Topac. 2013. Dyswebxia 2.0!: more accessible text for people with dyslexia. In *Proceedings of the 10th International Cross-Disciplinary Conference on Web Accessibility*, page 25.

J.F. Richard, J. Barcenilla, B. Brie, E. Charmet, E. Clement, and P. Reynard. 1993. Le traitement de documents administratifs par des populations de bas niveau de formation. *Le Travail Humain*, 56(4):345–367.

H. Saggion, E. Martínez, E. Etayo, A. Anula, and L. Bourg. 2011. Text simplification in simplext. making text more accessible. *Procesamiento del lenguaje natural*, 47:341–342.

V. Seretan. 2012. Acquisition of syntactic simplification rules for french. In *LREC*, pages 4019–4026.

A. Siddharthan. 2006. Syntactic Simplification and Text Cohesion. *Research on Language & Computation*, 4(1):77–109, jun.

L. Specia. 2010. Translating from Complex to Simplified Sentences. In *Proceedings of the 9th International Conference on Computational Processing of the Portuguese Language (Propor-2010).*, pages 30–39.

S. Williams and E. Reiter. 2008. Generating basic skills reports for low-skilled readers. *Natural Language Engineering*, 14(4):495–525.

J.D. Willms. 2003. Literacy proficiency of youth: Evidence of converging socioeconomic gradients. *International Journal of Educational Research*,

39(3):247–252.

K. Woodsend and M. Lapata. 2011. Learning to Simplify Sentences with Quasi-Synchronous Grammar and Integer Programming. In *Proceedings of EMNLP*, pages 409–420.

Z. Zhu, D. Bernhard, and I. Gurevych. 2010. A Monolingual Tree-based Translation Model for Sentence Simplification. In *Proceedings of COLING 2010*, pages 1353–1361.

Medical text simplification using synonym replacement: Adapting assessment of word difficulty to a compounding language

Emil Abrahamsson[1] **Timothy Forni**[1] **Maria Skeppstedt**[1] **Maria Kvist**[1,2]
[1]Department of Computer and Systems Sciences (DSV)
Stockholm University, Sweden
{emab6827, tifo6794, mariask}@dsv.su.se
[2]Department of Learning, Informatics, Management and Ethics (LIME)
Karolinska Institutet, Sweden
maria.kvist@karolinska.se

Abstract

Medical texts can be difficult to understand for laymen, due to a frequent occurrence of specialised medical terms. Replacing these difficult terms with easier synonyms can, however, lead to improved readability. In this study, we have adapted a method for assessing difficulty of words to make it more suitable to medical Swedish. The difficulty of a word was assessed not only by measuring the frequency of the word in a general corpus, but also by measuring the frequency of substrings of words, thereby adapting the method to the compounding nature of Swedish. All words having a MeSH synonym that was assessed as easier, were replaced in a corpus of medical text. According to the readability measure LIX, the replacement resulted in a slightly more difficult text, while the readability increased according to the OVIX measure and to a preliminary reader study.

1 Introduction

Our health, and the health of our family and friends, is something that concerns us all. To be able to understand texts from the medical domain, e.g. our own health record or texts discussing scientific findings related to our own medical problems, is therefore highly relevant for all of us.

Specialised terms, often derived from latin or greek, as well as specialised abbreviations, are, however, often used in medical texts (Kokkinakis and Toporowska Gronostaj, 2006). This has the effect that medical texts can be difficult to comprehend (Keselman and Smith, 2012). Comprehending medical text might be particularly challenging for those laymen readers who are not used to looking up unknown terms while reading. A survey of Swedish Internet users showed, for instance, that users with a long education consult medical information available on the Internet to a much larger extent than users with a shorter education (Findahl, 2010, pp. 28–35). This discrepancy between different user groups is one indication that methods for simplifying medical texts are needed, to make the medical information accessible to everyone.

Previous studies have shown that replacing difficult words with easier synonyms can reduce the level of difficulty in a text. The level of difficulty of a word was, in these studies, determined by measuring its frequency in a general corpus of the language; a measure based on the idea that frequent words are easier than less frequent, as they are more familiar to the reader. This synonym replacement method has been evaluated on medical English text (Leroy et al., 2012) as well as on Swedish non-medical text (Keskisärkkä and Jönsson, 2012). To the best of our knowledge, this method has, however, not previously been evaluated on medical text written in Swedish. In addition, as Swedish is a compounding language, laymen versions of specialised medical terms are often constructed by compounds of every-day Swedish words. Whether a word consists of easily understandable constituents, is a factor that also ought to be taken into account when assessing the difficulty of a word.

The aim of our study was, therefore, to investigate if synonym replacement based on term frequency could be successfully applied also on Swedish medical text, as well as if this method could be further developed by adapting it to the compounding nature of Swedish.

2 Background

The level of difficulty varies between different types of medical texts (Leroy et al., 2006), but studies have shown that even brochures intended for patients, or websites about health issues, can be difficult to comprehend (Kokkinakis et al., 2012; Leroy et al., 2012). Bio-medical texts, such as medical journals, are characterised by sentences that have high informational and structural complexity, thus containing a lot of technical terms (Friedman et al., 2002). An abundance of medical terminology and a frequent use of abbreviations form, as previously mentioned, a strong barrier for comprehension when laymen read medical text. Health literacy is a much larger issue than only the frequent occurrence of specialised terms; an issue that includes many socio-economic factors. The core of the issue is, however, the readability of the text, and adapting word choice to the reader group (Zeng et al., 2005; Leroy et al., 2012) is a possible method to at least partly improve the readability of medical texts.

Semi-automatic adaption of word choice has been evaluated on English medical text (Leroy et al., 2012) and automatic adaption on Swedish non-medical text (Keskisärkkä and Jönsson, 2012). Both studies used synonym lexicons and replaced words that were difficult to understand with more easily understandable synonyms. The level of difficulty of a word was determined by measuring its frequency in a general corpus. The English study based its figures for word frequency on the number of occurrences of a word in Google's index of English language websites, while the Swedish study used the frequency of a word in the Swedish Parole corpus (Gellerstam et al., 2000), which is a corpus compiled from several sources, e.g. newspaper texts and fiction.

The English study used English WordNet as the synonym resource, and difficult text was transformed by a medical librarian, who chose easier replacements for difficult words among candidates that were presented by the text simplification system. Also hypernyms from semantic categories in WordNet, UMLS and Wiktionary were used, but as clarifications for difficult words (e.g. in the form: '*difficult word*, a kind of *semantic category*'). A frequency cut-off in the Google Web Corpus was used for distinguishing between easy and difficult words. The study was evaluated by letting readers 1) assess perceived difficulty in 12 sentences extracted from medical texts aimed at patients, and 2) answer multiple choice questions related to paragraphs of texts from the same resource, in order to measure actual difficulty. The evaluations showed that perceived difficulty was significantly higher before the transformation, and that actual difficulty was significantly higher for one combination of medical topic and test setting.

The Swedish study used the freely available SynLex as the resource for synonyms, and one of the studied methods was synonym replacement based on word frequency. The synonym replacement was totally automatic and no cut-off was used for distinguishing between familiar and rare words. The replacement algorithm instead replaced all words which had a synonym with a higher frequency in the Parole corpus than the frequency of the original word. The effect of the frequency-based synonym replacement was automatically evaluated by applying the two Swedish readability measures LIX and OVIX on the original and on the modified text. Synonym replacement improved readability according to these two measures for all of the four studied Swedish text genres: newspaper texts, informative texts from the Swedish Social Insurance Agency, articles from a popular science magazine and academic texts.

For synonym replacement to be a meaningful method for text simplification, there must exist synonyms that are near enough not to change the content of what is written. Perfect synonyms are rare, as there is typically at least one aspect in which two separate words within a language differ; if it is not a small difference in meaning, it might be in the context in which they are typically used (Saeed, 1997). For describing medical concepts, there is, however, often one set of terms that are used by health professionals, whereas another set of laymen's terms are used by patients (Leroy and Chen, 2001; Kokkinakis and Toporowska Gronostaj, 2006). This means that synonym replacement could have a large potential for simplifying medical text, as there are many synonyms within this domain, for which the difference mainly lies in the context in which they are typically used.

The availability of comprehensive synonym resources is another condition for making it possible to implement synonym replacement for text simplification. For English, there is a consumer health vocabulary initiative connecting laymen's expressions to technical terminology (Keselman et al., 2008), as well as several medical termi-

Original	Med röntgen kan man se en ökad trabekulering, *osteoporos* samt pseudofrakturer.
Transformed	Med röntgen kan man se en ökad trabekulering, *benskörhet* samt pseudofrakturer.
Translated original	With X-ray, one can see an increased trabeculation, *osteoporosis* and pseudo-fractures.
Translated transformed	With X-ray, one can see an increased trabeculation, *bone-brittleness* and pseudo-fractures.

Table 1: An example of how the synonym replacement changes a word in a sentence.

nologies containing synonymic expressions, e.g. MeSH[1] and SNOMED CT[2]. Swedish, with fewer speakers, also has fewer lexical resources than English, and although SNOMED CT was recently translated to Swedish, the Swedish version does not contain any synonyms. MeSH on the other hand, which is a controlled vocabulary for indexing biomedical literature, is available in Swedish (among several other languages), and contains synonyms and abbreviations for medical concepts (Karolinska Institutet, 2012).

Swedish is, as previously mentioned, a compounding language, with the potential to create words expressing most of all imaginable concepts. Laymen's terms for medical concepts are typically descriptive and often consist of compounds of words used in every-day language. The word *humerusfraktur (humerus fracture)*, for instance, can also be expressed as *överarmsbenbrott*, for which a literal translation would be *upper-arm-bone-break*. That a compound word with many constituents occurring in standard language could be easier to understand than the technical terms of medical terminology, forms the basis for our adaption of word difficulty assessment to medical Swedish.

3 Method

We studied simplification of one medical text genre; medical journal text. The replacement method, as well as the main evaluation method, was based on the previous study by Keskisärkkä and Jönsson (2012). The method for assessing word difficulty was, however, further developed compared to this previous study.

As medical journal text, a subset of the journal Läkartidningen, the Journal of the Swedish Medical Association (Kokkinakis, 2012), was used. The subset consisted of 10 000 randomly selected sentences from issues published in 1996. As synonym lexicon, the Swedish version of MeSH was used. This resource contains 10 771 synonyms, near synonyms, multi-word phrases with a very similar meaning and abbreviation/expansion pairs (all denoted as *synonyms* here), belonging to 8 176 concepts.

Similar to the study by Keskisärkkä and Jönsson (2012), the Parole corpus was used for frequency statistics. For each word in the Läkartidningen subset, it was checked whether the word had a synonym in MeSH. If that was the case, and if the synonym was more frequently occurring in Parole than the original word, then the original word was replaced with the synonym. An example of a sentence changed by synonym replacement is shown in Table 1.

There are many medical words that only rarely occur in general Swedish, and therefore are not present as independent words in a corpus of standard Swedish, even if constituents of the words frequently occur in the corpus. The method used by Keskisärkkä and Jönsson was further developed to handle these cases. This development was built on the previously mentioned idea that a compound word with many constituents occurring in standard language is easier to understand than a rare word for which this is not the case. When neither the original word, nor the synonym, occurred in Parole, a search in Parole was therefore instead carried out for substrings of the words. The original word was replaced by the synonym, in cases when the synonym consisted of a larger number of substrings present in Parole than the original word. To insure that the substrings were relevant words, they had to consist of a least four characters.

Exemplified by a sentence containing the word *hemangiom (hemangioma)*, the extended replacement algorithm would work as follows: The al-

[1] www.nlm.nih.gov/mesh/
[2] www.ihtsdo.org

gorithm first detects that *hemangiom* has the synonym *blodkärlstumör (blood-vessel-tumour)* in MeSH. It thereafter establishes that neither *hemangiom* nor *blodkärlstumör* is included in the Parole corpus, and therefore instead tries to find substrings of the two words in Parole. For *hemangiom*, no substrings are found, while four substrings are found for *blodkärlstumör* (Table 2), and therefore *hemangiom* is replaced by *blodkärlstumör*.

Word	1	2	3	4
hemangiom	-	-	-	-
blodkärlstumör	blod	kärl	blodkärl	tumör

Table 2: Example of found substrings

As the main evaluation of the effect of the synonym replacement, the two readability measures used by Keskisärkkä and Jönsson were applied, on the original as well as on the modified text. LIX (läsbarhetsindex, readability measure) is the standard metric used for measuring readability of Swedish texts, while OVIX (ordvariationsindex, word variation index) measures lexical variance, thereby reflecting the size of vocabulary in the text (Falkenjack et al., 2013).

The two metrics are defined as follows (Mühlenbock and Johansson Kokkinakis, 2009):

$$\text{LIX} = \frac{O}{M} + \frac{L \cdot 100}{O}$$

Where:

- O = number of words in the text
- M = number of sentences in the text
- L = number of long words in the text (more than 6 characters)

$$\text{OVIX} = \frac{log(O)}{log(2 - \frac{log(U)}{log(O)})}$$

Where:

- O = number of words in the text
- U = number of unique words in the text

The interpretation of the LIX value is shown in Table 3, while OVIX scores ranging from 60 to 69 indicate easy-to-read texts (Mühlenbock and Johansson Kokkinakis, 2009).

LIX-value	**Genre**
less than 25	Children's books
25-30	Easy texts
30-40	Normal text/fiction
40-50	Informative texts
50-60	Specialist literature
more than 60	Research, dissertations

Table 3: The LIX-scale, from Mühlenbock and Johansson Kokkinakis (2009)

To obtain preliminary results from non-automatic methods, a very small manual evaluation of correctness and perceived readability was also carried out. A randomly selected subset of the sentences in which at least one term had been replaced were classified into three classes by a physician: 1) The original meaning was retained after the synonym replacement, 2) The original meaning was only slightly altered after the synonym replacement, and 3) The original meaning was altered more than slightly after the synonym replacement. Sentences classified into the first category by the physician were further categorised for perceived readability by two other evaluators; both with university degrees in non-life science disciplines. The original and the transformed sentence were presented in random order, and the evaluators were only informed that the simplification was built on word replacement. The following categories were used for the evaluation of perceived readability: 1) The two presented sentences are equally easy/difficult to understand, 2) One of the sentences is easier to understand than the other. In the second case, the evaluator indicated which sentence was easier.

4 Results

In the used corpus subset, which contained 150 384 tokens (26 251 unique), 4 909 MeSH terms for which there exist a MeSH synonym were found. Among these found terms, 1 154 were replaced with their synonym. The 15 most frequently replaced terms are shown in Table 4, many of them being words typical for a professional language that have been replaced with compounds of every-day Swedish words, or abbreviations that have been replaced by an expanded form.

The total number of words increased from 150 384 to 150 717 after the synonym replace-

Original term	(English)	Replaced with	(Literal translation)	n
aorta	(aorta)	kroppspulsåder	(body-artery)	34
kolestas	(cholestasis)	gallstas	(biliary-stasis)	33
angioödem	(angioedema)	angioneurotiskt ödem	(angio-neurotic-oedema)	29
stroke	(stroke)	slaganfall	(strike-seizure)	29
TPN	(TPN)	parenteral näring, total	(parenteral nutrition, total)	26
GCS	(GCS)	Glasgow Coma Scale	(Glasgow Coma Scale)	20
mortalitet	(mortality)	dödlighet	(deathrate)	20
ödem	(oedema)	svullnad	(swelling)	20
legitimation	(licensure)	licens	(certificate)	18
RLS	(RLS)	rastlösa ben-syndrom	(restless legs-syndrome)	18
anemi	(anemia)	blodbrist	(blood-shortage)	17
anhöriga	(family)	familj	(family)	17
ekokardiografi	(echocardiography)	hjärtultraljuds-undersökning	(heart-ultrasound -examination)	17
artrit	(arthritis)	ledinflammation	(joint-inflammation)	16
MHC	(MHC)	histokompatibilitets-komplex	(histocompatibility-complex)	15

Table 4: The 15 most frequently replaced terms. As the most frequent synonym (or synonym with most known substrings) is always chosen for replacement, the same choice among a number of synonyms, or a number of abbreviation expansions, will always be made. The column **n** contains the number of times the original term was replaced with this synonym.

ment. Also the number of long words (more than six characters) increased from 51 530 to 51 851. This resulted in an increased LIX value, as can be seen in Table 5. Both before and after the transformation, the LIX-value lies on the border between the difficulty levels of informative texts and non-fictional texts. The replacement also had the effect that the number of unique words decreased with 138 words, which resulted in a lower OVIX, also to be seen in Table 5.

For the manual evaluation, 195 sentences, in which at least one term had been replaced, were randomly selected. For 17% of these sentences, the original meaning was slightly altered, and for 10%, the original meaning was more than slightly altered. The rest of the sentences, which retained their original meaning, were used for measuring perceived readability, resulting in the figures shown in Table 6. Many replaced terms occurred more than once among the evaluated sentences. Therefore, perceived difficulty was also measured for a subset of the evaluation data, in which it was ensured that each replaced term occurred exactly once, by only including the sentence in which it first appeared. These subset figures (denoted *Unique* in Table 6) did, however, only differ marginally from the figures for the entire set. Although there was a large difference between the two evaluators in how they assessed the effect of the synonym replacement, they both classified a substantially larger proportion of the sentences as easier to understand after the synonym replacement.

	LIX	OVIX
Original text	50	87.2
After synonym replacement	51	86.9

Table 5: LIX and OVIX before and after synonym replacement

5 Discussion

According to the LIX measure, the medical text became slightly more difficult to read after the transformation, which is the opposite result to that achieved in the study by Keskisärkkä and Jönsson (2012). Similar to this previous study, however, the text became slightly easier to read according to the OVIX measure, as the number of unique words decreased. As words longer than six characters result in a higher LIX value, a very plausible explanation for the increased LIX-value, is that short words derived from Greek or Latin have been replaced with longer compounds

Perceived effect of replacement	Evaluator 1 All (Unique)	Evaluator 2 All (Unique)
No difference	51% (52%)	29% (28%)
Easier	42% (42%)	54% (52%)
More difficult	7% (7%)	17% (21%)

Table 6: Results for the manual classification of perceived difficulty. Evaluator 1 classified 143 sentences and Evaluator 2 classified 140 sentences. The (Unique) column contains results when only the first a occurrence of a replacement of a particular term is included. A binomial sign test (Newbold et al., 2003, p. 532) was performed on the effect of the replacement, with the null hypothesis that the probability of creating a more difficult sentence was equal to that of creating an easier one. This hypothesis could be rejected for both evaluators; when including all sentences and also when only including the (Unique) subset, showing that the differences were statistically significant ($p \ll 0.01$).

of every-day words. Replacing an abbreviation or an acronym with its expanded long form has the same effect. Expanding acronyms also increases the number of words per sentence, which also results in a higher LIX value.

Studies on English medical text indicate, however, that simple surface measures do not accurately reflect the readability (Zeng-Treitler et al., 2007; Wu et al., 2013), and user studies have been performed to construct readability measures better adapted to the domain of medical texts (Kim et al., 2007; Leroy and Endicott, 2012). Therefore, although the manual evaluation was very limited in scope, the results from this evaluation might give a better indication of the effects of the system. This evaluation showed that the perceived readability often improved with synonym replacement, although there were also replacements that resulted in a decrease of perceived readability. Further studies are required to determine whether these results are generalisable to a larger group of readers. Such studies should also include an evaluation of actual readability, using methods similar to those of Leroy et al. (2012). The cases, in which the synonym replacement resulted in a perceived decrease in readability should also be further studied. It might, for instance, be better to use a frequency cut-off for distinguishing between rare and frequent words, as applied by Leroy et al. (2012), rather than always replacing a word with a more frequent synonym.

The manual evaluation also showed that the original semantic meaning had been at least slightly altered in almost a third of the sentences, which shows that the set of synonyms in Swedish MeSH might need to be adapted to make the synonyms suitable to use in a text simplification system. The replacements in Table 4 show three types of potential problems. First, there are also distant synonyms, as exemplified by *oedema* and *swelling*, where *oedema* means a specific type of swelling in the form of increased amount of liquid in the tissues, as opposed to e.g. increased amount of fat. Second, the MeSH terms are not always written in a form that is appropriate to use in running text, such as the term *parenteral nutrition, total*. Such terms need to be transformed to another format before they can be used for automatic synonym replacement. Third, although the abbreviations included in the manual evaluation were all expanded to the correct form, abbreviations within the medical domain are often overloaded with a number of different meanings (Liu et al., 2002). For instance, apart from being an acronym for *restless legs syndrome*, RLS can also mean *reaction level scale* (Cederblom, 2005). Therefore, in order to include abbreviations and acronyms in the synonym replacement method studied here, an abbreviation disambiguation needs to be carried out first (Gaudan et al., 2005; Savova et al., 2008). An alternative could be to automatically detect which abbreviations and acronyms that are defined in the text when they first are mentioned (Dannélls, 2006), and restrict the replacement method to those.

The sentence in Table 1 shows an example of a successful synonym replacement, replacing a word typically used by health professionals (*osteoporosis*) with a word typically used in everyday language (*bone-brittleness*). This sentence also gives an example of when not enough is replaced in the sentence for it to be easy to understand. Neither *trabeculation*, nor *pseudofractures*, are included in MeSH, which shows the importance of having access to comprehensive terminological resources for the method of synonym replacement to be successful. Extracting terms that are frequently occurring within the text genre that is to be simplified, but which are neither included in the used terminology, nor in a corpus of standard language such as Parole, could be a method for finding candidates for expanding the terminological resources. Semi-automatic methods could be applied for finding synonyms to these new candidate terms, as well as to existing terms within the terminology for which no synonyms are provided (Henriksson et al., 2013).

Table 1 also exemplifies a further issue not addressed here, namely the frequent occurrence of inflected words in Swedish text. No morphologic normalisation, e.g. lemmatisation, was performed of the text that was to be simplified or of the terms in MeSH (e.g. normalising *pseudo-fractures* to *pseudo-fracture*). Such a normalisation would have the potential of matching, and thereby replacing, a larger number of words, but it would also require that the replaced word is inflected to match the grammatical form of the original word.

An alternative to using frequency in the Parole corpus, or occurrence of substrings in a word in Parole, for determining when a synonym is to be replaced, is to use the frequency in a medical corpus. That corpus then has to be targeted towards laymen, as word frequency in texts targeted towards health professionals would favour word replacements with words typical to the professional language. Examples of such patient corpora could be health related web portals for patients (Kokkinakis, 2011). However, as also texts targeted towards patients have been shown to be difficult to understand, the method of searching for familiar words in substrings of medical terms might be relevant for assessing word difficulty also if easy medical corpora would be used.

6 Future work

A number of points for future work have already been mentioned, among which evaluating the method on a large set of target readers has the highest priority. Adapting the method to handle inflected words, studying how near synonyms and ambiguity of abbreviations affect the content of the transformed sentences, as well as studying methods for semi-automatic expansion of terminologies, are other topics that have already been mentioned.

It might also be the case that what synonym replacements are suitable are dependent on the context in which a word occurs. Methods for adapting assessment of word difficulty to context have been studied within the Semeval-2012 shared task on English lexical simplification (Specia et al., 2012), although it was shown that infrequent words are generally perceived as more difficult, regardless of context.

In addition to these points, it should be noted that we in this study have focused on one type medical text, i.e. medical journal text. As mentioned in the introduction, there is, however, another medical text type on which applying text simplification would also be highly relevant, namely health record text (Kvist and Velupillai, 2013; Kandula et al., 2010). The electronic health record is nowadays made available to patients via e-services in a number of countries, and there is also an on-going project constructing such a service in Sweden. Apart from health record text also containing many words derived from greek and latin, there are additional challenges associated with this type of text. As health record text is written under time pressure, it is often written in a telegraphic style with incomplete sentences and many abbreviations (Friedman et al., 2002; Aantaa, 2012). As was exemplified among the top 15 most frequently replaced words, abbreviations is one of the large problems when using the synonym replacement method for text simplification, as they are often overloaded with a number of meanings.

Future work, therefore, also includes the evaluation of synonym replacement on health record text. It also includes the study of writing tools for encouraging health professionals to produce text that is easier to understand for the patient, or at least easier to transform into more patient-friendly texts with methods similar to the method studied here (Ahltorp et al., 2013).

7 Conclusion

A method used in previous studies for assessing difficulty of words in Swedish text was further developed. The difficulty of a word was assessed not only by measuring the frequency of the word in a general corpus, but also by measuring the frequency of substrings of words, thereby adapting the method to the compounding nature of Swedish. The replacement was mainly evaluated by the two readability measures LIX and OVIX, showing a slightly decreased OVIX but a slightly increased LIX. A preliminary study on readers showed, however, an increased perceived readability after the synonym replacement. Studies on a larger reader group are required to draw any conclusions on the general effect of the method for assessment of word difficult. The preliminary results are, however, encouraging, showing that a method that replaces specialised words derived from latin and greek by compounds of every-day Swedish words can result in a increase of the perceived readability.

Acknowledgements

We would like to thank the three reviewers for many useful comments. This work was partly supported by a grant from the Vårdal Foundation

References

Kirsi Aantaa. 2012. Mot patientvänligare epikriser, en kontrastiv undersökning [towards more patient friendly discharge letters, a contrastive study]. Master's thesis, Department of Nordic Languages, University of Turku.

Magnus Ahltorp, Maria Skeppstedt, Hercules Dalianis, and Maria Kvist. 2013. Using text prediction for facilitating input and improving readability of clinical text. *Stud Health Technol Inform*, 192:1149.

Staffan Cederblom. 2005. *Medicinska förkortningar och akronymer (In Swedish)*. Studentlitteratur, Lund.

Dana Dannélls. 2006. Automatic acronym recognition. In *Proceedings of the 11th conference on European chapter of the Association for Computational Linguistics (EACL)*.

Johan Falkenjack, Katarina Heimann Mühlenbock, and Arne Jönsson. 2013. Features indicating readability in Swedish text. In *Proceedings of the 19th Nordic Conference of Computational Linguistics (NODALIDA 2013)*, pages 27–40.

Olle Findahl. 2010. *Svenskarna och Internet*. .se.

Carol Friedman, Pauline Kra, and Andrey Rzhetsky. 2002. Two biomedical sublanguages: a description based on the theories of zellig harris. *J Biomed Inform*, 35(4):222–35, Aug.

S. Gaudan, H. Kirsch, and D. Rebholz-Schuhmann. 2005. Resolving abbreviations to their senses in medline. *Bioinformatics*, 21(18):3658–3664, September.

M Gellerstam, Y Cederholm, and T Rasmark. 2000. The bank of Swedish. In *LREC 2000. The 2nd International Conference on Language Resources and Evaluation*, pages 329–333, Athens, Greece.

Aron Henriksson, Mike Conway, Martin Duneld, and Wendy W. Chapman. 2013. Identifying synonymy between SNOMED clinical terms of varying length using distributional analysis of electronic health records. In *Proceedings of the Annual Symposium of the American Medical Informatics Association (AMIA 2013)*, Washington DC, USA.

Sasikiran Kandula, Dorothy Curtis, and Qing Zeng-Treitler. 2010. A semantic and syntactic text simplification tool for health content. *AMIA Annu Symp Proc*, 2010:366–70.

Karolinska Institutet. 2012. Hur man använder den svenska MeSHen (In Swedish, translated as: How to use the Swedish MeSH). http://mesh.kib.ki.se/swemesh/manual_se.html. Accessed 2012-03-10.

Alla Keselman and Catherine Arnott Smith. 2012. A classification of errors in lay comprehension of medical documents. *Journal of Biomedical Informatics*, 45(6):1151–1163.

Alla Keselman, Robert Logan, Catherine Arnott Smith, Gondy Leroy, and Qing Zeng-Treitler. 2008. Developing informatics tools and strategies for consumer-centered health communication. In *J Am Med Inform Assoc*, volume 15:4, pages 473–483.

Robin Keskisärkkä and Arne Jönsson. 2012. Automatic text simplification via synonym replacement. In *Proceedings of Swedish Language Technology Conference 2012*.

Hyeoneui Kim, Sergey Goryachev, Graciela Rosemblat, Allen Browne, Alla Keselman, and Qing Zeng-Treitler. 2007. Beyond surface characteristics: a new health text-specific readability measurement. *AMIA Annu Symp Proc*, pages 418–422.

Dimitrios Kokkinakis and Maria Toporowska Gronostaj. 2006. Lay language versus professional language within the cardiovascular subdomain - a contrastive study. In *Proceedings of the 2006 WSEAS Int. Conf. on Cellular & Molecular Biology, Biophysics & Bioengineering*.

Dimitrios Kokkinakis, Markus Forsberg, Sofie Johansson Kokkinakis, Frida Smith, and Joakim Öhlén. 2012. Literacy demands and information to cancer patients. In *Proceedings of the 15th International Conference on Text, Speech and Dialogue*, pages 64–71.

Dimitrios Kokkinakis. 2011. Evaluating the coverage of three controlled health vocabularies with focus on findings, signs and symptoms. In NEALT Proceedings Series, editor, *NODALIDA*, volume 12, pages 27–31.

Dimitrios Kokkinakis. 2012. The journal of the Swedish medical association - a corpus resource for biomedical text mining in Swedish. In *The Third Workshop on Building and Evaluating Resources for Biomedical Text Mining (BioTxtM), an LREC Workshop. Turkey*.

Maria Kvist and Sumithra Velupillai. 2013. Professional language in swedish radiology reports – characterization for patient-adapted text simplification. In *Scandinavian Conference on Health Informatics*, Copenhagen, Denmark, August.

Gondy Leroy and Hsinchun Chen. 2001. Meeting medical terminology needs-the ontology-enhanced medical concept mapper. *IEEE Transactions on Information Technology in Biomedicine*, 5(4):261–270.

Gondy Leroy and James E. Endicott. 2012. Combining nlp with evidence-based methods to find text metrics related to perceived and actual text difficulty. In *IHI*, pages 749–754.

Gondy Leroy, Evren Eryilmaz, and Benjamin T. Laroya. 2006. Health information text characteristics. In *AMIA Annu Symp Proc*, pages 479–483.

Gondy Leroy, James E Endicott, Obay Mouradi, David Kauchak, and Melissa L Just. 2012. Improving perceived and actual text difficulty for health information consumers using semi-automated methods. *AMIA Annu Symp Proc*, 2012:522–31.

Hongfang Liu, Alan R Aronson, and Carol Friedman. 2002. A study of abbreviations in medline abstracts. *Proc AMIA Symp*, pages 464–8.

Katarina Mühlenbock and Sofie Johansson Kokkinakis. 2009. Lix 68 revisited - an extended readability measure. In *Proceedings of Corpus Linguistics 2009*.

Paul Newbold, William L. Carlson, and Betty Thorne. 2003. *Statistics for business and economics*. Prentice-Hall, Upper Saddle River, N. J., 5. ed. edition.

John I. Saeed. 1997. *Semantics*. Blackwell Publishers, Oxford.

Guergana K. Savova, Anni Coden, Igor L. Sominsky, Rie Johnson, Philip V. Ogren, Piet C. de Groen, and Christopher G. Chute. 2008. Word sense disambiguation across two domains: Biomedical literature and clinical notes. *Journal of Biomedical Informatics*, 41(6):1088–1100.

Lucia Specia, Sujay Kumar Jauhar, and Rada Mihalcea. 2012. Semeval-2012 task 1: English lexical simplification. In **SEM, First Joint Conference on Lexical and Computational Semantics*, pages 347–355, Montréal, Canada.

Danny T Y Wu, David A Hanauer, Qiaozhu Mei, Patricia M Clark, Lawrence C An, Jianbo Lei, Joshua Proulx, Qing Zeng-Treitler, and Kai Zheng. 2013. Applying multiple methods to assess the readability of a large corpus of medical documents. *Stud Health Technol Inform*, 192:647–51.

Qing T. Zeng, Tony Tse, Jon Crowell, Guy Divita, Laura Roth, and Allen C. Browne. 2005. Identifying consumer-friendly display (cfd) names for health concepts. In *Proceedings of AMIA Annual Symposium*, pages 859–863.

Qing Zeng-Treitler, Hyeoneui Kim, Sergey Goryachev, Alla Keselman, Laura Slaughter, and Catherine. A. Smith. 2007. Text characteristics of clinical reports and their implications for the readability of personal health records. *Medinfo*, 12(Pt 2):1117–1121.

Segmentation of patent claims for improving their readability

Gabriela Ferraro[1 2], **Hanna Suominen**[1–4], **Jaume Nualart**[1 3]
[1]NICTA / Locked Bag 8001, Canberra ACT 2601, Australia
[2]The Australian National University
[3]University of Canberra
[4]University of Turku
firstname.lastname@nicta.com.au

Abstract

Good readability of text is important to ensure efficiency in communication and eliminate risks of misunderstanding. Patent claims are an example of text whose readability is often poor. In this paper, we aim to improve claim readability by a clearer presentation of its content. Our approach consist in segmenting the original claim content at two levels. First, an entire claim is segmented to the components of preamble, transitional phrase and body, using a rule-based approach. Second, a conditional random field is trained to segment the components into clauses. An alternative approach would have been to modify the claim content which is, however, prone to also changing the meaning of this legal text. For both segmentation levels, we report results from statistical evaluation of segmentation performance. In addition, a qualitative error analysis was performed to understand the problems underlying the clause segmentation task. Our accuracy in detecting the beginning and end of preamble text is 1.00 and 0.97, respectively. For the transitional phase, these numbers are 0.94 and 1.00 and for the body text, 1.00 and 1.00. Our precision and recall in the clause segmentation are 0.77 and 0.76, respectively. The results give evidence for the feasibility of automated claim and clause segmentation, which may help not only inventors, researchers, and other laypeople to understand patents but also patent experts to avoid future legal cost due to litigations.

1 Introduction

Clear language is important to ensure efficiency in communication and eliminate risks of misunderstanding. With written text, this clarity is measured by readability. In the last years, we have witnessed an increasing amount work towards *improving text readability*. In general, these efforts focus on making general text easier to understand to non-native speakers and people with special needs, poor literacy, aphasia, dyslexia, or other language deficits.

In this paper, we address making *technical text* more readable to *laypeople*, defined as those without professional or specialised knowledge in a given field. Technical documentation as scientific papers or legal contracts are two genres of written text that are difficult to understand (Alberts et al., 2011). An extreme example that takes the worst from both these worlds is the *claim section of patent documents*: it defines the boundaries of the legal protection of the invention by describing complex technical issues and using specific legal jargon (Pressman, 2006). Moreover, due to international conventions, each patent claim must be written into a single sentence. This leads to very long sentences with complex syntactic structures that are hard to read and comprehend not only for laypeople but also for technical people who are not trained to read patent claims.

As an example of other efforts with similar goals to improve the readability of technical text to laypeople, we mention the CLEF eHealth shared tasks in 2013 and 2014 (Suominen et al., 2013). However, instead of inventors, researchers, and other claim readers, they target patients and their next-of-kins by developing and evaluating technologies to improve the readability of clinical reports and help them in finding further information related to their condition in the Internet.

Some proposals have also been made in order to improve claim readability, for example, by applying simplification, paraphrasing, and summarisation methods (see Section 2). However, these approaches *modify the claim content*. This increases the risk of changing also the meaning, which is not desirable in the context of patent claims and other legal documents.

In this paper, we propose an alternative method that focuses on *clarifying the presentation* of the claim content rather than its modification. Since readability strongly affects text comprehension (Inui et al., 2003), the aim of this study is to make the content of the patent claims more legible and consequently make them easier to comprehend.

As the first steps towards this improved presentation of the patent claims, we propose to *segment the original text*. Our approach is data driven and we perform the segmentation at two levels: first, an *entire claim* is segmented *into three components* (i.e., preamble, transition, and body text) and second, the components are further segmented *into clauses*. At the first level, we use a *rule-based* method and at the second level, we apply a *conditional random field*.

We evaluate segmentation performance *statistically* at both levels and in addition, we analyse errors in clause segmentation *qualitatively*; because our *performance at the first level is almost perfect* (i.e., for detecting the beginning and end of the preamble, the accuracy percentages are 100 and 97 and these numbers are 94 and 100 for the transition and 100 and 100 for the body text), we focus on the errors at the second level alone. In comparison, we have the precision of 77 per cent and recall of 76 per cent in clause segmentation. Even though this performance *at the second level* is not perfect, it is *significantly better than* the respective percentages of 41 and 29 (0.2 and 0.3) for *a baseline* based on both punctuation and keywords (punctuation only).

The rest of the paper is organised as follows: Section 2 describes as background information of this study includes an explanation about what patent claims are, how to read them, and what kind of related work exists on claim readability. Section 3 outlines our materials and methods. Section 4 presents the experiments results and discussion. Finally, conclusions and ideas for future work are presented in Section 5.

2 Background

2.1 Patent claims

Patent documents have a predefined document structure that consists of *several sections*, such as the title, abstract, background of the invention, description of the drawings, and claims. As already mentioned, the claims can be seen as the most important section as they define the scope of legal protection of the invention. In most modern patent laws, patent applications must have at least one claim (Pressman, 2006).

The claims are written into a *single sentence* because of international conventions. Figure 1 provides an example claim.

> [Toolholder]$_p$, [comprising]$_t$ [a holder body with an insert site at its forward end comprising a bottom surface and at least one side wall where there projects a pin from said bottom surface upon which there is located an insert having a central bore, a clamping wedge for wedging engagement between a support surface of the holder and an adjacent edge surface of said insert and an actuating screw received in said wedge whilst threadably engaged in a bore of said holder, said support surface and said edge surface are at least partially converging downwards said wedge clamp having distantly provided protrusions for abutment against the top face and the edge surface of said insert, characterised in that the wedge consists of a pair of distantly provided first protrusions for abutment against a top face of the insert, and a pair of distantly provided second protrusions for abutment against an adjacent edge surface]$_b$.

Figure 1: An example patent claim. We have used brackets to illustrate claim components and the sub-scripts *p*, *t*, and *b* correspond to the preamble, transition, and body text, respectively.

Furthermore, a claim should be composed by, at least, the following parts,

1. *Preamble* is an introduction, which describes the class of the invention.

2. *Transition* is a phrase or linking word that relates the preamble with the rest of the claim. The expressions *comprising*, *containing*, *including*, *consisting of*, *wherein* and *characterise in that* are the most common transitions.

3. *Body text* describes the invention and recites its limitations.

We have also included an illustration of these claim components in Figure 1.

Because a claim is a single sentence, special *punctuation conventions* have been developed and are being used by patent writers. Modern claims follow a format where the preamble is separated

Table 1: Per claim demographics

		Training set	Test set
# tokens	mean	60	66
	min	7	8
	max	440	502
# boundaries	mean	5	5
	min	1	1
	max	53	41

from the transition by a comma, the transition from the body text by a colon, and each invention element in the body text by a semicolon (Radack, 1995). Other specifications regarding punctuation are the following text elaboration and element combination conventions:

- A claim should contain a period only in the end.
- A comma should be used in all natural pauses.
- The serial comma[1] should be used to separate the elements of a list.
- Dashes, quotes, parentheses, and abbreviations should be avoided.

Because a claim takes the form of a single sentence, long sentences are common. Meanwhile, in the general discourse (e.g., news articles) sentences are composed of twenty to thirty words, claim sentences with over a hundred words are very frequent (see, e.g., Table 1 related to materials used in this paper). As a consequence, claims usually contain several *subordinate and coordinate clauses*, as they enable the aforementioned elaboration and the combination of elements of equal importance, respectively.

As claims are difficult to read and interpret, several books and tutorials suggest how claims should be *read* (Radack, 1995; Pressman, 2006). The first step towards reading a claim is to identify its components (i.e., preamble, transition, and body text). Another suggestion is to identify and highlight the different elements of the invention spelled out in the body text of the claims.

[1]The serial comma (also known as the Oxford comma) is the comma used mediately before a coordination conjunction (e.g., *CDs, DVDs, and magnetic tapes* where the last comma indicates that *DVDs* and *magnetic tapes* are not mixed). `http://oxforddictionaries.com` (accessed 28 Feb, 2014)

The clear punctuation marks and lexical markers enable the claim component segmentation, as suggested above. Moreover, the predominance of intra-sentential syntactic structures (e.g., subordinate and coordinate constructions) favours segmenting patent claims into clauses. These clauses can then be presented as a sequence of segments which is likely to improve claim readability.

2.2 Related work

So far, not many studies have addressed the problem of improving the readability of patents claims. In particular, to the best of our knowledge, there is no research that specifically targets the problem of presenting the claims in a more readable layout. Consequently, we focus on efforts devoted to claim readability in general with an emphasis on text segmentation.

We begin by discussing three studies that address *text simplification in patent claims*. Note that these approaches modify the claim content which may also change their meaning. This is riskier in the context of patent documents and other legal text than our approach of clarifying the presentation. Moreover, in order achieve a reasonable performance, the methods of these studies require sophisticated tools for discourse analysis and syntactic parsing. Usually these tools also need to be tailored to the genre of claim text.

First, a *parsing methodology* to simplify sentences in *US patent documents* has been proposed (Sheremetyeva, 2003). The resulting analysis structure is a syntactic dependency tree and the simplified sentences are generated based on the intermediate chunking structure of the parser. However, neither the tools used to simplify sentences nor the resulting improvement in readability has been formally measured.

Second, simplification of *Japanese claim sentences* has been addressed through a rule-based method (Shinmori et al., 2003). It identifies the *discourse structure* of a claim using cue phrases and lexico-syntactic patterns. Then it *paraphrases* each discourse segment.

Third, a claim simplification method to *paraphrase* and *summarise* text has been introduced (Bouayad-Agha et al., 2009). It is *multilingual* and consists of claim segmentation, coreference resolution, and discourse tree derivation. In claim segmentation, a rule-based system is compared to machine learning with the conclusion of the former approach outperforming the latter. The machine learning approach is, however, very similar to the clause segmentation task described in this paper. They differ in the features used to characterized the clause boundaries and in evaluation. For the evaluation, these authors use the cosine similarity to calculate a 1:1 term overlap between the automated solution and gold standard set whereas we assess whether a token is an accurate segment boundary or not.

We continue by discussing a *complementary method* to our approach of improving the readability of claims through their clearer presentation without modifying the text itself. This work by Shinmori et al. (2012) is inspired by the fact that claims must be understood in the light of the definitions provided in the description section of the patents. It aims to enrich the content by *aligning claim phrases with relevant text from the description section*. For the evaluation, the authors have inspected 38 patent documents. The automated method generates 35 alignments for these documents (i.e., twenty correct and fifteen false) and misses only six. It would be interesting to test if this alignment method and the claim segmentation proposed in this paper complement each other.

We end by noting that the task of segmenting claim phrases is similar to the task of *detecting phrase boundaries* by Sang and Déjean (2001) in the sense that the segments we want to identify are intra-sentential. However, the peculiar syntactic style of claims makes the phrase detection strategies not applicable (see Ferraro (2012) for a detailed study on the linguistic idiosyncrasy of patent claims).

3 Materials and methods

In this paper, we performed *statistical experiments* and *qualitative error analyses* related to two segmentation tasks (see Figure 2):

1. Segmenting claims section to the components for preamble, transition, and body text.

2. Segmenting each claim to subordinate and coordinate clauses.

For Task 1, we developed a *rule-based method* using the *General Architecture for Text Engineering* (GATE) (Cunningham et al., 2011). The system had three rules, one for each of the claim parts we were interested in identifying. The rules were

Table 2: Dataset demographics

	# claims	# segments	# words
Training set	811	4397	48939
Development set	10	15	260
Test set	80	491	5517

written in terms of JAPE grammars.[2] In order to process the rules, the GATE pipeline illustrated in Figure 3 was applied. Because transitions should match with the first instance of a closed set of keywords (we used *comprise*, *consist*, *wherein*, *characterize*, *include*, *have*, and *contain*), our first rule identified a transition and, using its boundary indices, we restricted the application of our further rules. This resulted in the following application order:

$$\text{transition} \longrightarrow \text{preamble} \longrightarrow \text{body text.}$$

Our two other rules relied on lexico-syntactic patterns and punctuation marks. Note that even though punctuation conventions have been developed for claim writing (see Section 2.1), their following is not mandatory. This led us to experiment these more complex rules. The first task was applied to the complete dataset (training, development, and test sets merged into one single dataset) described in Table 2.

For Task 2, our method was based on *supervised machine learning* (ML). To train this ML classifier, we used a patent claim corpus annotated with clause boundaries. This corpus was provided by the TALN Research Group from Universitat Pompeu Fabra. The aim of the segmentation classifier was to decide whether a claim token is a segment boundary or not, given a context. Thus, every token was seen as a candidate for placing a segment boundary. Following standard ML traditions, we split the dataset in *training*, *development*, and *test sets* (Tables 2 and 1).

The corpus was analysed with a transitional[3] version of *Bohnet's parser* (Bohnet and Kuhn, 2012). It was one of the best parsers in the CoNLL Shared Task 2009 (Hajič et al., 2009).

[2]JAPE, a component of GATE, is a finite state transducer that operates over annotations based on regular expressions.

[3]Patent claim sentences can be very long which implies long-distance dependencies. Therefore, transition-based parsers, which typically have a linear or quadratic complexity (Nivre and Nilsson, 2004; Attardi, 2006), are better suited for parsing patent sentences than graph-based parsers, which usually have a cubic complexity.

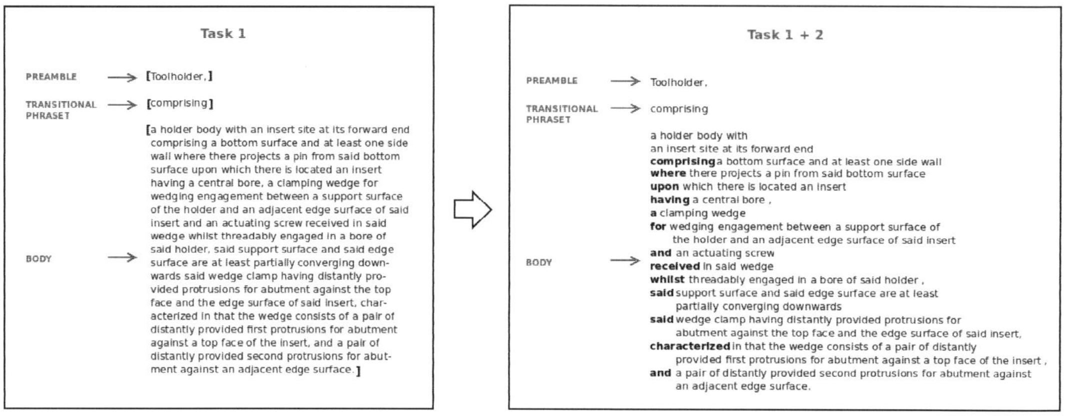

Figure 2: Example of the claim segmentation experiments

ANNI Tokenizer	⟶	RegEx Sentence Splitter	⟶	OpenNLP
POS Tagger	⟶	Noun Phrase Chunker	⟶	JAPE

Figure 3: GATE pipeline for Task 1

In order to characterise the clause boundaries, the following *features* were used for each token in the corpus:

- lemma of the current token,
- part-of-speech (POS) tag[4] of the current token as well as POS-tags of the two immediately preceding and two immediately subsequent words,
- syntactic head and dependent of the current token, and
- syntactic dependency relation between the current token and its head and dependent tokens.

Moreover, the fifteen most frequent lemmas and five most frequent POS-tags and punctuation marks were used as features we called segmentation keywords (Table 3).

For classification we used the *CRF++ toolkit*, an open source implementation of conditional random fields (Lafferty et al., 2001). This framework for building probabilistic graphical models to segment and label sequence data has been successfully applied to solve chunking (Sha and Pereira, 2003), information extraction (Smith, 2006), and other sequential labelling problems. We compared the results obtained by CRF++ with the following baselines:

- *Baseline 1*: each punctuation mark is a segment boundary, and
- *Baseline 2*: each punctuation mark and keyword is a segment boundary.

Table 3: The most frequent lemmas and POS-tags in the beginning of a segment.

Rank	Lemmas	Abs. Freq.	Rel. Freq.
1	and	675	0.137
2	wherein	554	0.112
3	for	433	0.088
4	which	174	0.035
5	have	158	0.032
6	to	155	0.031
7	characterize	152	0.031
8	a	149	0.030
9	the	142	0.028
10	say	140	0.028
11	is	64	0.013
12	that	62	0.012
13	form	59	0.012
14	in	58	0.011
15	when	56	0.011
Rank	POS-tag	Abs. Freq.	Rel. Freq.
1	IN	739	0.150
2	CC	686	0.139
3	VBN	511	0.104
4	VBG	510	0.104
5	WRB	409	0.083

[4]The POS-tag corresponds to the Peen Tree Bank tag set (Marcus et al., 1993) whereas IN = preposition or conjunction, subordinating; CC = Coordinating Conjunction; VBN = Verb, past participle; VBG = verb, gerund or present participle; WRB = Wh-adverb.

Table 4: Evaluation of claim components

		Correct	Incorrect
Preamble	Beginning	100%	0%
	End	97%	3%
Transition	Beginning	94%	6%
	End	100%	0%
Body text	Beginning	100%	0%
	End	100%	0%

Performance in Task 1 was assessed using the *accuracy*. Due to the lack of a corpus annotated with claims components, we selected twenty claims randomly and performed the annotation ourselves (i.e., one of the authors annotated the claims). The annotator was asked to assess whether the beginning and ending of a claim component was successfully identified.

Performance in Task 2 was evaluated using the *precision*, *recall*, and *F-score* on the test set. We considered that clause segmentation is a precision oriented task, meaning that we emphasised the demand for a high precision at the expense of a possibly more modest recall.

In order to better understand errors in clause segmentation, we analysed errors qualitatively using *content analysis* (Stemler, 2001). This method is commonly used in evaluation of language technologies. Fifty segmentation errors were randomly selected and manually analysed by one of the authors.

4 Results and discussion

4.1 Statistical performance evaluation in Tasks 1 and 2

We achieved a substantial accuracy in Task 1, claim component segmentation (Table 4). That is, the resulting segmentation was almost perfect. This was not surprising since we were processing simple and well defined types of segments. However, there was a small mismatch in the boundary identification for the preamble and the transition segments.

Our ML method clearly outperformed both its baselines in Task 2 (Table 5). It had the precision of 77 per cent and recall of 76 per cent in clause segmentation. The respective percentages were 41 and 29 for the baseline based on both punctuation and keywords. If punctuation was used alone, both the precision and recall were almost zero.

Table 5: Evaluation of claim clauses

	Precision	Recall	F-score
Baseline 1	0.2%	0.3%	2.6%
Baseline 2	41%	29%	34%
CRF++	77%	76%	76%

4.2 Qualitative analysis of errors in Task 2

The most common errors in clause segmentation were due to two reasons: first, ambiguity in coordinating conjunctions (e.g., commas as wll as *and*, *or*, and other particles) and second, consecutive segmentation keywords.

Segmentation errors caused by ambiguous coordinating conjunctions were due to the fact that not all of them were used as segment delimiters. Let us illustrate this with the following automatically segmented claim fragment with two coordinating conjunctions (a segment is a string between square brackets, the integer sub-script indicating the segment number, and the conjunctions in italics):

...[said blade advancing member comprises a worm rotatable by detachable handle]$_1$ [*or* key]$_2$ [*and* meshingeorm wheel secured to a shift]$_3$ ...

In this example, the two conjunctions were considered as segment delimiters which resulted in an incorrect segmentation. The correct analysis would have been to maintain the fragment as a single segment since simple noun phrases are not annotated as individual segments in our corpus.

Segmentation errors due to consecutive segmentation keywords resulted in undesirable segments only once in our set of fifty cases. This happened because the classifier segmented every encounter with a segmentation keyword, even when the keywords were consecutive. We illustrate this case with the following example, which contains two consecutive keywords, a verb in past participle (*selected*) and a subordinate conjunction (*for*). Example (a) shows a wrong segmentation, while example (b) shows its correct segmentation.

...(a) [said tool to be]$_1$ [selected]$_2$ [for the next working operation]$_3$ ...

...(b) [said tool to be selected]$_1$ [for working]$_2$ ...

In general, correcting both these error types should be relatively straightforward. First, to solve the problem of ambiguous commas, a possible solution could be to constrain their application as keywords, for example, by combining commas with other context features. Second, segmentation errors caused by consecutive segmentation keywords could be solved, for example, by applying a set of correction rules after the segmentation algorithm (Tjong and Sang, 2001).

5 Conclusion and future work

In this paper we have presented our on-going research on claim readability. We have proposed a method that focuses on presenting the claims in a clearer way rather than modifying their text content. This claim clarity is an important characteristic for inventors, researchers, and other laypeople. It may also be useful for patent experts, because clear clauses may help them to avoid future legal cost due to litigations. Moreover, better capabilities to understand patent documents contribute to democratisation of the invention and, therefore, to human knowledge.

For future work, we plan to conduct a user-centered evaluation study on claim readability. We wish to ask laypeople and patents experts to assess the usability and usefulness of our approach. Furthermore, we plan to consider text highlighting, terminology linking to definitions, and other content enrichment functionalities as ways of improving claim readability.

Acknowledgments

NICTA is funded by the Australian Government through the Department of Communications and the Australian Research Council through the ICT Centre of Excellence Program. We also express our gratitude to the TALN Research Group from Universitat Pompeu Fabra for their corpus development. Finally, we thank the anonymous reviewers of The 3rd Workshop on Predicting and Improving Text Readability for Target Reader Populations (PITR 2014), held in conjunction with the 14th Conference of the European Chapter of the Association for Computational Linguistics (EACL 2014), for their comments and suggestions.

References

D. Alberts, C. Barcelon Yang, D. Fobare-DePonio, K. Koubek, S. Robins, M. Rodgers, E. Simmons, and D. DeMarco. 2011. Introduction to patent searching. In M Lupu, J Tait, . Mayer, and A J Trippe, editors, *Current Challenges in Patent Information Retrieval*, pages 3–44, Toulouse, France. Springer.

G. Attardi. 2006. Experiments with a multilanguage non-projective dependency parser. In *Proceedings of the Tenth Conference on Computational Natural Language Learning*, CoNLL-X '06, pages 166–170, Stroudsburg, PA, USA. Association for Computational Linguistics.

B. Bohnet and J. Kuhn. 2012. The best of both worlds: a graph-based completion model for transition-based parsers. In *Proceedings of the 13th Conference of the European Chapter of the Association for Computational Linguistics*, EACL '12, pages 77–87, Stroudsburg, PA, USA. Association for Computational Linguistics.

N. Bouayad-Agha, G. Casamayor, G. Ferraro, S. Mille, V. Vidal, and Leo Wanner. 2009. Improving the comprehension of legal documentation: the case of patent claims. In *Proceedings of the 12th International Conference on Artificial Intelligence and Law*, ICAIL '09, pages 78–87, New York, NY, USA. Association for Computing Machinery.

H. Cunningham, D. Maynard, K. Bontcheva, V. Tablan, N. Aswani, I. Roberts, G. Gorrell, A. Funk, A. Roberts, D. Damljanovic, T. Heitz, M. A. Greenwood, H. Saggion, J. Petrak, Y. Li, and W. Peters. 2011. *Text Processing with GATE (Version 6)*. Gateway Press CA, Shefield. UK.

G. Ferraro. 2012. *Towards Deep Content Extraction: The Case of Verbal Relations in Patent Claims. PhD Thesis*. Department of Information and Communication Technologies, Pompeu Fabra Univesity, Barcelona. Catalonia. Spain.

J. Hajič, M. Ciaramita, R. Johansson, D. Kawahara, M. A. Mart, L. Márquez, A. Meyers, J. Nivre, S. Pad, J. Stepanek, et al. 2009. The CoNLL-2009 shared task: syntactic and semantic dependencies in multiple languages. In *Proceedings of the Thirteenth Conference on Computational Natural Language Learning: Shared Task*, page 118, Stroudsburg, PA, USA. Association for Computational Linguistics.

K. Inui, A. Fujita, T. Takahashi, R. Iida, and T. Iwakura. 2003. Text simplification for reading assistance: A project note. In *In Proceedings of the 2nd International Workshop on Paraphrasing: Paraphrase Acquisition and Applications*, IWP '03, pages 9–16, Stroudsburg, PA, USA. Association for Computational Linguistics.

D. Lafferty, A. McCallum, and F. C. N. Pereira. 2001. Conditional random fields: Probabilistic models for segmenting and labeling sequence data. In *Proceedings of the Eighteenth International Conference on Machine Learning*, ICML '01, pages 282–289, San Francisco, CA, USA. Morgan Kaufmann Publishers Inc.

M. P. Marcus, B. Santorini, and M. A. Marcinkiewicz. 1993. Building a large annotated corpus of English: The Penn Treebank. *Computational Linguistics*, 19(2):313–330.

J. Nivre and J. Nilsson. 2004. Memory-based dependency parsing. In *Proceedings of the Eight Conference on Computational Natural Language Learning*, CoNLL '04, Stroudsburg, PA, USA. Association for Computational Linguistics.

D. Pressman. 2006. *Patent It Yourself*. Nolo, Berkeley, CA.

D. V. Radack. 1995. Reading and understanding patent claims. *JOM*, 47(11):69–69.

E. T. K. Sang and H. Déjean. 2001. Introduction to the CoNLL-2001 shared task: Clause identification. In W. Daelemans and R. Zajac, editors, *Proceedings of the Fith Conference on Computational Natural Language Learning*, volume 7 of *CoNLL '01*, pages 53–57, Toulouse, France.

F. Sha and F. Pereira. 2003. Shallow parsing with conditional random fields. In *Proceedings of the 2003 Conference of the North American Chapter of the Association for Computational Linguistics on Human Language Technology*, volume 1 of *NAACL '03*, pages 134–141, Stroudsburg, PA, USA. Association for Computational Linguistics.

S. Sheremetyeva. 2003. Natural language analysis of patent claims. In *Proceedings of the ACL 2003 Workshop on Patent Processing*, ACL '03, Stroudsburg, PA, USA. Association for Computational Linguistics.

A. Shinmori, M. Okumura, Y. Marukawa, and M. Iwayama. 2003. Patent claim processing for readability: structure analysis and term explanation. In *Proceedings of the ACL-2003 Workshop on Patent Corpus Processing*, volume 20 of *PATENT '03*, pages 56–65, Stroudsburg, PA, USA. Association for Computational Linguistics.

A. Shinmori, M. Okumura, and Marukawa. 2012. Aligning patent claims with the "detailed description" for readability. *Journal of Natural Language Processing*, 12(3):111–128.

A. Smith. 2006. Using Gazetteers in discriminative information extraction. In *Proceedings of the Tenth Conference on Computational Natural Language Learning*, CoNLL '06, pages 10–8, Stroudsburg, PA, USA. Association for Computational Linguistics.

S. Stemler. 2001. An overview of content analysis. *Practical Assessment, Research and Evaluation*, 7(17).

H. Suominen, S. Salantera, S. Velupillai, W. W. Chapman, G. Savova, N. Elhadad, S. Pradhan, B. R. South, D. L. Mowery, G. J. F. Jones, J. Leveling, L. Kelly, L. Goeuriot, Da Martinez, and Gu Zuccon. 2013. Overview of the ShARe/CLEF eHealth Evaluation Lab 2013. In Pa Forner, H Müller, R Parades, P Rosso, and B Stein, editors, *Information Access Evaluation: Multilinguality, Multimodality, and Visualization. Proceedings of the 4th International Conference of the CLEF Initiative*, volume 8138 of *Lecture Notes in Computer Science*, pages 212–231, Heidelberg, Germany. Springer.

E. F. Tjong and Kim Sang. 2001. Memory-based clause identification. In *Proceedings of the 2001 workshop on Computational Natural Language Learning - Volume 7*, ConLL '01, Stroudsburg, PA, USA. Association for Computational Linguistics.

Improving Readability of Swedish Electronic Health Records through Lexical Simplification: First Results

Gintarė Grigonytė[a], Maria Kvist[bc], Sumithra Velupillai[b], Mats Wirén[a]
[a]Department of Linguistics, Stockholm University, Sweden
[b]Department of Computer and Systems Sciences, Stockholm University, Sweden
[c]Department of Learning, Informatics, Management and Ethics, Karolinska Institutet, Sweden
gintare@ling.su.se, maria.kvist@karolinska.se,
sumithra@dsv.su.se, mats.wiren@ling.su.se

Abstract

This paper describes part of an ongoing effort to improve the readability of Swedish electronic health records (EHRs). An EHR contains systematic documentation of a single patient's medical history across time, entered by healthcare professionals with the purpose of enabling safe and informed care. Linguistically, medical records exemplify a highly specialised domain, which can be superficially characterised as having telegraphic sentences involving displaced or missing words, abundant abbreviations, spelling variations including misspellings, and terminology. We report results on lexical simplification of Swedish EHRs, by which we mean detecting the unknown, out-of-dictionary words and trying to resolve them either as compounded known words, abbreviations or misspellings.

1 Introduction

An electronic health record (EHR; Swedish: *patientjournal*) contains systematic documentation of a single patient's medical history across time, entered by healthcare professionals with the purpose of enabling safe and informed care. The value of EHRs is further increased by the fact that they provide a source of information for statistics and research, and a documentation for the patient through the Swedish Patient Data Act. EHRs collect information from a range of sources, such as administration of drugs and therapies, test results, preoperative notes, operative notes, progress notes, discharge notes, etc.

EHRs contain both structured parts (such as details about the patient, lab results, diagnostic codes, etc.) and unstructured parts (in the form of free text). The free-text part of EHRs is referred to as clinical text, as opposed to the kind of general medical text found in medical journals, books or web pages containing information about health care. Clinical texts have many subdomains depending on the medical speciality of the writer and the intended reader. There are more formal kinds of EHRs, such as discharge summaries and radiology reports, directed to other physicians, and more informal kinds such as daily notes, produced by nurses and physicians (as memory notes for themselves or for the team). In spite of the Patient Data Act, the patient is seldom seen as a receiver or reader of the document.

Linguistically, health records exemplify a highly specialised domain, which can be superficially characterised as having telegraphic sentences involving displaced or missing words, abundant abbreviations, undisputed misspellings, spelling variation which may or may not amount to misspellings depending on the degree of prescriptivism, and terminology. While this specialised style has evolved as an efficient means of communication between healthcare professionals, it presents formidable challenges for laymen trying to decode it.

In spite of this, there has been no previous work on the problem of automatically improving the readability of Swedish EHRs. As an initial attempt in this direction, we provide an automatic approach to the problem of lexical simplification, by which we mean detecting the unknown, out of dictionary words and trying to resolve them either as compounds generated from known words, as abbreviations or as misspellings. As an additional result, we obtain a distribution of how prevalent these problems are in the clinical domain.

2 Lexical challenges to readability of EHRs

A major reason for the obstacles to readability of EHRs for laymen stems from the fact that they are written under time pressure by professionals, for professionals (Kvist et al., 2011). This results in a telegraphic style, with omissions, abbreviations and misspellings, as reported for several languages including Swedish, Finnish, English, French, Hungarian and German (Laippala et al., 2009; Friedman et al., 2002; Hagège et al., 2011; Surján and Héja, 2003; Bretschneider et al., 2013). The omitted words are often subjects, verbs, prepositions and articles (Friedman et al., 2002; Bretschneider et al., 2013).

Unsurprisingly, medical terminology abounds in EHRs. What makes this problem an even greater obstacle to readability is that many medical terms (and their inflections) originate from Latin or Greek. Different languages have adapted these terms differently (Bretschneider et al., 2013). The Swedish medical terminology went through a change during the 1990s due to a *swedification* of diagnostic expressions performed in the 1987 update of the Swedish version of ICD, the International Classification of Diseases[1]. For this version, the Swedish National Board of Health and Welfare decided to partly change the terminology of traditional Latin- and Greek-rooted words to a spelling compatible to Swedish spelling rules, as well as abandoning the original rules for inflection (Smedby, 1991). In this spelling reform, *c* and *ch* pronounced as *k* was changed to *k*, *ph* was changed to *f*, *th* to *t*, and *oe* was changed to *e*. For example, the technical term for cholecsystitis (inflammation of the gall bladder) is spelled *kolecystit* in contemporary Swedish, thus following the convention of changing *ch* to *k* and removing the Latin ending of *-is*. The results[2] of exact matching to *kolecystit* (English: cholecystitis) and some presumed spelling variants clearly demonstrate the slow progress (Table 1).

As medical literature is predominantly written in English nowadays, physicians increasingly get exposed to the English spelling of Latin and Greek words rather than the Swedish one. This has resulted in a multitude of alternate spellings of several medical terms. For example, *tachycardia* (rapid heart) is correctly spelled *takykardi*, but is also frequently found as *tachycardi*, *tachykardi*, and *takycardi* (Kvist et al., 2011). A similar French study found this kind of spelling variation to be abundant as well (Ruch et al., 2003).

Term	KORP	DAY	X-RAY
kolecystit	**51**	**48**	**84**
colecystit	0	1	8
cholecystit	4	88	1613

Table 1: Alternate spellings of the Swedish medical term *kolecystit* (eng. cholecystitis) in the Swedish corpus collection Korp, daily notes (DAY) and radiology reports (X-RAY), respectively. Correct spelling in bold.

EHRs also contain neologisms. These are often verbs, typically describing events relating to the patient in active form, such as "the patient is infarcting" (Swedish: *patienten infarcerar*) instead of the unintentional "the patient is having a myocardial infarction". Similar phenomena are described by Josefsson (1999).

Abbreviations and acronyms in EHRs can follow standardised writing rules or be *ad hoc* (Liu et al., 2001). They are often domain-specific and may be found in medical dictionaries such as MeSH[3] and Snomed CT[4]. For instance, 18 of the 100 most common words in Swedish radiology reports were abbreviations, and 10 of them were domain-specific (Kvist and Velupillai, 2013). Because many medical terms are multiword expressions that are repeated frequently in a patient's EHR, the use of acronyms is very common. Skeppstedt et al. (2012) showed that 14% of diagnostic expressions were abbreviated in Swedish clinical text.

Abbreviations are often ambiguous. As an example, 33% of the short abbreviations in the UMLS terminology are ambiguous (Liu et al., 2001). Pakhomov et al. (2005) found that the abbreviation RA had more than 20 expansions in the UMLS terminology alone. Furthermore, a certain word or expression can be shortened in several different ways. For instance, in a Swedish intensive care unit, the drug Noradrenalin was creatively written in 60 different ways by the nurses (Allvin et al., 2011).

It should be noted that speech recognition, although common in many hospitals around the

[1] http://www.who.int/classifications/icd/en/

[2] Based on a subset of the Stockholm Electronic Patient Record Corpus (Dalianis et al., 2012) of 100,000 daily notes (DAY) written by physicians of varying disciplines (4 mill. tokens) and 435,000 radiology reports (X-RAY) written by radiologists (20 mill. tokens). KORP: http://spraakbanken.gu.se/korp/

[3] www.ncbi.nlm.nih.gov

[4] http://www.ihtsdo.org/

world, has not been introduced in Sweden, and many physicians and all nurses type the notes themselves. This is one explanation to the variation with respect to abbreviations.

User studies have shown that the greatest barriers for patients lie mainly in the frequent use of abbreviations, jargon and technical terminology (Pyper et al., 2004; Keselman et al., 2007; Adnan et al., 2010). The most common comprehension errors made by laymen concern clinical concepts, medical terminology and medication names. Furthermore, there are great challenges for higher-level processing like syntax and semantics (Meystre et al., 2008; Wu et al., 2013). The research presented in this paper focuses on lexical simplification of clinical text.

3 Related research

We are aware of several efforts to construct automated text simplification tools for clinical text in English (Kandula et al., 2010; Patrick et al., 2010). For Swedish, there are few studies on medical language from a readability perspective. Borin et al. (2009) present a thorough investigation on Swedish (and English) medical language, but EHR texts are explicitly not included. This section summarizes research on Swedish (clinical) text with respect to lexical simplification by handling of abbreviations, terminology and spelling correction.

3.1 Abbreviation detection

Abbreviation identification in English biomedical and clinical texts has been studied extensively (e.g. Xu et al. (2007), Liu et al. (2001)). For detection of Swedish medical abbreviations, there are fewer studies. Dannélls (2006) reports detection of acronyms in medical journal text with 98% recall and 94% precision by using part of speech information and heuristic rules. Clinical Swedish presents greater problems than medical texts, because of *ad hoc* abbreviations and noisier text. By using lexicons and a few heuristic rules, Isenius et al. (2012) report the best *F-score* of 79% for abbreviation detection in clinical Swedish.

3.2 Compound splitting

Good compound analysis is critical especially for languages whose orthographies concatenate compound components. Swedish is among those languages, in which every such concatenation thus corresponds to a word. The most common approach to compound splitting is to base it on a lexicon providing restrictions on how different word forms can be used for generating compounds. For example, Sjöbergh and Kann (2006) used a lexicon derived from SAOL (the Swedish Academy word list), and Östling and Wirén (2013) used the SALDO lexicon of Swedish morphology (Borin and Forsberg, 2009). With this kind of approach, compound splitting is usually very reliable for genres like newspaper text, with typical accuracies for Swedish around 97%, but performs poorer in domain specific genres.

3.3 Terminology detection

The detection of English medical terminology is a widely researched area. An example of term detection in English clinical texts is Wang and Patrick (2009) work based on rule-based and machine learning methods, reporting 84% precision.

For Swedish clinical text, Kokkinakis and Thurin (2007) have employed domain terminology matching and reached 98% precision and 87% recall in detecting terms of disorders. Using similar approaches, Skeppstedt et al. (2012), reached 75% precision and 55% recall in detecting terms of disorders. With a machine learning based approach, improved results were obtained: 80% precision, 82% recall (Skeppstedt et al., 2014). Skeppstedt et al. (2012) have also demonstrated the negative influence of abbreviations and multiword expressions in their findings.

3.4 Spelling correction

A system for general spelling correction of Swedish is described by Kann et al. (1998), but we are not aware of any previous work related to spelling correction of Swedish clinical text. An example of spelling correction of clinical text for other languages is Tolentino et al. (2007), who use several algorithms for word similarity detection, including phonological homonym lookup and n-grams for contextual disambiguation. They report a precision of 64% on English medical texts. Another example is Patrick et al. (2010) and Patrick and Nguyen (2011), who combine a mixture of generation of spelling candidates based on orthographic and phonological edit distance, and a 2-word window of contextual information for ranking the spelling candidates resulting in an accuracy of 84% on English patient records. Siklóski et al. (2013) use a statistical machine translation model

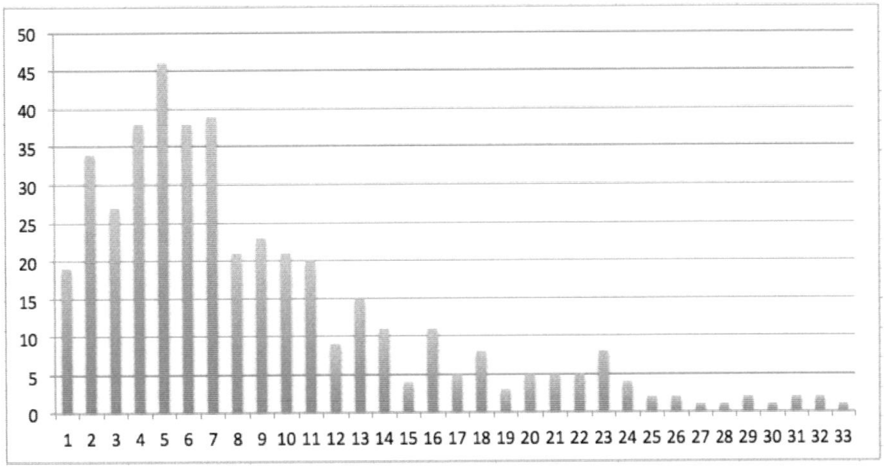

Figure 1: Distribution of 100 PR dataset sentences by length (number of sentences on the y-axis and number of tokens on the x-axis).

(with 3-grams) for spelling correction, achieving 88% accuracy on Hungarian medical texts.

4 Experimental data

This study uses clinical notes[5] from the Stockholm Electronic Patient Record corpus containing more than 600,000 patients of all ages from more than 500 health units during 2006–2013 (Dalianis et al., 2012).

A randomly selected subset of 100 daily notes from different EHRs written by physicians between 2009–2010 was used as a gold standard dataset for evaluating abbreviation detection, compound splitting and spelling corrections. This 100 daily notes dataset contains 433 sentences and 3,888 tokens, as determined by Stagger (Östling, 2013), a Swedish tokenizer and POS tagger. The majority of sentences contain between 4–11 tokens (see Figure 1.)

The text snippet in Figure 2 provides an illustrative example of the characteristics of a health record. What is immediately striking is the number of misspellings, abbreviations, compounds and words of foreign origin. But also the syntax is peculiar, alternating between telegraphic clauses with implicit arguments, and long sentences with complex embeddings.

[5]Approved by the Regional Ethical Review Board in Stockholm (Etikprövningsnämnden i Stockholm), permission number 2012/2028-31/5

5 Lexical normalization of EHRs

Normalization of lexis in clinical text relies heavily on the lookup in available lexicons, corpora and domain terminologies. Although these resources usually cover the majority of words (i.e. tokens) in texts, however due to the ever evolving language and knowledge inside the domain, medical texts, when analysed with the NLP tools, also contain *unknown*[6] words. These remaining words that are not covered by any lexicon, or corpora resource, can be misspellings, abbreviations, compounds (new word formations), words in foreign languages (Latin, Greek, English), or new terms.

Our approach to dealing with *unknown* words combines a rule-based abbreviation detection and Swedish statistical language model-based compound analysis and misspelling resolution.

The following sections describe three methods that are applied in a pipeline manner. That is, first, all known abbreviations are detected and marked; second the unknown words are checked whether they are compounds; finally, for the remaining unknown words, context dependent word corrections are made.

5.1 Detecting abbreviations

This section describes the heuristics and lexicon lookup-based abbreviation detection method. The Swedish Clinical Abbreviation and Medical Terminology Matcher (SCATM) is based on

[6]By unknown words we mean words that cannot be looked up in available lexical resources or linguistically analyzed by POS tokenizer.

Original:

Cirk och **resp** stabil, **pulm** **ausk** något nedsatt **a-ljud** **bilat**, cor **RR** **HF** 72, **sat** 91% på 4 **l** **O2**. Följer *Miktionslista*. I samråd med <title> bakjour <First name> <Second name>, som bedömmer **pat** som komplicerad *sjukdomsbild*, så följer vi vitala parametrar, samt svara han ej på *smärtlindring*, så går vi vidare med **CT** **BÖS**.

Swedish with expanded abbreviations and corrected misspellings:

Cirkulatoriskt och respiratoriskt stabil, pulmonales auskulteras något nedsatt andningsljud bilateralt, cor regelbunden rytm hjärtfrekvens 72, saturation 91 procent på 4 liter syrgas. Följer miktionslista. I samråd med <title> bakjour <First name> <Second name> , som bedömer patienten som komplicerad sjukdomsbild, så följer vi vitala parametrar, samt svarar han ej på smärtlindring, så går vi vidare med computed tomography buköversikt.

Literal translation to English:

Circ and **resp** stable, **pulm** **ausc** somewhat weak **resp** sound **bilat**, cor **RR** **HF** 72, **sat** 91% on 4 **l** **O2**. Following list for micturation. Consulting <title> senior **dr** on call <First name> <Second name> , who aseses **pat** as complicated condition, so we follow vital parameters, and anwers he not to *pain-relief*, so we go on to **CT** **ABD**.

English translation with expanded abbreviations (extended with missing words):

Circulatory and respiratory stable, pulmonary auscultated somewhat weak respiratory sound bilaterally, heart regular rythm frequency 72, saturation 91% on 4 liter oxygen. Following list for micturation. In consultation with <title> senior doctor on call <First name> <Second name> , who assesses patient as having complex condition, we monitor vital parameters, and if he doesn't respond to pain relief, we proceed with computed tomography of abdomen.

Figure 2: Characteristics of a health record: misspellings (underline), **abbreviations** (bold), *compounds* (italic) and words of foreign origin (red).

SCAN (Isenius et al., 2012). The SCATM method uses domain-adapted Stagger (Östling, 2013) for the tokenization and POS-tagging of text. The adapted version of Stagger handles clinical-specific[7] abbreviations from three domains, i.e. radiology, emergency, and dietology. SCATM also uses several lexicons to determine whether a word is a common word (in total 122,847 in the lexicon), an abbreviation (in total 7,455 in the lexicon), a medical term (in total 17,380 in the lexicon), or a name (both first and last names, in total 404,899 in the lexicon). All words that are at most 6 characters long, or contains the characters "-" and/or "." are checked against these lexicons in a specific order in order to determine whether it is an abbreviation or not.

The SCATM method uses various lexicons[8] of Swedish medical terms, Swedish abbreviations, Swedish words and Swedish names (first and last).

5.2 Compound splitting

For compound splitting, we use a collection of lexical resources, the core of which is a full-form dictionary produced by Nordisk språkteknologi holding AS (NST), comprising 927,000 entries[9]. In addition, various resources from the medical domain have been mined for vocabulary: Swedish SNOMED[10] terminology, the Läkartidningen medical journal[11] corpus, and Swedish Web health-care guides/manuals[12].

A refinement of the basic lexicon-driven technique described in the related research section is that our compound splitting makes use of contextual disambiguation. As the example of *hjärteko* illustrates, this compound can be hypothetically split into[13]:

hjärt+eko (en. cardiac+echo)

[7]Abbreviations that do not follow conventional orthography styles, e.g. a typical abbreviation *p.g.a.* (en. due to) can have the following variants *p g a*, *pga*, *p. G. A.*, *p. gr. a.*

[8]the sources of lexicons are: anatomin.se, neuro.ki.se smittskyddsinstitutet.se, medicinskordbok.se, runeberg.org, g3.spraakdata.gu.se/saob, sv.wikipedia.org/wiki/Lista_ver_frkortningar, karolinska.se/Karolinska-Universitetslaboratoriet/Sidor-om-PTA/Analysindex-alla-enheter/Forkortningar/ and the list of Swedish names (Carlsson and Dalianis, 2010).

[9]Available at: www.nb.no/Tilbud/Forske/Spraakbanken/Tilgjengelege-ressursar/Leksikalske-ressursar

[10]www.socialstyrelsen.se/nationellehalsa/nationelltfacksprak/

[11]http://spraakbanken.gu.se/eng/research/infrastructure/korp

[12]www.1177.se and www.vardguiden.se

[13]Korp (http://spraakbanken.gu.se/korp) is a collection of Swedish corpora, comprising 1,784,019,272 tokens, as of January 2014.

```
KORP freq.: 642 + 5,669
```

```
hjärte+ko     (en. beloved+cow)
 KORP freq.:  8     + 8,597
```

For choosing the most likely composition in the given context, we use the Stockholm Language Model with Entropy (SLME) (Östling, 2012) which is a simple n-gram language model.

The max probability defines the correct word formation constituents:

```
hjärt+eko   2.3e-04
hjärte+ko   5.1e-07
```

The SMLE is described in the following section.

5.3 Misspelling detection

The unknown words that are not abbreviations or compounds can very likely be misspellings. Misspellings can be a result of typing errors or the lack of knowledge of the correct spelling.

Our approach to clinical Swedish misspellings is based on the best practices of spell checkers for Indo-European languages, namely the phonetic similarity key method combined with a method to measure proximity between the strings. In our spelling correction method, the Edit distance (Levenshtein, 1966) algorithm is used to measure the proximity of orthographically possible candidates. The Soundex algorithm (Knuth, 1973) shortlists the spelling candidates which are phonologically closest to the misspelled word. Further, the spelling correction candidates are analyzed in a context by using the SLME n-gram model.

The SLME employs the Google Web 1T 5-gram, 10 European Languages, Version 1, dataset for Swedish, which is the largest publically available Swedish data resource. The SLME is a simple n-gram language model, based on the Stupid Backoff Model (Brants et al., 2007). The n-gram language model calculates the probability of a word in a given context:

$$P(w_1^L) = \prod_{i=1}^{L} P(w_i|w_1^{i-1}) \approx \prod_{i=1}^{L} \hat{P}(w_i|w_{i-n+1}^{i-1}) \tag{1}$$

The maximum-likelihood probability estimates for the n-grams are calculated by their relative frequencies:

$$r(w_i|w_{i-n+1}^{i-1}) = \frac{f(w_{i-n+1}^{i})}{f(w_{i-n+1}^{i-1})} \tag{2}$$

The smoothing is used when the complete n-gram is not found. If $r(w_{i-n+1}^{i-1})$ is not found, then the model looks for $r(w_{i-n+2}^{i-1})$, $r(w_{i-n+3}^{i-1})$, and so on. The Stupid backoff (Brants et al., 2007) smoothing method uses relative frequencies instead of normalized probabilities and context-dependent discounting. Equation (3) shows how score S is calculated:

$$S(w_i|w_{i-k+1}^{i-1}) = \\ = \begin{cases} \frac{f(w_{i-k+1}^{i})}{f(w_{i-k+1}^{i-1})} & \text{if} f(w_{i-k+1}^{i})) > 0 \\ \alpha S(w_i|w_{i-k+2}^{i-1}) & \text{otherwise} \end{cases} \tag{3}$$

The backoff parameter α is set to 0.4, which was heuristically determined by (Brants et al., 2007). The recursion stops when the score for the last context word is calculated. N is the size of the corpus.

$$S(w_i) = \frac{f(w_i)}{N} \tag{4}$$

The SLME n-gram model calculates the probability of a word in a given context: $p(word|context)$. The following example[14] shows the case of spelling correction:

```
Original:
 Vpl på onsdag.  UK tortdag.
(en. Vpl on wednesday. UK thsday.)

torgdag (en. marketday): 4.2e-10
torsdag (en. Thursday):   1.1e-06

Corrected:
 Vpl på onsdag.  UK torsdag.
```

6 Experiments and results

Our approach to lexical normalization was tested against a gold standard, namely, the 100 EHR daily notes dataset. The dataset was annotated for abbreviations, compounds including abbreviations and misspellings by a physician.

We carried out the following experiments (see Table 2):

1. SCATM to mark abbreviations and terms;

[14]Vpl stands for *Vårdplanering* (en. planning for care), UK stands for *utskrivningsklar* (en. ready for discharge).

Method	Lexical normalization task	Gold-standard, occurences	Precision, %	Recall, %
SCATM 1	Abbreviation detection	550	**91.1**	**81.0**
SCATM 1a	Abbreviations included in compounds only	78	89.74	46.15
NoCM 1	Out-of-dictionary compound splitting	97	**83.5**	-
NoCM 1a	Out-of-dictionary compounds which include abbreviations	44	59.1	-
NoCM 2	Spelling correction	41	**54.8**	**63.12**
SCATM+NoCM	Spelling correction	41	**83.87**	**76.2**

Table 2: Results of lexical normalization.

2. NoCM (lexical normalization of compounds and misspellings as described in sections 5.2 and 5.3) to resolve compounds and misspellings;

3. The combined experiment SCATM+NoCM to resolve misspellings.

The last experimental setting was designed as a solution to deal with compounds that include abbreviations. Marking abbreviations prior to the spelling correction can help to reduce the number of false positives.

The 433 sentences contained a total of 550 abbreviations (78 of these were constituents of compound words), and 41 misspellings of which 13 were misspelled words containing abbreviations. Due to the tokenization errors, a few sentence boundaries were detected incorrectly, e.g. interrupted dates and abbreviations. Because of this some abbreviations were separated into different sentences and thus added to false negatives and false positives.

The first experiment (SCATM 1 and 1a) of detecting abbreviations achieved both high precision and recall. As a special case of demonstrating the source of errors (see SCATM 1a) is the evaluation of detecting abbreviations which are part of compounds only. The low recall is due to the design of the SCATM which does not handle words longer than 6 characters, thus resulting in compounded abbreviations like *kärlkir* or *övervak* to go undetected.

The evaluation of the second experiment (NoCM 1, 1a and 2) showed that the majority of out-of-dictionary compounds was resolved correctly (NoCM 1) and reached 83.5% precision. Errors mainly occurred due to spelling candidate ranking, e.g. even+tull instead of eventuell and compounds containing abbreviations and misspelled words. As a special case of demonstrating the source of errors of the latter (see NoCM 1a) is the evaluation of those compounds[15] only which contain abbreviations. The task of spelling correction (NoCM 2) performed poorly, reaching only 54.8% precision. This can be explained by failing to resolve misspellings in compounds where abbreviations are compounded together with a misspelled words, e.g. *aciklocvirkonc* (*aciklovir koncentrate*).

The third experiment (SCATM+NoCM) combined abbreviation detection followed by the out-of-dictionary word normalization (spelling correction and compound splitting). This setting helped to resolve the earlier source of errors, i.e. words that contain both misspelling(s) and abbreviation(s). The overall precision of spelling correction is 83.87%.

7 Conclusions

Our attempt to address the problem of lexical simplification, and, in the long run, improve readability of Swedish EHRs, by automatically detecting and resolving out of dictionary words, achieves 91.1% (abbreviations), 83.5% (compound splitting) and 83.87% (spelling correction) precision, respectively. These results are comparable to those

[15]This number of compounds is derived from the number of abbreviations included in compounds (from SCATM 1a) by selecting only those out-of -dictionary words which do not contain punctuation.

reported in similar studies on English and Hungarian patient records (Patrick et al., 2010; Siklósi et al., 2013).

Furthermore, the analysis of the gold standard data revealed that around 14% of all words in Swedish EHRs are abbreviations. More specifically, 2% of all the words are compounds including abbreviations. In contrast, and somewhat unexpectedly, only 1% are misspellings. This distribution result is an important finding for future studies in lexical simplification and readability studies of EHRs, as it might be useful for informing automatic processing approaches.

We draw two conclusions from this study. First, to advance research into the field of readability of EHRs, and thus to develop suitable readability measures it is necessary to begin by taking these findings into account and by relating abbreviations, spelling variation, misspellings, compounds and terminology to reading comprehension.

Second, as a future guideline for the overall pipeline for detecting and resolving unknown, out-of-dictionary words, we suggest handling abbreviations in a first step, and then taking care of misspellings and potential compounds. The most urgent area for future improvement of the method is to handle compound words containing both abbreviations and misspellings.

Acknowledgements

The authors wish to thank the anonymous reviewers for valuable feedback. Maria Kvist and Sumithra Velupillai were in part funded by the Vårdal Foundation, Sumithra also by the Swedish Research Council and the Swedish Fulbright commission. We thank Robert Östling who provided the POS tagger and the Stockholm Language Model with Entropy.

References

M. Adnan, J. Warren, and M. Orr. 2010. Assessing text characteristics of electronic discharge summaries and their implications for patient readability. In *Proceedings of the Fourth Australasian Workshop on Health Informatics and Knowledge Management - Volume 108*, HIKM '10, pages 77–84, Darlinghurst, Australia, Australia. Australian Computer Society, Inc.

H. Allvin, E. Carlsson, H. Dalianis, R. Danielsson-Ojala, V. Daudaravicius, M. Hassel, D. Kokkinakis, H. Lundgren-Laine, G.H. Nilsson, Ø. Nytrø, S. Salanterä, M. Skeppstedt, H. Suominen, and S. Velupillai. 2011. Characteristics of Finnish and Swedish intensive care nursing narratives: a comparative analysis to support the development of clinical language technologies. *Journal of Biomedical Semantics*, 2(Suppl 3):S1, doi:10.1186/2041-1480-2-S3-S1, July.

L. Borin and M. Forsberg. 2009. All in the family: A comparison of SALDO and WordNet. In *Proceedings of the Nodalida 2009 Workshop on WordNets and other Lexical Semantic Resources*, pages 7–12. NEALT.

L. Borin, N. Grabar, M. Gronostaj, C. Hallett, D. Hardcastle, D. Kokkinakis, S. Williams, and A. Willis. 2009. Semantic Mining Deliverable D27.2: Empowering the patient with language technology. Technical report, Semantic Mining (NOE 507505).

T. Brants, A. C. Popat, P. Xu, F. J. Och, and J. Dean. 2007. Large language models in machine translation. In *In Proceedings of the 2007 Joint Conference EMNLP-CoNLL*, pages 858–867.

C. Bretschneider, S. Zillner, and M. Hammon. 2013. Identifying pathological findings in German radiology reports using a syntacto-semantic parsing approach. In *Proceedings of the 2013 Workshop on Biomedical Natural Language Processing (BioNLP 2013)*. ACL.

E. Carlsson and H. Dalianis. 2010. Influence of Module Order on Rule-Based De-identification of Personal Names in Electronic Patient Records Written in Swedish. In *Proceedings of the Seventh International Conference on Language Resources and Evaluation, LREC 2010*, pages 3071–3075, Valletta, Malta, May 19–21.

H. Dalianis, M. Hassel, A. Henriksson, and M. Skeppstedt. 2012. Stockholm EPR Corpus: A Clinical Database Used to Improve Health Care. In Pierre Nugues, editor, *Proc. 4th SLTC, 2012*, pages 17–18, Lund, October 25-26.

D. Dannélls. 2006. Automatic acronym recognition. In *Proceedings of the 11th conference on European chapter of the Association for Computational Linguistics (EACL)*.

C. Friedman, P. Kra, and A. Rzhetsky. 2002. Two biomedical sublanguages: a description based on the theories of Zellig Harris. *Journal of Biomedical Informatics*, 35(4):222–235.

C. Hagège, P. Marchal, Q. Gicquel, S. Darmoni, S. Pereira, and M. Metzger. 2011. Linguistic and temporal processing for discovering hospital acquired infection from patient records. In *Proceedings of the ECAI 2010 Conference on Knowledge Representation for Health-care*, KR4HC'10, pages 70–84, Berlin, Heidelberg. Springer-Verlag.

N. Isenius, S. Velupillai, and M. Kvist. 2012. Initial results in the development of scan: a swedish clinical abbreviation normalizer. In *Proceedings of the*

CLEF 2012 Workshop on Cross-Language Evaluation of Methods, Applications, and Resources for eHealth Document Analysis - CLEFeHealth2012, Rome, Italy, September. CLEF.

G. Josefsson. 1999. Få feber eller tempa? Några tankar om agentivitet i medicinskt fackspråk.

S. Kandula, D. Curtis, and Q. Zeng-Treitler. 2010. A Semantic and Syntactic Text Simplification Tool for Health Content. In *Proc AMIA 2010*, pages 366–370.

V. Kann, R. Domeij, J. Hollman, and M. Tillenius. 1998. Implementation Aspects and Applications of a Spelling Correction Algorithm. . Technical Report TRITA-NA-9813, NADA, KTH.

A. Keselman, L. Slaughter, CA. Smith, H. Kim, G. Divita, A. Browne, and et al. 2007. Towards consumer-friendly PHRs: patients experience with reviewing their health records. In *AMIA Annu Symp Proc 2007*, pages 399–403.

D. E. Knuth, 1973. *The Art of Computer Programming: Volume 3, Sorting and Searching*, pages 391–392. Addison-Wesley.

D. Kokkinakis and A. Thurin. 2007. Identification of Entity References in Hospital Discharge Letters. In *Proceedings of the 16th Nordic Conference of Computational Linguistics (NODALIDA) 2007*, pages 329–332, Tartu, Estonia.

M. Kvist and S. Velupillai. 2013. Professional Language in Swedish Radiology Reports – Characterization for Patient-Adapted Text Simplification. In *Proceedings of the Scandinavian Conference on Health Informatics 2013*, Copenhagen, Denmark, August. Linköping University Electronic Press, Linköpings universitet.

M. Kvist, M. Skeppstedt, S. Velupillai, and H. Dalianis. 2011. Modeling human comprehension of swedish medical records for intelligent access and summarization systems, a physician's perspective. In *Proc. 9th Scandinavian Conference on Health Informatics, SHI*, Oslo, August.

V. Laippala, F. Ginter, S. Pyysalo, and T. Salakoski. 2009. Towards automated processing of clinical Finnish: Sublanguage analysis and a rule-based parser. *Int journal of medical informatics*, 78:e7–e12.

VI Levenshtein. 1966. Binary Codes Capable of Correcting Deletions, Insertions and Reversals. *Soviet Physics Doklady*, 10:707–710.

H. Liu, Y. A. Lussier, and C. Friedman. 2001. Disambiguating Ambiguous Biomedical Terms in Biomedical Narrative Text: An Unsupervised Method. *Journal of Biomedical Informatics*, 34:249–261.

S. M. Meystre, G. K. Savova, K. C. Kipper-Schuler, and John E. Hurdle. 2008. Extracting information from textual documents in the electronic health record: a review of recent research. *IMIA Yearbook of Medical Informatics 2008. 47 Suppl 1:138-154.*

R. Östling and M. Wirén, 2013. *Compounding in a Swedish Blog Corpus*, pages 45–63. Stockholm Studies in Modern Philology. New series 16. Stockholm university.

R. Östling. 2012. http://www.ling.su.se/english/nlp/tools/slme/stockholm-language-model-with-entropy-slme-1.101098 .

R. Östling. 2013. Stagger: an Open-Source Part of Speech Tagger for Swedish. *Northern European Journal of Language Technology*, 3:1–18.

S. Pakhomov, T. Pedersen, and C. G. Chute. 2005. Abbreviation and Acronym Disambiguation in Clinical Discourse. In *Proc AMIA 2005*, pages 589–593.

J. Patrick and D. Nguyen. 2011. Automated Proof Reading of Clinical Notes. In Helena Hong Gao and Minghui Dong, editors, *PACLIC*, pages 303–312. Digital Enhancement of Cognitive Development, Waseda University.

J. Patrick, M. Sabbagh, S. Jain, and H. Zheng. 2010. Spelling correction in Clinical Notes with Emphasis on First Suggestion Accuracy. In *2nd Workshop on Building and Evaluating Resources for Biomedical Text Mining*, pages 2–8.

C. Pyper, J. Amery, M. Watson, and C. Crook. 2004. Patients experiences when accessing their on-line electronic patient records in primary care. *The British Journal of General Practice*, 54:38–43.

P. Ruch, R. Baud, and A. Geissbühler. 2003. Using lexical disambiguation and named-entity recognition to improve spelling correction in the electronic patient record. *Artificial Intelligence in Medicine*, 29(1-2):169–184.

B. Siklósi, A. Novák, and G. Prószéky, 2013. *Context-Aware Correction of Spelling Errors in Hungarian Medical Documents*, pages 248–259. Number Lecture Notes in Computer Science 7978. Springer Berlin Heidelberg.

J. Sjöbergh and V. Kann. 2006. Vad kan statistik avslöja om svenska sammansättningar? *Språk och stil*, 1:199–214.

M. Skeppstedt, M. Kvist, and H Dalianis. 2012. Rule-based Entity Recognition and Coverage of SNOMED CT in Swedish Clinical Text. In *Proceedings of the Eighth International Conference on Language Resources and Evaluation, LREC 2012*, pages 1250–1257, Istanbul, Turkey, May 23–25.

M. Skeppstedt, M. Kvist, G. H. Nilsson, and H. Dalianis. 2014. Automatic recognition of disorders, findings, pharmaceuticals and body structures from clinical text: An annotation and machine learning study. *Journal of Biomedical Informatics*, http://dx.doi.org/10.1016/j.jbi.2014.01.012.

B. Smedby. 1991. Medicinens Språk: språket i sjukdomsklassifikationen – mer konsekvent försvenskning eftersträvas [Language of Medicine: the language of diagnose classification - more consequent Swedification sought]. *Läkartidningen*, pages 1519–1520.

G. Surján and G. Héja. 2003. About the language of Hungarian discharge reports. *Stud Health Technol Inform*, 95:869–873.

H. D. Tolentino, M. D. Matters, W. Walop, B. Law, W. Tong, F. Liu, P. A. Fontelo, K. Kohl, and D. C. Payne. 2007. A UMLS-based spell checker for natural language processing in vaccine safety. *BMC Med. Inf. & Decision Making*, 7.

Y. Wang and J. Patrick. 2009. Cascading classifiers for named entity recognition in clinical notes. In *Proceedings of the Workshop on Biomedical Information Extraction*, WBIE '09, pages 42–49, Stroudsburg, PA, USA. Association for Computational Linguistics.

D. T. Y. Wu, D. A. Hanauer, Q. Mei, P. M. Clark, L. C. An, J. Lei, J. Proulx, Q. Zeng-Treitler, and K. Zheng. 2013. Applying Multiple Methods to Assess the Readability of a Large Corpus of Medical Documents. *Stud Health Technol Inform*, 192:647–651.

H. Xu, P. D. Stetson, and C. Friedman. 2007. A Study of Abbreviations in Clinical Notes. In *Proc AMIA 2007*, pages 821–825.

An Open Corpus of Everyday Documents for Simplification Tasks

David Pellow and **Maxine Eskenazi**
Language Technologies Institute, Carnegie Mellon University
Pittsburgh PA USA
dpellow@cs.cmu.edu, max@cs.cmu.edu

Abstract

In recent years interest in creating statistical automated text simplification systems has increased. Many of these systems have used parallel corpora of articles taken from Wikipedia and Simple Wikipedia or from Simple Wikipedia revision histories and generate Simple Wikipedia articles. In this work we motivate the need to construct a large, accessible corpus of everyday documents along with their simplifications for the development and evaluation of simplification systems that make everyday documents more accessible. We present a detailed description of what this corpus will look like and the basic corpus of everyday documents we have already collected. This latter contains everyday documents from many domains including driver's licensing, government aid and banking. It contains a total of over 120,000 sentences. We describe our preliminary work evaluating the feasibility of using crowdsourcing to generate simplifications for these documents. This is the basis for our future extended corpus which will be available to the community of researchers interested in simplification of everyday documents.

1 Introduction

People constantly interact with texts in everyday life. While many people read for enjoyment, some texts must be read out of necessity. For example, to file taxes, open a bank account, apply for a driver's license or rent a house, one must read instructions and the contents of forms, applications, and other documents. For people with limited reading ability - whether because they are not native speakers of the language, have an incomplete education, have a disability, or for some other reason - the reading level of these everyday documents can limit accessibility and affect their well-being.

The need to present people with texts that are at a reading level which is suitable for them has motivated research into measuring readability of any given text in order to assess whether automatic simplification has rendered a more difficult text into a more readable one. Readability can be measured using tools which assess the reading level of a text. We define simplification as the process of changing a text to lower its reading level without removing necessary information or producing an ungrammatical result. This is similar to the definition of (cf. (Zhu et al., 2010)), except that we avoid defining a specific, limited, set of simplification operations. The Related Work section details research into measures of readability and work on automatic simplification systems.

We have begun to construct a large, accessible corpus of everyday documents. This corpus will eventually contain thousands of these documents, each having statistics characterising its contents, and multiple readability measures. Multiple different simplifications will be collected for the original documents and their content statistics and readability measures will be included in the corpus. This type of large and accessible corpus is of vital importance in driving development of automated text simplification. It will provide training material for the systems as well as a common basis of evaluating results from different systems.

Thus far, we have collected a basic corpus of everyday documents from a wide variety of sources. We plan to extend this basic corpus to create the much larger and more structured corpus that we describe here. We have also carried out a preliminary study to evaluate the feasibility of using crowdsourcing as one source of simplifications in the extended corpus. We have used Amazon Mechanical Turk (AMT) and collected 10 simplifications each for 200 sentences from the basic corpus to determine feasibility, a good experimental design, quality control of the simplifications, and time and cost effectiveness.

In the next section we discuss related work relevant to creating and evaluating a large corpus of everyday documents and their simplifications. In Section 3 we further demonstrate the need for a corpus of everyday documents. Section 4 presents a description of our existing basic corpus. Section 5 describes the details of the extended corpus and presents our evaluation of the feasibility of using crowdsourcing to generate human simplifications for the corpus. Section 6 shows how the extended corpus will be made accessible. Section 7 concludes and outlines the future work that we will undertake to develop the extended corpus.

2 Related Work

2.1 Readability Evaluation

Measures of readability are important because they help us assess the reading level of any document, provide a target for simplification systems, and help evaluate and compare the performance of different simplification systems. Several measures of readability have been proposed; DuBay (2004) counted 200 such measures developed by the 1980s and the number has grown, with more advanced automated measures introduced since then.

Early measures of readability such as the Flesch-Kincaid grade level formula (Kincaid et al., 1975) use counts of surface features of the text such as number of words and number of sentences. While these older measures are less sophisticated than more modern reading level classifiers, they are still widely used and reported and recent work has shown that they can be a good first approximation of more complex measures (Štajner et al., 2012).

More recent approaches use more complicated features and machine learning techniques to learn classifiers that can predict readability. For example, Heilman et al. (2007) combine a naive Bayes classifier that uses a vocabulary-based language model with a k-Nearest Neighbors classifier using grammatical features and interpolate the two to predict reading grade level. Feng et al. (2010) and François and Miltsakaki (2012) examine a large number of possible textual features at various levels and compare SVM and Linear Regression classifiers to predict grade level. Vajjala and Meurers (2012) reported significantly higher accuracy on a similar task using Multi-level Perceptron classification.

The above two methods of measuring readability can be computed directly using the text of a document itself. To evaluate the performance of a simplification system which aims to make texts easier to read and understand, it is also useful to measure improvement in individuals' reading and comprehension of the texts. Siddharthan and Katsos (2012) recently studied sentence recall to test comprehension; and Temnikova and Maneva (2013) evaluated simplifications using the readers' ability to answer multiple choice questions about the text.

2.2 Automated Text Simplification Systems

Since the mid-90s several systems have been developed to automatically simplify texts. Early systems used hand-crafted syntactic simplification rules; for example, Chandrasekar et al. (1996), one of the earliest attempts at automated simplification. Rule-based systems continue to be used, amongst others, Siddharthan (2006), Aluisio and Gasperin (2010), and Bott et al. (2012).

Many of the more recent systems are statistically-based adapting techniques developed for statistical machine translation. Zhu et al. (2010) train a probabilistic model of a variety of sentence simplification rules using expectation maximization with a parallel corpus of aligned sentences from Wikipedia and Simple Wikipedia. Woodsend and Lapata (2011) present a system that uses quasi-synchronous grammar rules learned from Simple Wikipedia edit histories. They solve an integer linear programming (ILP) problem to select both which sentences are simplified (based on a model learned from aligned Wikipedia-Simple Wikipedia articles) and what the best simplification is. Feblowitz and Kauchak (2013) use parallel sentences from Wikipedia and Simple Wikipedia to learn synchronous tree substitution grammar rules.

2.3 Corpora for Text Simplification

Presently there are limited resources for statistical simplification methods that need to train on a parallel corpus of original and simplified texts. As mentioned in the previous section, common data sources are Simple Wikipedia revision histories and aligned sentences from parallel Wikipedia and Simple Wikipedia articles. Petersen and Ostendorf

(2007) present an analysis of a corpus of 104 original and abridged news articles, and Barzilay and Elhadad (2003) present a system for aligning sentences trained on a corpus of parallel Encyclopedia Britannica and Britannica Elementary articles. Other work generates parallel corpora of original and simplified texts in languages other than English for which Simple Wikipedia is not available. For example, Klerke and Søgaard (2012) built a sentence-aligned corpus from 3701 original and simplified Danish news articles, and Klaper et al. (2013) collected 256 parallel German and simple German articles.

2.4 Crowdsourcing for Text Simplification and Corpus Generation

Crowdsourcing uses the aggregate of work performed by many non-expert workers on small tasks to generate high quality results for some larger task. To the best of our knowledge crowdsourcing has not previously been explored in detail to generate text simplifications. Crowdsourcing has, however, been used to evaluate the quality of automatically generated simplifications. Feblowitz and Kauchak (2013) used AMT to collect human judgements of the simplifications generated by their system and De Clercq et al. (2014) performed an extensive evaluation of crowdsourced readability judgements compared to expert judgements.

Crowdsourcing has also been used to generate translations. The recent statistical machine translation-inspired approaches to automated simplification motivate the possibility of using crowdsourcing to collect simplifications. Ambati and Vogel (2010) and Zaidan and Callison-Burch (2011) both demonstrate the feasibility of collecting quality translations using AMT. Post et al. (2012) generated parallel corpora between English and six Indian languages using AMT.

3 The Need for a Corpus of Everyday Documents

A high quality parallel corpus is necessary to drive research in automated text simplification and evaluation. As shown in the Related Work section, most statistically driven simplification systems have used parallel Wikipedia - Simple Wikipedia articles and Simple Wikipedia edit histories. The resulting systems take Wikipedia articles as input and generate simplified versions of those articles. While this demonstrates the possibility of automated text simplification, we believe that a primary goal for simplification systems should be to increase accessibility for those with poor reading skills to the texts which are most important to them. Creating a corpus of everyday documents will allow automated simplification techniques to be applied to texts from this domain. In addition, systems trained using Simple Wikipedia only target a single reading level - that of Simple Wikipedia. A corpus containing multiple different simplifications at different reading levels for any given original will allow text simplification systems to target specific reading levels.

The research needs that this corpus aims to meet are:

- A large and accessible set of original everyday documents to:
  - provide a training and test set for automated text simplification
- A set of multiple human-generated simplifications at different reading levels for the same set of original documents to provide:
  - accessible training data for automated text simplification systems
  - the ability to model how the same document is simplified to different reading levels
- An accessible location to share simplifications of the same documents that have been generated by different systems to enable:
  - comparative evaluation of the performance of several systems
  - easier identification and analysis of specific challenges common to all systems

4 Description of the Basic Corpus of Everyday Documents

We have collected a first set of everyday documents. This will be extended to generate the corpus described in the following section. The present documents are heavily biased to the domain of driving since they include driving test preparation materials from all fifty U.S. states. This section presents the information collected about each document and its organisation in the basic corpus. The basic corpus is available at: `https://dialrc.org/simplification/data.html`.

4.1 Document Fields

Each document has a name which includes information about the source, contents, and type of document. For example the name of the Alabama Driver Manual document is `al_dps_driver_man`. The corpus entry for each document also includes the full title, the document source (url for documents available online), the document type and domain, the date retrieved, and the date added to the corpus. For each document the number of sentences, the number of words, the average sentence length, the Flesch-Kincaid grade level score, and the lexical (L) and grammatical (G) reading level scores described in Heilman et al. (2007) are also reported. An example of an entry for the Alabama Driver Manual is shown in Table 1. The documents are split so that each sentence is on a separate line to enable easy alignments between the original and simplified versions of the documents.

Document Name	al_dps_driver_man
Full Title	Alabama Driver Manual
Document Type	Manual
Domain	Driver's Licensing
# Sentences	1,626
# Words	28,404
Avg. # words/sent	17.47
F-K Grade Level	10.21
Reading Level (L)	10
Reading Level (G)	8.38
Source	http://1.usa.gov/1jjd4vw
Date Added	10/01/2013
Date Accessed	10/01/2013

Table 1: Example basic corpus entry for Alabama Driver Manual

4.2 Corpus Statistics

There is wide variation between the different documents included in the corpus, across documents from different domains and also for documents from the same domain. This includes variability in both document length and reading level. For example, the driving manuals range from a lexical reading level of 8.2 for New Mexico to 10.4 for Nebraska. Table 2 shows the statistics for the different reading levels for the documents which have been collected, using the lexical readability measure and rounding to the nearest grade level. Table 3 shows the different domains for which documents have been collected and the statistics for the documents in those domains.

Reading Level (L)	# Documents	# Sentences
4	1	23
5	0	0
6	4	200
7	1	695
8	6	1,869
9	30	36,783
10	54	83,123
11	4	1,457
12	1	461

Table 2: Corpus statistics by lexical reading level

5 Description of an Extended Corpus of Everyday Documents

To meet the needs described in Section 3 the basic corpus will be extended significantly. We are starting to collect more everyday documents from each of the domains in the basic corpus and to extend the corpus to other everyday document domains including prescription instructions, advertising materials, mandatory educational testing, and operating manuals for common products. We are also collecting human-generated simplifications for these documents. We will open up the corpus for outside contributions of more documents, readability statistics and simplifications generated by various human and automated methods. This section describes what the extended corpus will contain and the preliminary work to generate simplified versions of the documents we presently have.

5.1 Document Fields

The extended corpus includes both original documents and their simplified versions. The original documents will include all the same information as the basic corpus, listed in Section 4.1. Novel readability measures for each document can be contributed. For each readability measure that is contributed, the name of the measure, document score, date added, as well as relevant references to the system used to calculate it will be included.

Multiple simplified versions of each original document can be contributed. The simplification for each sentence in the original document will be on the same line in the simplified document as the corresponding sentence in the original document. Each simplified version will include a brief description of how it was simplified and relevant references to the simplification method. As with the original documents, the date added, optional comments and the same document statistics and read-

Domain	# Documents	Avg. # Sentences	Avg. # Words	Avg. # words/sent	Total # Sentences	Total # Words	Avg. F-K Grade Level	Avg. Readability (L)	Avg. Readability (G)
Driver's Licensing	60	1927.6	30,352.6	16.1	115,657	1,821,155	9.54	9.6	7.9
Vehicles	3	46.7	1,118.3	22.5	140	3355	13.3	8.2	7.9
Government Documents	11	150	2,242.8	16.4	1650	24,671	10.5	8.6	8.4
Utilities	5	412.8	8,447.2	21.5	2,064	42,236	13.4	9.8	8.9
Banking	3	158	2,900	17.6	474	8,700	11.4	10.5	8.9
Leasing	4	101	2,386.8	23.8	404	9,547	13.7	9.0	8.7
Government Aid	10	317.4	5,197.5	17.4	3,174	51,975	10.7	9.2	8.8
Shopping	3	281	5,266.7	19.7	843	15,800	12.2	9.9	9.0
Other	2	102.5	1,634	16.0	205	3268	9.7	8.8	8.2
All	101	1,233.8	19,611.0	17.2	124,611	1,980,707	10.4	9.4	8.2

Table 3: Corpus statistics for the basic corpus documents

ability metrics will be included. Additional readability metrics can also be contributed and documented.

5.2 Generating Simplifications Using Crowdsourcing

We conducted a preliminary study to determine the feasibility of collecting simplifications using crowdsourcing. We used AMT as the crowdsourcing platform to collect sentence-level simplification annotations for sentences randomly selected from the basic corpus of everyday documents.

5.2.1 AMT Task Details

We collected 10 simplification annotations for each of the 200 sentences which we posted in two sets of Human Intelligence Tasks (HITs) to AMT. Each HIT included up to four sentences and included an optional comment box that allowed workers to submit comments or suggestions about the HIT. Workers were paid $0.25 for each HIT, and 11 workers were given a $0.05 bonus for submitting comments which helped improve the task design and remove design errors in the first iteration of the HIT design. The first set of HITs was completed in 20.5 hours and the second set in only 6.25 hours. The total cost for all 2000 simplification annotations was $163.51 for 592 HITs, each with up to four simplifications. The breakdown of this cost is shown in Table 4.

Item	Cost
592 HITs	$148.00
11 bonuses	$0.55
AMT fees	$14.96
Total	$163.51

Table 4: Breakdown of AMT costs

5.2.2 Quality Control Measures

To ensure quality, we provided a training session which shows workers explanations, examples, and counter-examples of multiple simplification techniques. These include lexical simplification, reordering, sentence splitting, removing unnecessary information, adding additional explanations, and making no change for sentences that are already simple enough. One of the training examples is the following:

Original Sentence: "Do not use only parking lights, day or night, when vehicle is in motion."

Simplification: "When your vehicle is moving do not use only the parking lights. This applies both at night and during the day."

The explanations demonstrated how lexical simplification, sentence splitting, and reordering techniques were used.

The training session also tested workers' abilities to apply these techniques. Workers were given four test sentences to simplify. Test 1 required lexical simplification. Test 2 was a counter-example of a sentence which did not require simplification. Test 3 required sentence splitting. Test 4 required either moving or deleting an unclear modifying clause. We chose the test sentences directly from the corpus and modified them where necessary to ensure that they contained the features being tested. Workers could take the training session and submit answers as many times as they wanted, but could not work on a task without first successfully completing the entire session. After completing the training session once, workers could complete as many HITs as were available to them.

In addition to the training session, we blocked submissions with empty or garbage answers (defined as those with more than 15% of the words not in a dictionary). We also blocked copy-paste functions to discourage worker laziness. Workers who submitted multiple answers that were either very close to or very far from the original sentence were flagged and their submissions were manually reviewed to determine whether to approve them. Similarity was measured using the ratio of Levenshtein distance to alignment length; Levenshtein distance is a common, simple metric for measuring the edit distance between two strings. The Levenshtein ratio $\left(1 - \frac{Levenshtein\ dist.}{alignment\ length}\right)$ provides a normalised similarity measure which is robust to length differences in the inputs. We also asked workers to rate their confidence in each simplification they submitted on a five point scale ranging from "Not at all" to "Very confident".

5.2.3 Effectiveness of Quality Control Measures

To determine the quality of the AMT simplifications, we examine the effectiveness of the quality control measures described in the previous section.

Training: In addition to providing training and simplification experience to workers who worked on the task, the training session effectively blocked workers who were not able to complete it and spammers. Of the 358 workers who looked at the training session only 184 completed it (51%) and we found that no bots or spammers had completed the training session. Tables 5 and 6 show the performance on the four tests in the training session for workers who completed the training session and for those who did not, respectively.

# of workers	181
Avg. # Attempts Test 1	1.1
Avg. # Attempts Test 2	1.5
Avg. # Attempts Test 3	1.6
Avg. # Attempts Test 4	1.4

Table 5: Training statistics for workers who completed training

# of workers	174
# Completed Test 1	82
# Completed Test 2	47
# Completed Test 3	1

Table 6: Training statistics for workers who did not complete training

Blocking empty and garbage submissions: Empty simplifications and cut-paste functions were blocked using client-side scripts and we did not collect statistics of how many workers attempted either of these actions. One worker submitted a comment requesting that we do not block copy-paste functions. In total only 0.6% of submissions were detected as garbage and blocked.

Manual reviews: We (the first author) reviewed workers who were automatically flagged five or more times. We found that this was not an effective way to detect work to be rejected since there were many false positives and workers who did more HITs were more likely to get flagged. None of the workers flagged for review had submitted simplifications that were rejected.

5.2.4 Evaluating Simplification Quality

To determine whether it is feasible to use crowdsourced simplifications to simplify documents for the extended corpus, we examine the quality of the simplifications submitted. The quality control measures described in the previous sections are designed to ensure that workers know what is meant by simplification and how to apply some simplification techniques, to block spammers, and to limit worker laziness. However, workers were free to simplify sentences creatively and encouraged to use their judgement in applying any techniques that seem best to them.

It is difficult to verify the quality of the simplification annotations that were submitted or to determine how to decide what simplification to chose as the "correct" one for the corpus. For any given sentence there is no "right" answer for what the simplification should be; there are many different possible simplifications, each of which could be valid. For example, below is an original sentence taken from a driving manual with two of the simplifications that were submitted for it.

> Original Sentence: "Vehicles in any lane, except the right lane used for slower traffic, should be prepared to move to another lane to allow faster traffic to pass."
> Simplification 1: "Vehicles that are not in the right lane should be prepared to move to another lane in order to allow faster traffic to pass."
> Simplification 2: "Vehicles not in the right lane should be ready to move to another lane so faster traffic can pass them. The right lane is for slower traffic."

There are a number of heuristics that could be used to detect which simplifications are most likely to be the best choice to use in the corpus.

The average time for workers to complete one HIT of up to four simplifications was 3.85 minutes. This includes the time to complete the training session during a worker's first HIT; excluding this, we estimate the average time per HIT is approximately 2.75 minutes. Simplifications which are completed in significantly less time, especially when the original sentence is long, can be flagged for review or simply thrown out if there are enough other simplifications for the sentence.

Workers' confidence in their simplifications can also be used to exclude simplifications which were submitted with low confidence (using worker confidence as a quality control filter was explored by Parent and Eskenazi (2010)). Table 7 shows the statistics for the worker-submitted confidences. Again, simplifications with very low confidence

Confidence Level	# of answers
1 (Not at all)	9
2 (Somewhat confident)	143
3 (Neutral)	251
4 (Confident)	1030
5 (Very confident)	567

Table 7: Self-assessed worker confidences in their simplifications

can either be reviewed or thrown out if there are enough other simplifications for the sentence.

Worker agreement can also be used to detect simplifications that are very different from those submitted by other workers. Using the similarity ratio of Levenshtein distance to alignment length, we calculated which simplifications had at most one other simplification with which they have a similarity ratio above a specific threshold (here referred to as 'outliers'). Table 8 reports how many simplifications are outliers while varying the similarity threshold. Since there are many different

Threshold	90%	85%	75%	65%	50%
# Outliers	1251	927	500	174	12

Table 8: Number of outlier simplifications with similarity ratio above the threshold for at most one other simplification

valid simplifications possible for any given sentence this is not necessarily the best way to detect poor quality submissions. For example, one of the outliers, using the 50% threshold, was a simplification of the sentence "When following a tractor-trailer, observe its turn signals before trying to pass" which simplified by using a negative - "Don't try to pass ... without ...". This outlier was the only simplification of this sentence which used the negative but it is not necessarily a poor one. However, the results in Table 7 do show that there are many simplifications which are similar to each other, indicating that multiple workers agree on one simplification. One of these similar simplifications could be used in the corpus, or multiple different possible simplifications could be included.

To further verify that usable simplifications can be generated using AMT the first author manually reviewed the 1000 simplifications of 100 sentences submitted for the first set of HITs. We judged whether each simplification was grammatical and whether it was a valid simplification. This is a qualitative judgement, but simplifications were judged to be invalid simplifications if they had significant missing or added information compared to the original sentence or added significant extra grammatical or lexical complexity for no apparent reason. The remaining grammatical, valid simplifications were judged as more simple, neutral, or less simple than the original for each of the following features: length, vocabulary, and grammatical structure. The results of this review are shown in Table 9. These results show that approximately 15% of the simplifications were ungrammatical or invalid, further motivating the need to use the other features, such as worker agreement and confidence, to automatically remove poor simplifications.

5.2.5 Extending the Corpus Using Crowdsourcing

The preliminary work undertaken demonstrates that it is feasible to quickly collect multiple simplifications for each sentence relatively inexpensively. We have also presented an evaluation of the quality of the crowdsourced simplifications and several methods of determining which simplifications could be used in the extended corpus. More work is still needed to determine the most cost effective way of getting simplification results that are of sufficient quality to use without gathering overly redundant simplifications for each sentence. Additionally, simplifications of more sentences are needed to assess improvements in reading level since the reading level measures we use are not accurate for very short input texts.

Un-grammatical	Invalid (excludes ungrammatical)	Simpler vocabulary	Less simple vocabulary	Equivalent vocabulary	Grammatically simpler	Less grammatically simple	Equivalent grammar	Longer	Shorter	Same length
35	122	383	21	596	455	21	524	99	537	364

Table 9: Manual evaluation of 1000 AMT simplifications. Numbers of simplifications with each feature.

6 Contributing to & Accessing the Corpus

6.1 Contributing to the Extended Corpus

The following items can be contributed to the corpus: original everyday copyright-free documents, manual or automated simplifications of the original documents (or parts of the documents), and readability scores for original or simplified documents.

Original documents submitted to the corpus can be from any domain. Our working definition of an everyday document is any document which people may have a need to access in their everyday life. Examples include government and licensing forms and their instructions, banking forms, prescription instructions, mandatory educational testing, leasing and rental agreements, loyalty program sign-up forms and other similar documents. We excluded Wikipedia pages because we found that many article pairs actually had few parallel sentences. Documents should be in English and of North American origin to avoid dialect-specific issues.

Hand generated or automatically generated simplifications of everyday documents are also welcome. They should be accompanied the information detailed in Section 5.1. The document statistics listed in Sections 4 and 5 will be added for each simplified document.

Readability scores can be contributed for any of the documents.They should also include the information detailed in Section 5.1 and pertinent information about the system that generated the scores.

6.2 Accessing the Extended Corpus

The extended corpus will be made publicly accessible at the same location as the basic corpus. The names and statistics of each of the documents will be tabulated and both the original and simplified documents, and their statistics, will be available to download. Users will submit their name or organizational affiliation along with a very brief description of how they plan to use the data. This will allow us to keep track of how the corpus is being used and how it could be made more useful to those researching simplification.

The goal of this corpus is to make its contents as accessible as possible. However, many of the original documents from non-governmental sources may not be freely distributed and will instead be included under a data license, unlike the remainder of the corpus and the simplifications[1].

7 Conclusions & Future Work

In this paper we have given the motivation for creating a large and publicly accessible corpus of everyday documents and their simplifications. This corpus will advance research into automated simplification and evaluation for everyday documents. We have already collected a basic corpus of everyday documents and demonstrated the feasibility of collecting large numbers of simplifications using crowdsourcing. We have defined what information the extended corpus will contain and how contributions can be made to it.

There is significantly more work which must be completed in the future to create an extended corpus which meets the needs described in this paper. There are three tasks that we plan to undertake in order to complete this corpus: we will collect significantly more everyday documents; we will manage a large crowdsourcing task to generate simplifications for thousands of the sentences in these documents; and we will create a website to enable access and contribution to the extended simplification corpus. By making this work accessible we hope to motivate others to contribute to the corpus and to use it to advance automated text simplification and evaluation techniques for the domain of everyday documents.

Acknowledgments

The authors would like to thank the anonymous reviewers for their detailed and helpful feedback and comments on the paper.

[1]Thanks to Professor Jamie Callan for explaining some of the issues with including these types of documents in our dataset.

References

Sandra Aluisio and Caroline Gasperin. 2010. Fostering digital inclusion and accessibility: The porsimples project for simplification of portuguese texts. In *Proc. of the NAACL HLT 2010 Young Investigators Workshop on Computational Approaches to Languages of the Americas*, pages 46–53. Association for Computational Linguistics.

Vamshi Ambati and Stephan Vogel. 2010. Can crowds build parallel corpora for machine translation systems? In *Proc. of the NAACL HLT 2010 Workshop on Creating Speech and Language Data with Amazon's Mechanical Turk*, pages 62–65. Association for Computational Linguistics.

Regina Barzilay and Noemie Elhadad. 2003. Sentence alignment for monolingual comparable corpora. In *Proc. of the 2003 Conference on Empirical Methods in Natural Language Processing*, EMNLP '03, pages 25–32. Association for Computational Linguistics.

Stefan Bott, Horacio Saggion, and David Figueroa. 2012. A hybrid system for spanish text simplification. In *Proc. of the Third Workshop on Speech and Language Processing for Assistive Technologies*, pages 75–84. Association for Computational Linguistics.

R. Chandrasekar, Christine Doran, and B. Srinivas. 1996. Motivations and methods for text simplification. In *Proc. of the 16th Conference on Computational Linguistics - Volume 2*, COLING '96, pages 1041–1044. Association for Computational Linguistics.

Orphée De Clercq, Veronique Hoste, Bart Desmet, Philip van Oosten, Martine De Cock, and Lieve Macken. 2014. Using the crowd for readability prediction. *Natural Language Engineering*, FirstView:1–33.

William H. DuBay. 2004. *The Principles of Readability*. Costa Mesa, CA: Impact Information, http://www.impact-information.com/impactinfo/readability02.pdf.

Dan Feblowitz and David Kauchak. 2013. Sentence simplification as tree transduction. In *Proc. of the Second Workshop on Predicting and Improving Text Readability for Target Reader Populations*, pages 1–10. Association for Computational Linguistics.

Lijun Feng, Martin Jansche, Matt Huenerfauth, and Noémie Elhadad. 2010. A comparison of features for automatic readability assessment. In *Coling 2010: Posters*, pages 276–284. Coling 2010 Organizing Committee.

Thomas François and Eleni Miltsakaki. 2012. Do nlp and machine learning improve traditional readability formulas? In *Proc. of the First Workshop on Predicting and Improving Text Readability for target reader populations*, pages 49–57. Association for Computational Linguistics.

Michael Heilman, Kevyn Collins-Thompson, Jamie Callan, and Maxine Eskenazi. 2007. Combining lexical and grammatical features to improve readability measures for first and second language texts. In *HLT-NAACL 2007: Main Proceedings*, pages 460–467. Association for Computational Linguistics.

J. Peter Kincaid, Robert P. Fishburne Jr., Richard L. Rogers, and Brad S. Chissom. 1975. Derivation of new readability formulas (automated readability index, fog count and flesch reading ease formula) for navy enlisted personnel. Technical report, Naval Technical Training Command, Millington Tn.

David Klaper, Sarah Ebling, and Martin Volk. 2013. Building a german/simple german parallel corpus for automatic text simplification. In *Proc. of the Second Workshop on Predicting and Improving Text Readability for Target Reader Populations*, pages 11–19. Association for Computational Linguistics.

Sigrid Klerke and Anders Søgaard. 2012. Dsim, a danish parallel corpus for text simplification. In *Proc. of the Eighth Language Resources and Evaluation Conference (LREC 2012)*, pages 4015–4018. European Language Resources Association (ELRA).

Gabriel Parent and Maxine Eskenazi. 2010. Toward better crowdsourced transcription: Transcription of a year of the let's go bus information system data. In *SLT*, pages 312–317. IEEE.

Sarah E Petersen and Mari Ostendorf. 2007. Text simplification for language learners: a corpus analysis. In *Proc. of Workshop on Speech and Language Technology for Education*, pages 69–72.

Matt Post, Chris Callison-Burch, and Miles Osborne. 2012. Constructing parallel corpora for six indian languages via crowdsourcing. In *Proc. of the Seventh Workshop on Statistical Machine Translation*, pages 401–409. Association for Computational Linguistics.

Advaith Siddharthan and Napoleon Katsos. 2012. Offline sentence processing measures for testing readability with users. In *Proc. of the First Workshop on Predicting and Improving Text Readability for target reader populations*, pages 17–24. Association for Computational Linguistics.

Advaith Siddharthan. 2006. Syntactic simplification and text cohesion. *Research on Language and Computation*, 4(1):77–109.

Irina Temnikova and Galina Maneva. 2013. The c-score – proposing a reading comprehension metrics as a common evaluation measure for text simplification. In *Proc. of the Second Workshop on Predicting and Improving Text Readability for Target Reader Populations*, pages 20–29. Association for Computational Linguistics.

Sowmya Vajjala and Detmar Meurers. 2012. On improving the accuracy of readability classification using insights from second language acquisition. In *Proc. of the Seventh Workshop on Building Educational Applications Using NLP*, pages 163–173. Association for Computational Linguistics.

Sanja Štajner, Richard Evans, Constantin Orasan, , and Ruslan Mitkov. 2012. What can readability measures really tell us about text complexity? In *Proc. of the Workshop on Natural Language Processing for Improving Textual Accessibility (NLP4ITA)*.

Kristian Woodsend and Mirella Lapata. 2011. Wikisimple: Automatic simplification of wikipedia articles. In *Proc. of the Twenty-Fifth AAAI Conference on Artificial Intelligence*, pages 927–932.

Omar F. Zaidan and Chris Callison-Burch. 2011. Crowdsourcing translation: Professional quality from non-professionals. In *Proc. of the 49th Annual Meeting of the Association for Computational Linguistics: Human Language Technologies*, pages 1220–1229. Association for Computational Linguistics.

Zhemin Zhu, Delphine Bernhard, and Iryna Gurevych. 2010. A monolingual tree-based translation model for sentence simplification. In *Proc. of the 23rd International Conference on Computational Linguistics (Coling 2010)*, pages 1353–1361.

EACL - Expansion of Abbreviations in CLinical text

Lisa Tengstrand*, Beáta Megyesi*, Aron Henriksson+, Martin Duneld+ and Maria Kvist+
*Department of Linguistics and Philology,
Uppsala University, Sweden
tengstrand@ling.su.se, beata.megyesi@lingfil.uu.se
+Department of Computer and System Sciences,
Stockholm University, Sweden
aronhen@dsv.su.se, xmartin@dsv.su.se, maria.kvist@karolinska.se

Abstract

In the medical domain, especially in clinical texts, non-standard abbreviations are prevalent, which impairs readability for patients. To ease the understanding of the physicians' notes, abbreviations need to be identified and expanded to their original forms. We present a distributional semantic approach to find candidates of the original form of the abbreviation, and combine this with Levenshtein distance to choose the correct candidate among the semantically related words. We apply the method to radiology reports and medical journal texts, and compare the results to general Swedish. The results show that the correct expansion of the abbreviation can be found in 40% of the cases, an improvement by 24 percentage points compared to the baseline (0.16), and an increase by 22 percentage points compared to using word space models alone (0.18).

1 Introduction

Abbreviations are prevalent in text, especially in certain text types where the author has either limited space or time to write the written message and therefore shortens some words or phrases. This might, however, make it difficult for the reader to understand the meaning of the actual abbreviation. Although some abbreviations are well-known, and frequently used by most of us (e.g., i.e., pm, etc.), most of the abbreviations used in specialized domains are often less known to the public. Interpreting them is not an easy task, as abbreviations are often ambiguous and their correct meaning depends on the context in which they appear. For example, military and governmental staff would naturally read EACL as Emergency Action Checklist, people in the food and beverage business might think of the company name EACL, linguists would probably interpret it as the European Chapter of Chinese Linguistics, while computational linguists would generally claim that EACL stands for the European Chapter of the Association for Computational Linguistics. However, the readers of this particular article know, as the title suggests, that the intended meaning here is the *Expansion of Abbreviations in CLinical text.*

It has been shown that abbreviations are frequently occurring in various domains and genres, such as in historical documents, messages in social media, as well as in different registers used by specialists within a particular field of expertise. Clinical texts produced by health care personnel is an example of the latter. The clinical texts are communication artifacts, and the clinical setting requires that information is expressed in an efficient way, resulting in short telegraphic messages. Physicians and nurses need to document their work to describe findings, treatments and procedures precisely and compactly, often under time pressure.

In recent years, governments and health care actors have started making electronic health records accessible, not only to other caretakers, but also to patients in order to enable them to participate actively in their own health care processes. However, several studies have shown that patients have difficulties to comprehend their own health care reports and other medical texts due to the different linguistic features that characterize these, aswell as to medical jargon and technical terminology (Elhadad, 2006; Rudd et al., 1999; Keselman et al., 2007). It has also been shown that physicians rarely adapt their writing style in order to produce documents that are accessible to lay readers (Allvin, 2010). Besides the use of different terminologies and technical terms, an important obstacle for patients to comprehend medical texts is the frequent use of – for the patients unknown – abbreviations (Keselman et al., 2007; Adnan et al., 2010).

In health records, abbreviations, which constitute linguistic units that are inherently difficult to decode, are commonly used and often non standard (Skeppstedt, 2012). An important step in order to increase readability for lay readers is to translate abbreviated words into their corresponding full length words.

The aim of this study is to explore a distributional semantic approach combined with word normalization, measured by Levenshtein distance, to abbreviation expansion. Using distributional semantic models, which can be applied to large amounts of data, has been shown to be a viable approach to extracting candidates for the underlying, original word of an abbreviation. In order to find the correct expansion among the semantically related candidates, we apply the Levenshtein distance measure. We report on experiments on comparative studies of various text types in Swedish, including radiology reports, medical journals and texts taken from a corpus of general Swedish.

2 Background

An abbreviation is a shorter – abbreviated – form of a word or phrase, often originating from a technical term or a named entity. Abbreviations are typically formed in one of three ways: by (i) clipping the last character sequence of the word (e.g., *pat* for *patient* or *pathology*), (ii) merging the initial letter(s) of the words to form an acronym (e.g., *UU* for *Uppsala University*), or (iii) merging some of the letters – often the initial letter of the syllables – in the word (e.g., *msg* for *message*). Abbreviations can also be formed as a combination of these three categories (e.g., *EACL* for *Expansion of Abbreviations in CLinical text*).

Automatically expanding abbreviations to their original form has been of interest to computational linguists as a means to improve text-to-speech, information retrieval and information extraction systems. Rule-based systems as well as statistical and machine learning methods have been proposed to detect and expand abbreviations. A common component of most solutions is their reliance on the assumption that an abbreviation and its corresponding definition will appear in the same text.

Taghva and Gilbreth (1999) present a method for automatic acronym-definition extraction in technical literature, where acronym detection is based on case and token length constraints. The surrounding text is subsequently searched for possible definitions corresponding to the detected acronym using an inexact pattern-matching algorithm. The resulting set of candidate definitions is then narrowed down by applying the Longest Common Subsequence (LCS) algorithm (Nakatsu et al., 1982) to the candidate pairs. They report 98% precision and 93% recall when excluding acronyms of two or fewer characters.

Park and Byrd (2001), along somewhat similar lines, propose a hybrid text mining approach for abbreviation expansion in technical literature. Orthographic constraints and stop lists are first used to detect abbreviations; candidate definitions are then extracted from the adjacent text based on a set of pre-specified conditions. The abbreviations and definitions are converted into patterns, for which transformation rules are constructed. An initial rule-base comprising the most frequent rules is subsequently employed for automatic abbreviation expansion. They report 98% precision and 94% recall as an average over three document types.

In the medical domain, most approaches to abbreviation resolution also rely on the co-occurrence of abbreviations and definitions in a text, typically by exploiting the fact that abbreviations are sometimes defined on their first mention. These studies extract candidate abbreviation-definition pairs by assuming that either the definition or the abbreviation is written in parentheses (Schwartz and Hearst, 2003). The process of determining which of the extracted abbreviation-definition pairs are likely to be correct is then performed either by rule-based (Ao and Takagi, 2005) or machine learning (Chang et al., 2002; Movshovitz-Attias and Cohen, 2012) methods. Most of these studies have been conducted on English corpora; however, there is one study on Swedish medical text (Dannélls, 2006). There are problems with this popular approach to abbreviation expansion: Yu et al. (2002) found that around 75% of all abbreviations in the biomedical literature are never defined.

The application of this method to clinical text is even more problematic, as it seems highly unlikely that abbreviations would be defined in this way. The telegraphic style of clinical narrative, with its many non-standard abbreviations, is reasonably explained by time constraints in the clinical setting. There has been some work on identifying such undefined abbreviations in clinical text (Isenius et al., 2012), as well as on finding the intended abbreviation expansion among candidates in an abbreviation dictionary (Gaudan et al., 2005).

Henriksson et al. (2012; 2014) present a method for expanding abbreviations in clinical text that does not require abbreviations to be defined, or even co-occur, in the text. The method is based on distributional semantic models by effectively treating abbreviations and their corresponding definition as synonymous, at least in the sense of sharing distributional properties. Distributional semantics (see Cohen and Widdows (2009) for an overview) is based on the observation that words that occur in similar contexts tend to be semantically related (Harris, 1954). These relationships are captured in a Random Indexing (RI) word space model (Kanerva et al., 2000), where semantic similarity between words is represented as proximity in high-dimensional vector space. The RI word space representation of a corpus is obtained by assigning to each unique word an initially empty, n-dimensional context vector, as well as a static, n-dimensional index vector, which contains a small number of randomly distributed non-zero elements (-1s and 1s), with the rest of the elements set to zero[1]. For each occurrence of a word in the corpus, the index vectors of the surrounding words are added to the target word's context vector. The semantic similarity between two words can then be estimated by calculating, for instance, the cosine similarity between their context vectors. A set of word space models are induced from unstructured clinical data and subsequently combined in various ways with different parameter settings (i.e., sliding window size for extracting word contexts). The models and their combinations are evaluated for their ability to map a given abbreviation to its corresponding definition. The best model achieves 42% recall. Improvement of the post-processing of candidate definitions is suggested in order to obtain enhanced performance on this task.

The estimate of word relatedness that is obtained from a word space model is purely statistical and has no linguistic knowledge. When word pairs should not only share distributional properties, but also have similar orthographic representations – as is the case for abbreviation-definition pairs – normalization procedures could be applied. Given a set of candidate definitions for a given abbreviation, the task of identifying *plausible* candidates can be viewed as a normalization problem. Petterson et al. (2013) utilize a string distance measure, Levenshtein distance (Levenshtein, 1966), in order to normalize historical spelling of words into modern spelling. Adjusting parameters, i.e., the maximum allowed distance between source and target, according to observed distances between known word pairs of historical and modern spelling, gives a normalization accuracy of 77%. In addition to using a Levenshtein distance weighting factor of 1, they experiment with context free and context-sensitive weights for frequently occurring edits between word pairs in a training corpus. The context-free weights are calculated on the basis of one-to-one standard edits involving two characters; in this setting the normalization accuracy is increased to 78.7%. Frequently occurring edits that involve more than two characters, e.g., substituting two characters for one, serve as the basis for calculating context-sensitive weights and gives a normalization accuracy of 79.1%. Similar ideas are here applied to abbreviation expansion by utilizing a normalization procedure for candidate expansion selection.

3 Method

The current study aims to replicate and extend a subset of the experiments conducted by Henriksson et al. (2012), namely those that concern the abbreviation expansion task. This includes the various word space combinations and the parameter optimization. The evaluation procedure is similar to the one described in (Henriksson et al., 2012). The current study, however, focuses on post-processing of the semantically related words by introducing a filter and a normalization procedure in an attempt to improve performance. An overview of the approach is depicted in Figure 1.

Abbreviation expansion can be viewed as a two-step procedure, where the first step involves detection, or extraction, of abbreviations, and the second step involves identifying plausible expansions. Here, the first step is achieved by extracting abbreviations from a clinical corpus with clinical abbreviation detection software and using a list of known medical abbreviations. The second step is performed by first extracting a set of semantically

[1]Generating sparse vectors of a sufficiently high dimensionality in this manner ensures that the index vectors will be *nearly* orthogonal.

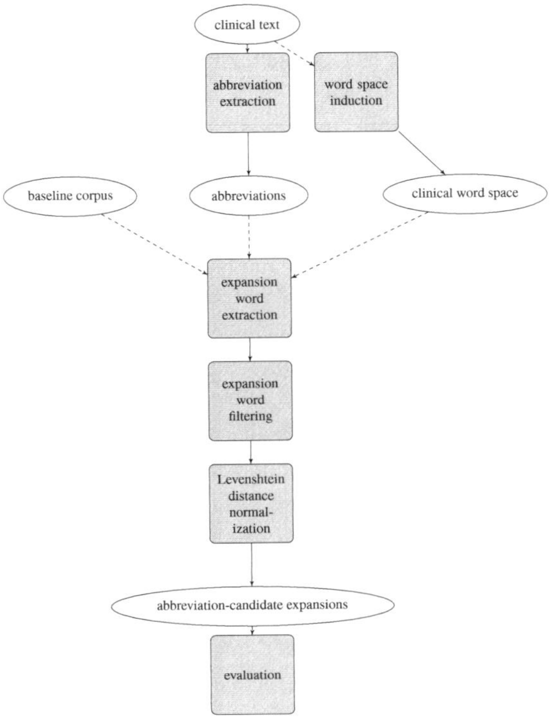

Figure 1: The abbreviation expansion process of the current study.

similar words for each abbreviation and treating these as initial expansions. More plausible expansions of each abbreviation are then obtained by filtering the expansion words and applying a normalization procedure.

3.1 Data

3.1.1 Corpora

Four corpora are used in the experiments: two clinical corpora, a medical (non-clinical) corpus and a general Swedish corpus (Table 1).

The clinical corpora are subsets of the Stockholm EPR Corpus (Dalianis et al., 2009), comprising health records for over one million patients from 512 clinical units in the Stockholm region over a five-year period (2006-2010)[2]. One of the clinical corpora contains records from various clinical units, for the first five months of 2008, henceforth referred to as SEPR, and the other contains radiology examination reports, produced in 2009 and 2010, the Stockholm EPR X-ray Corpus (Kvist and Velupillai, 2013) henceforth referred to as SEPR-X. The clinical corpora were lemmatized using Granska (Knutsson et al., 2003).

[2]This research has been approved by the Regional Ethical Review Board in Stockholm (Etikprövningsnamnden i Stockholm), permission number 2012/2028-31/5

The experiments in the current study also include a medical corpus. The electronic editions of Läkartidningen (Journal of the Swedish Medical Association), with issues from 1996 to 2010, have been compiled into a corpus (Kokkinakis, 2012), here referred to as LTK.

To compare the medical texts to general Swedish, the third version of the Stockholm Umeå Corpus (SUC 3.0) (Källgren, 1998) is used. It is a balanced corpus and consists of written Swedish texts from the early 1990's from various genres.

Corpus	#Tokens	#Types	#Lemmas
SEPR	109,663,052	853,341	431,932
SEPR-X	20,290,064	200,703	162,387
LTK	24,406,549	551,456	498,811
SUC	1,166,593	97,124	65,268

Table 1: Statistical descriptions of the corpora

3.1.2 Reference standards

A list of medical abbreviation-definition pairs is used as test data and treated as the reference standard in the evaluation. The list is derived from Cederblom (2005) and comprises 6384 unique abbreviations from patient records, referrals and scientific articles. To increase the size of the test data, the 40 most frequent abbreviations are extracted by a heuristics-based clinical abbreviation detection tool called SCAN (Isenius et al., 2012). A domain expert validated these abbreviations and manually provided the correct expansion(s).

An inherent property of word space models is that they model semantic relationships between unigrams. There are, however, abbreviations that expand into multiword expressions. Ongoing research on modeling semantic composition with word space models exists, but, in the current study abbreviations that expanded to multiword definitions were simply removed from the test data set. The two sets of abbreviation-expansion pairs were merged into a single test set, containing 1231 unique entries in total.

In order to obtain statistically reliable semantic relations in the word space, the terms of interest must be sufficiently frequent in the data. As a result, only abbreviation-expansion pairs with frequencies over 50 in SEPR and SEPR-X, respectively, were included in each test set. The SEPR test set contains 328 entries and the SEPR-X test set contains 211 entries. Each of the two test data sets is split into a development set (80%) for model selection, and a test set (20%) for final performance estimation.

3.2 Expansion word extraction

For the experiments where semantically related words were used for extraction of expansion words, the top 100 most correlated words for each of the abbreviations were retrieved from each of the word space model configurations that achieved the best results in the parameter optimization experiments.

The optimal parameter settings of a word space vary with the task and data at hand. It has been shown that when modeling paradigmatic (e.g., synonymous) relations in word spaces, a fairly small context window size is preferable (Sahlgren, 2006). Following the best results of Henriksson et al. (2012), we experiment with window sizes of 1+1, 2+2, and 4+4.

Two word space algorithms are explored: Random Indexing (RI), to retrieve the words that occur in a similar context as the query term, and Random Permutation (RP), which also incorporates word order information when accumulating the context vectors (Sahlgren et al., 2008). In order to exploit the advantages of both algorithms, and to combine models with different parameter settings, RI and RP model combinations are also evaluated. The models and their combinations are:

- Random Indexing (RI): words with a contextually high similarity are returned; word order within the context window is ignored.
- Random Permutation (RP): words that are contextually similar and used in the same relative positions are returned; these are more likely to share grammatical properties.
- RP-filtered RI candidates (RI_RP): returns the top ten terms in the RI model that are among the top thirty terms in the RP model.
- RI-filtered RP candidates (RP_RI): returns the top ten terms in the RP model that are among the top thirty terms in the RI model.
- RI and RP combination of similarity scores (RI+RP): sums the cosine similarity scores from the two models for each candidate term and returns the candidates with the highest aggregate score.

All models are induced with three different context window sizes for the two clinical corpora, SEPR and SEPR-X. For each corpus, two variants are used for word space induction, one where stop words are removed and one where stop words are retained. All word spaces are induced with a dimensionality of 1000.

For parameter optimization and model selection, the models and model combinations are queried for semantically similar words. For each of the abbreviations in the development set, the ten most similar words are retrieved. Recall is computed with regard to this list of candidate words, whether the correct expansion is among these ten candidates. Since the size of the test data is rather limited, 3-fold cross validation is performed on the development set for the parameter optimization experiments. For both SEPR and SEPR-X development sets, a combination of a RI model with a context window size of 4+4 and a RP model with 4+4 context window size in the summing similarity scores setting were among the most successful with recall scores of 0.25 for SEPR and 0.17 for SEPR-X.

3.3 Filtering expansion words

Given the expansion words, extracted from clinical word spaces or baseline corpora (the baselines are more thoroughly accounted for in 3.5), a filter was applied in order to generate candidate expansions. The filter was defined as a set of requirements, which had to be met in order for the expansion word to be extracted as a candidate expansion. The requirements were that the intitial letter of the abbreviation and expansion word had to be identical. All the letters of the abbreviation also had to be present in the expansion word in the same order.

String length difference was also a part of the requirements: the expansion word had to be at least one character longer than the abbreviation. In order to define an upper bound for expansion token length, string length differences of the SEPR and SEPR-X development sets were obtained. The distribution of string length differences for abbreviation-expansion pairs in the SEPR development set ranged from 1 to 21 characters. If a maximum string length difference of 14 was allowed, 95.2% of the abbreviation-expansion pairs were covered. As for the string length differences in the SEPR-X development set, the distribution ranged from 1 to 21 characters. If a string length difference of up to and including 14 characters was allowed, 96.3% of the abbreviation-expansion pairs were covered. Thus, a maximum difference in string length of 14 was also required for the expansion word to be extracted as a candidate expansion.

3.4 Levenshtein distance normalization

Given the set of filtered candidate expansions for the abbreviations, choosing the correct one can be seen as a normalization problem. The goal is to map a source word to a target word, similarly to for instance methods for spelling correction. The target word is chosen from a list of words, and the choice is based on the distance between the source and the target where a small distance implies high plausibility. However, we cannot adopt the same assumptions as for the problem of spelling correction, where the most common distance between a source word and the correct target word is 1 (Kukich, 1992). Intuitively, we can expect that there are abbreviations that expand to words within a larger distance than 1. It would seem somewhat useless to abbreviate words by one character only, although it is not entirely improbable.

Similarly to measuring the string length difference in order to define an upper bound for filtering candidate expansions, the Levenshtein distances for abbreviation-expansion pairs in the development sets were obtained.

For the SEPR and SEPR-X development sets, allowing a Levenshtein distance up to and including 14 covers 97.8% and 96.6% of the abbreviation-expansion pairs, as shown in Table 2.

Given the filtered candidate expansions, the Levenshtein distance for the abbreviation and each of the candidate expansions were computed. For each one of the candidate expansions, the Levenshtein distance beween the entry and the abbreviation was associated with the entry. The resulting list was sorted in ascending order according to Levenshtein distance.

Going through the candidate expansion list, if the Levenshtein distance was less than or identical to the upper bound for Levenshtein distance (14), the candidate expansion was added to the expansion list that was subsequently used in the evaluation. In the Levenshtein distance normalization experiments, a combination of semantically related words and words from LTK was used. When compiling the expansion list, semantically related words were prioritized. This implied that word space candidate expansion would occupy the top positions in the expansion list, in ascending order

LD	SEPR Avg %	SEPR SDev	SEPR-X Avg %	SEPR-X SDev
1	1	0.3	0.4	0.2
2	4.6	0.4	5	0.6
3	13	1.2	14.7	1.3
4	12.2	1	15.1	0.6
5	12.7	1.3	14.5	2.2
6	12.7	0.8	12.9	0.9
7	8.4	0.7	7.8	0.3
8	10.4	1.5	9.8	2
9	5.7	0.7	4.9	0.5
10	4.1	0.7	2.9	0.3
11	3	0.5	2.6	0.4
12	3	0.6	2.6	0.4
13	3.8	5.5	1.3	0.5
14	3.5	1.1	2.2	0.8
15	1.3	0.5	1.3	0.5
16	1.6	0.4	0.4	0.2
17	0.2	0.1		
18	0.8	0.3	1	0.1
20	0.2	0.1		
21	0.2	0.1	0.5	0

Table 2: Levenshtein distance distribution for abbreviation-expansion pairs. Average proportion over 5 folds at each Levensthein distance with standard deviation (SDev) in SEPR and SEPR-X development sets.

according to Levenshtein distance. The size of the list was restricted to ten, and the remaining positions, if there were any, were populated by LTK candidate expansions in ascending order according to Levenshtein distance to the abbreviation. If there were more than one candidate expansion at a specific Levenshtein distance, ranking of these was randomized.

3.5 Evaluation

The evaluation procedure of the abbreviation expansion implied assessing the ability of finding the correct expansions for abbreviations. In order to evaluate the performance gain of using semantic similarity to produce the list of candidate expansions over using the filtering and normalization procedure alone, a baseline was created. For the baseline, expansion words were instead extracted from the baseline corpora, the corpus of general Swedish SUC 3.0 and the medical corpus LTK. A list of all the lemma forms from each baseline corpus (separately) was provided for each abbreviation as initial expansion words. The filter and normalization procedure was then applied to these expansion words.

The reference standard contained abbreviation-expansion pairs, as described in 3.1.2. If any of the correct expansions (some of the abbreviations had multiple correct expansions) was present in the expansion list provided for each abbreviation in the test set, this was regarded as a true positive. Precision was computed with regard to the position of the correct expansion in the list and the number of expansions in the expansion list, as suggested in Henriksson (2013). For an abbreviation that expanded to one word only, this implied that the expansion list besides holding the correct expansion, also contained nine incorrect expansions, which was taken into account when computing precision. The list size was static: ten expansions were provided for each abbreviation, and this resulted in an overall low precision. Few of the abbreviations in the development set expanded to more than one word, giving a precision of 0.17-0.18 for all experiments.

Results of baseline abbreviation expansion in the development sets are given in table 3. Recall is given as an average of 5 folds, as cross validation was performed. The baseline achieves overall low recall, with the lowest score of 0.08 for the SEPR-X development set using SUC for candidate expansion extraction. The rest of the recall results are around 0.11.

Corpus	SEPR Recall	SEPR SDev	SEPR-X Recall	SEPR-X SDev
SUC	0.10	0.05	0.08	0.06
LTK	0.11	0.06	0.11	0.11

Table 3: Baseline average recall for SEPR and SEPR-X development sets.

Results from abbreviation expansion using semantically related words with filtering and normalization to refine the selection of expansions on SEPR and SEPR-X development sets are shown in Table 4. Recall is given as an average of 5 folds, as cross validation was performed. The semantically related words are extracted from the word space model configuration that had the top recall scores in the parameter optimization experiments described in 3.2, namely the combination of an RI model and an RP model both with 4+4 context window sizes. Recall is increased by 14 percentage points for SEPR and 20 percentage points for SEPR-X when applying filtering and normalization to the semantically related words.

SEPR Recall	SEPR SDev	SEPR-X Recall	SEPR-X SDev
0.39	0.05	0.37	0.1

Table 4: Abbreviation expansion results for SEPR and SEPR-X development sets using the best model from parameter optimization experiments (RI.4+4+RP.4+4).

4 Results

4.1 Expansion word extraction

The models and model combinations that had the best recall scores in the word space parameter optimization were also evaluated on the test set. The models that had top recall scores in 3.2 achieved 0.2 and 0.18 for SEPR and SEPR-X test sets respectively, compared to 0.25 and 0.17 in the word space parameter optimization.

4.2 Filtering expansion words and Levenshtein normalization

Abbreviation expansion with filtering and normalization was evaluated on the SEPR and SEPR-X test sets. The results are summarized in Table 5.

	SEPR	SEPR-X
SUC	0.09	0.16
LTK	0.08	0.14
Expansion word extraction	0.20	0.18
Filtering and normalization	0.38	0.40

Table 5: SEPR and SEPR-X test set results in abbreviation expansion.

Baseline recall scores were 0.09 and 0.08 for SUC and LTK respectively, showing a lower score for LTK compared to the results on the SEPR development set. For abbreviation expansion (with filtering and normalization) using semantically related words in combination with LTK, the best recall score was 0.38 for the SEPR test set, compared to 0.39 for the same model evaluated on the SEPR development set. Compared to the results of using semantically related words only (expansion word extraction), recall increased by 18 percentage points for the same model when filtering and normalization was applied.

Evaluation on the SEPR-X test set gave higher recall scores for both baseline corpora compared to the baseline results for the SEPR-X development set: the SUC result increased by 8 percentage points for recall. For LTK, there was an increase in recall of 3 percentage points. For the SEPR-X test set, recall increased by 22 percentage points when filtering and normalization was applied to semantically related words extracted from the best model configuration.

In comparison to the results of Henriksson et al (2012), where recall of the best model is 0.31 without and 0.42 with post-processing of the expansion words for word spaces induced from the data set (i.e., an increase in recall by 11 percentage points), the filtering and normalization procedure for expansion words of the current study yielded an increase by 18 percentage points.

5 Discussion

The filter combined with the Levenshtein normalisation procedure to refine candidate expansion selection showed a slight improvement compared to using post-processing, although the normalization procedure should be elaborated in order to be able to confidently claim that Levenshtein distance normalization is a better approach to expansion candidate selection. A suggestion for future work is to introduce weights based on frequently occurring edits between abbreviations and expansions and to apply these in abbreviation normalization.

The approach presented in this study is limited to abbreviations that translate into *one* full length word. Future research should include handling multiword expressions, not only unigrams, in order to process acronyms and initialisms.

Recall of the development sets in the word space parameter optimization experiments showed higher scores for SEPR (0.25) compared to SEPR-X (0.17). An explanation to this could be that the amount of data preprocessing done prior to word space induction might have varied, in terms of excluding sentences with little or no clinical content. This will of course affect word space co-occurrence information, as word context is accumulated without taking sentence boundaries into account.

The lemmatization of the clinical text used for word space induction left some words in their original form, causing test data and semantically related words to be morphologically discrepant. Lemmatization adapted to clinical text might have improved results. Spelling errors were also frequent in the clinical text, and abbreviations were sometimes normalized into a misspelled variant of the correct expansion. In the future, spelling correction could be added and combined with abbreviation expansion.

The impact that this apporach to abbreviation expansion might have on readability of clinical texts should also be assessed by means of an extrinsic evaluation, a matter to be pursued in future research.

6 Conclusions

We presented automatic expansion of abbreviations consisting of unigram full-length words in clinical texts. We applied a distributional semantic approach by using word space models and combined this with Levenshtein distance measures to choose the correct candidate among the semantically related words. The results show that the correct expansion of the abbreviation can be found in 40% of the cases, an improvement by 24 percentage points compared to the baseline (0.16) and an increase by 22 percentage points compared to using word space models alone (0.18). Applying Levenshtein distance to refine the selection of semantically related candidate expansions yields a total recall of 0.38 and 0.40 for radiology reports and medical health records, respectively.

Acknowledgments

The study was partly funded by the Vårdal Fundation and supported by the Swedish Foundation for Strategic Research through the project High-Performance Data Mining for Drug Effect Detection (ref. no. IIS11-0053) at Stockholm University, Sweden. The authors would also like to direct thanks to the reviewers for valuable comments.

References

M. Adnan, J. Warren, and M. Orr. 2010. Assessing text characteristics of electronic discharge summaries and their implications for patient readability. In *Proceedings of the Fourth Australasian Workshop on Health Informatics and Knowledge Management-Volume 108*, pages 77–84. Australian Computer Society, Inc.

H. Allvin. 2010. Patientjournalen som genre: En text- och genreanalys om patientjournalers relation till patientdatalagen. Master's thesis, Stockholm University.

H. Ao and T. Takagi. 2005. ALICE: an algorithm to extract abbreviations from MEDLINE. *Journal of the American Medical Informatics Association*, 12(5):576–586.

S. Cederblom. 2005. *Medicinska förkortningar och akronymer (In Swedish)*. Studentlitteratur.

J.T. Chang, H. Schütze, and R.B. Altman. 2002. Creating an online dictionary of abbreviations from medline. *Journal of the American Medical Informatics Association*, 9:612–620.

T. Cohen and D. Widdows. 2009. Empirical distributional semantics: Methods and biomedical applications. *Journal of Biomedical Informatics*, 42(2):390–405.

H. Dalianis, M. Hassel, and S. Velupillai. 2009. The Stockholm EPR Corpus – Characteristics and some initial findings. In *Proceedings of the 14th International Symposium on Health Information Management Research*, pages 243–249.

D. Dannélls. 2006. Automatic acronym recognition. In *Proceedings of the 11th conference on European chapter of the Association for Computational Linguistics (EACL)*, pages 167–170.

N. Elhadad. 2006. *User-sensitive text summarization: Application to the medical domain*. Ph.D. thesis, Columbia University.

S. Gaudan, H. Kirsch, and D. Rebholz-Schuhmann. 2005. Resolving abbreviations to their senses in MEDLINE. *Bioinformatics*, 21(18):3658–3664, September.

Z.S. Harris. 1954. Distributional structure. *Word*, 10:146–162.

A. Henriksson, H. Moen, M. Skeppstedt, A. Eklund, V. Daudaravicius, and M. Hassel. 2012. Synonym Extraction of Medical Terms from Clinical Text Using Combinations of Word Space Models. In *Proceedings of Semantic Mining in Biomedicine (SMBM 2012)*, pages 10–17.

A. Henriksson, H. Moen, M. Skeppstedt, V. Daudaravicius, and M. Duneld. 2014. Synonym extraction and abbreviation expansion with ensembles of semantic spaces. *Journal of Biomedical Semantics*, 5(6).

A. Henriksson. 2013. *Semantic Spaces of Clinical Text: Leveraging Distributional Semantics for Natural Language Processing of Electronic Health Records*. Licentiate thesis, Department of Computer and Systems Sciences, Stockholm University.

N. Isenius, S. Velupillai, and M. Kvist. 2012. Initial Results in the Development of SCAN: a Swedish Clinical Abbreviation Normalizer. In *Proceedings of the CLEF 2012 Workshop on Cross-Language Evaluation of Methods, Applications, and Resources for eHealth Document Analysis (CLEFe-Health2012)*.

G. Källgren. 1998. Documentation of the Stockholm-Umeå corpus. *Department of Linguistics, Stockholm University*.

P. Kanerva, J. Kristoferson, and A. Holst. 2000. Random indexing of text samples for latent semantic analysis. In *Proceedings of the 22nd annual conference of the cognitive science society*, page 1036.

A. Keselman, L. Slaughter, C. Arnott-Smith, H. Kim, G. Divita, A. Browne, C. Tsai, and Q. Zeng-Treitler. 2007. Towards consumer-friendly PHRs: patients experience with reviewing their health records. In *AMIA Annual Symposium Proceedings*, volume 2007, pages 399–403.

O. Knutsson, J. Bigert, and V. Kann. 2003. A robust shallow parser for Swedish. In *Proceedings of Nodalida*.

D. Kokkinakis. 2012. The Journal of the Swedish Medical Association-a Corpus Resource for Biomedical Text Mining in Swedish. In *Proceedings of Third Workshop on Building and Evaluating Resources for Biomedical Text Mining Workshop Programme*, page 40.

K. Kukich. 1992. Techniques for automatically correcting words in text. *ACM Computing Surveys (CSUR)*, 24(4):377–439.

M. Kvist and S. Velupillai. 2013. Professional Language in Swedish Radiology Reports – Characterization for Patient-Adapted Text Simplification. In *Scandinavian Conference on Health Informatics 2013*, pages 55–59.

V.I. Levenshtein. 1966. Binary codes capable of correcting deletions, insertions and reversals. In *Soviet physics doklady*, volume 10, page 707.

D. Movshovitz-Attias and W.W. Cohen. 2012. Alignment-HMM-based Extraction of Abbreviations from Biomedical Text. In *Proceedings of the 2012 Workshop on Biomedical Natural Language Processing (BioNLP 2012)*, pages 47–55.

N. Nakatsu, Y. Kambayashi, and S. Yajima. 1982. A longest common subsequence algorithm suitable for similar text strings. *Acta Informatica*, 18(2):171–179.

Y. Park and R.J. Byrd. 2001. Hybrid text mining for finding abbreviations and their definitions. In *Proceedings of the 2001 conference on empirical methods in natural language processing*, pages 126–133.

E. Pettersson, B. Megyesi, and J. Nivre. 2013. Normalisation of historical text using context-sensitive weighted levenshtein distance and compound splitting. In *Proceedings of the 19th Nordic Conference of Computational Linguistics (NODALIDA 2013)*, pages 163–179.

R.E. Rudd, B.A. Moeykens, and T.C. Colton. 1999. Health and literacy: a review of medical and public health literature. *Office of Educational Research and Improvement*.

M. Sahlgren, A. Holst, and P. Kanerva. 2008. Permutations as a means to encode order in word space. In *Proceedings of the 30th Annual Meeting of the Cognitive Science Society*, pages 1300–1305.

M. Sahlgren. 2006. *The Word-space model*. Ph.D. thesis, Stockholm University.

A.S. Schwartz and M.A. Hearst. 2003. A simple algorithm for identifying abbreviation definitions in biomedical text. In *Proceedings of Pacific Symposium on Biocomputing*, pages 451–462.

M. Skeppstedt. 2012. *From Disorder to Order: Extracting clinical findings from unstructured text*. Licentiate thesis, Department of Computer and Systems Sciences, Stockholm University.

K. Taghva and J. Gilbreth. 1999. Recognizing acronyms and their definitions. *International Journal on Document Analysis and Recognition*, 1(4):191–198.

H. Yu, G. Hripcsak, and C. Friedman. 2002. Mapping abbreviations to full forms in biomedical articles. *Journal of the American Medical Informatics Association*, 9(3):262–272.

A Quantitative Insight into the Impact of Translation on Readability

Alina Maria Ciobanu, Liviu P. Dinu
Center for Computational Linguistics, University of Bucharest
Faculty of Mathematics and Computer Science, University of Bucharest
alina.ciobanu@my.fmi.unibuc.ro, ldinu@fmi.unibuc.ro

Abstract

In this paper we investigate the impact of translation on readability. We propose a quantitative analysis of several shallow, lexical and morpho-syntactic features that have been traditionally used for assessing readability and have proven relevant for this task. We conduct our experiments on a parallel corpus of transcribed parliamentary sessions and we investigate readability metrics for the original segments of text, written in the language of the speaker, and their translations.

1 Introduction

Systems for automatic readability assessment have been studied since the 1920s and have received an increasing attention during the last decade. Early research on readability assessment focused only on shallow language properties, but nowadays natural language processing technologies allow the investigation of a wide range of factors which influence the ease which a text is read and understood with. These factors correspond to different levels of linguistic analysis, such as the lexical, morphological, semantic, syntactic or discourse levels. However, readability depends not only on text properties, but also on characteristics of the target readers. Aspects such as background knowledge, age, level of literacy and motivation of the expected audience should be considered when developing a readability assessment system. Although most readability metrics were initially developed for English, current research has shown a growing interest in other languages, such as German, French, Italian or Portuguese.

Readability assessment systems are relevant for a wide variety of applications, both human- and machine-oriented (Dell'Orletta et al., 2011). Second language learners and people with disabilities or low literacy skills benefit from such systems, which provide assistance in selecting reading material with an appropriate level of complexity from a large collection of documents – for example, the documents available on the web (Collins-Thompson, 2011). Within the medical domain, the investigation of the readability level of medical texts helps developing well-suited materials to increase the level of information for preventing diseases (Richwald et al., 1989) and to automatically adapt technical documents to various levels of medical expertise (Elhadad and Sutaria, 2007). For natural language processing tasks such as machine translation (Stymne et al., 2013), text simplification (Aluisio et al., 2010), speech recognition (Jones et al., 2005) or document summarization (Radev and Fan, 2000), readability approaches are employed to assist the process and to evaluate and quantify its performance and effectiveness.

1.1 Related Work

Most of the traditional readability approaches investigate shallow text properties to determine the complexity of a text. These readability metrics are based on assumptions which correlate surface features with the linguistic factors which influence readability. For example, the average number of characters or syllables per word, the average number of words per sentence and the percentage of words not occurring among the most frequent n words in a language are correlated with the lexical, syntactic and, respectively, the semantic complexity of the text. The Flesch-Kincaid measure (Kincaid et al., 1975) employs the average number of syllables per word and the average number of words per sentence to assess readability, while the Automated Readability Index (Smith and Senter, 1967) and the Coleman-Liau metric (Coleman and Liau, 1975) measure word length based on character count rather than syllable count; they are functions of both the average number of characters per word and the average number of words per sentence. Gunning Fog (Gunning, 1952) and SMOG (McLaughlin, 1969) account also for the percentage of polysyllabic words and the Dale-Chall formula (Dale and Chall, 1995) relies on word frequency lists to assess readability. The traditional readability approaches are not computationally expensive, but they are only a coarse approximation of the linguistic factors which influence readability (Pitler and Nenkova, 2008). According to Si and Callan (2001), the shallow features employed by standard readability indices are based on assumptions about writing style that may not apply in all situations.

Along with the development of natural languages processing tools and machine learning techniques, factors of increasing complexity , corresponding to various levels of linguistic analysis, have been taken into account in the study of readability assessment. Si and Callan (2001) and Collins-Thompson and Callan (2004) use statistical language modeling and Petersen and Ostendorf (2009) combine features from statistical language models, syntactic parse trees and traditional metrics to estimate reading difficulty. Feng (2009) explores discourse level attributes, along with lexical and syntactic features, and emphasizes the value of the global semantic properties of the text for predicting text readability. Pitler and Nenkova (2008) propose and analyze two perspectives for the task of readability assessment: prediction and ranking. Using various features, they reach the conclusion that only discourse level features exhibit robustness across the two tasks. Vajjala and Meurers (2012) show that combining lexical and syntactic features with features derived from second language acquisition research leads to performance improvements.

Although most readability approaches developed so far deal with English, the development of adequate corpora for experiments and the study of readability features tailored for other languages have received increasing attention. For Italian, Franchina and Vacca (1986) propose the Flesch-Vacca formula, which is an adaptation of the Flesch index (Flesch, 1946). Another metric developed for Italian is Gulpease (Lucisano and Piemontese, 1988), which uses characters instead of syllables to measure word length and thus requires less resources. Dell'Orletta et al. (2011) combine traditional, morpho-syntactic, lexical and syntactic features for building a readability model for Italian, while Tonelli et al. (2012) propose a system for readability assessment for Italian inspired by the principles of Coh-Metrix (Graesser et al., 2004). For French, Kandel and Moles (1958) propose an adaptation of the Flesch formula and François and Miltsakaki (2012) investigate a wide range of classic and non-classic features to predict readability level using a dataset for French as a foreign language. Readability assessment was also studied for Spanish (Huerta, 1959) and Portuguese (Aluisio et al., 2010) using features derived from previous research on English.

1.2 Readability of Translation

According to Sun (2012), the reception of a translated text is related to cross-cultural readability. Translators need to understand the particularities of both the source and the target language in order to transfer the meaning of the text from one language to another. This process can be challenging, especially for languages with significant structure differences, such as English and Chinese. The three-step system of translation (analysis, transfer and restructuring) presented by Nida and Taber (1969) summarizes the process and emphasizes the importance of a proper understanding of the source and the target languages. While rendering the source language text into the target language, it is also important to maintain the style of the document. Various genres of text might be translated for different purposes, which influence the choice of the translation strategy. For example, for political speeches the purpose is to report exactly what is communicated in a given text (Trosborg, 1997).

Parallel corpora are very useful in studying the properties of translation and the relationships between source language and target language. Therefore, the corpus-based research has become more and more popular in translation research. Using the *Europarl* (Koehn, 2005) parallel corpus, van Halteren (2008) investigates the automatic identification of the source language of European Parliament speeches, based on frequency counts of word n-grams. Islam and Mehler (2012) draw attention to the absence of adequate corpora for studies on translation and propose a resource suited for this purpose.

2 Our Approach and Methodology

The problem that we address in this paper is whether human translation has an impact on readability. Given a text T_1 in a source language L_1 and its translations in various target languages $L_2, ..., L_n$, how does readability vary? Is the original text in L_1 easier to read and understand than its translation in a target language L_i? Which language is closest to the source language, in terms of readability? We investigate several shallow, lexical and morpho-syntactic features that have been widely used and have proven relevant for assessing readability. We are interested in observing the differences between the feature values obtained for the original texts and those obtained for their translations. Although some of the metrics (such as average word length) might be language-specific, most of them are language-independent and a comparison between them across languages is justified. The 10 readability metrics that we account for are described in Section 3.2.

We run our experiments on *Europarl* (Koehn, 2005), a multilingual parallel corpus which is described in detail in Section 3.1. We investigate 5 Romance languages (Romanian, French, Italian, Spanish and Portuguese) and, in order to excerpt an adequate dataset of parallel texts, we adopt a strategy similar to that of van Halteren (2008): given n languages $L_1, ..., L_n$, we apply the following steps:

1. we select L_1 as the source language
2. we excerpt the collection of segments of text T_1 for which L_1 is the source language
3. we identify the translations $T_2, ..., T_n$ of T_1 in the target languages $L_2, ..., L_n$
4. we compute the readability metrics for $T_1, ..., T_n$
5. we repeat steps $1 - 4$ using each language $L_2, ..., L_n$ as the source language, one at a time

We propose two approaches to quantify and evaluate the variation in the readability feature values from the original texts to their translations: a distance-based method and a multi-criteria technique based on rank aggregation.

3 Experimental Setup

3.1 Data

Europarl (Koehn, 2005) is a multilingual parallel corpus extracted from the proceedings of the European Parliament. Its main intended use is as aid for statistical machine translation research (Tiedemann, 2012). The corpus is tokenized and aligned in 21 languages. The files contain annotations for marking the document (*<chapter>*), the speaker (*<speaker>*) and the paragraph (*<p>*). Some documents have the attribute *language* for the *speaker* tag, which indicates the language used by the original speaker. Another way of annotating the original language is by having the language abbreviation written between parentheses at the beginning of each segment of text. However, there are segments where the language is not marked in either of the two ways. We account only for sentences for which the original language could be determined and we exclude all segments showing inconsistent values.

We use the following strategy: because for the Romance languages there are very few segments of text for which the *language* attribute is consistent across all versions, we take into account an attribute *L* if all other Romance languages mention it. For example, given a paragraph *P* in the Romanian subcorpus, we assume that the source language for this paragraph is Romanian if all other four subcorpora (Italian, French, Spanish and Portuguese) mark this paragraph *P* with the tag *RO* for language. Thus, we obtain a collection of segments of text for each subcorpus. We identify 4,988 paragraphs for which Romanian is the source language, 13,093 for French, 7,485 for Italian, 5,959 for Spanish and 8,049 for Portuguese. Because we need sets of approximately equal size for comparison, we choose, for each language, a subset equal with the size of the smallest subset, i.e., we keep 4,988 paragraphs for each language.

Note that in this corpus paragraphs are aligned across languages, but the number of sentences may be different. For example, the sentence *"UE trebuie să fie ambiţioasă în combaterea schimbărilor climatice, iar rolul energiei nucleare şi energiilor regenerabile nu poate fi neglijat."*[1], for which Romanian is the source language,

[1]Translation into English: *"The EU must be ambitious in the battle against climate change, which means that the role of nuclear power and renewable energy sources cannot be discounted."*

is translated into French in two sentences: *"L'UE doit se montrer ambitieuse dans sa lutte contre les changements climatiques."* and *"L'énergie nucléaire et les sources d'énergie renouvelables ne peuvent donc pas être écartées."*. Therefore, we match paragraphs, rather than sentences, across languages.

As a preprocessing step, we discard the transcribers' descriptions of the parliamentary sessions (such as *"Applause"*, *"The President interrupted the speaker"* or *"The session was suspended at 19.30 and resumed at 21.00"*).

According to van Halteren (2008), translations in the European Parliament are generally made by native speakers of the target language. Translation is an inherent part of the political activity (Schäffner and Bassnett, 2010) and has a high influence on the way the political speeches are perceived. The question posed by Schäffner and Bassnett (2010) *"What exactly happens in the complex processes of recontextualisation across linguistic, cultural and ideological boundaries?"* summarizes the complexity of the process of translating political documents. Political texts might contain complex technical terms and elaborated sentences. Therefore, the results of our experiments are probably domain-specific and cannot be generalized to other types of texts. Although parliamentary documents probably have a low readability level, our investigation is not negatively influenced by the choice of corpus because we are consistent across all experiments in terms of text gender and we report results obtained solely by comparison between source and target languages.

3.2 Features

We investigate several shallow, lexical and morpho-syntactic features that were traditionally used for assessing readability and have proven high discriminative power within readability metrics.

3.2.1 Shallow Features

Average number of words per sentence. The average sentence length is one of the most widely used metrics for determining readability level and was employed in numerous readability formulas, proving to be most meaningful in combined evidence with average word frequency. Feng et al. (2010) find the average sentence length to have higher predictive power than all the other lexical and syllable-based features they used.

Average number of characters per word. It is generally considered that frequently occurring words are usually short, so the average number of characters per word was broadly used for measuring readability in a robust manner. Many readability formulas measure word length in syllables rather than letters, but this requires additional resources for syllabication.

3.2.2 Lexical Features

Percentage of words from the basic lexicon. Based on the assumption that more common words are easier to understand, the percentage of words not occurring among the most frequent *n* in the language is a commonly used metric to approximate readability. To determine the percentage of words from the basic lexicon, we employ the representative vocabularies for Romance languages proposed by Sala (1988).

Type/Token Ratio. The proportion between the number of lexical types and the number of tokens indicates the range of use of vocabulary. The higher the value of this feature, the higher the variability of the vocabulary used in the text.

3.2.3 Morpho-Syntactic Features

Relative frequency of POS unigrams. The ratio for 5 parts of speech (verbs, nouns, pronouns, adjectives and adverbs), computed individually on a per-token basis. This feature assumes that the probability of a token is context-independent. For lemmatization and part of speech tagging we use the *DexOnline*[2] machine-readable dictionary for Romanian and the *FreeLing*[3] (Padró and Stanilovsky, 2012; Padró, 2011; Padró et al., 2010; Atserias et al., 2006; Carreras et al., 2004) language analysis tool suite for French, Italian, Spanish and Portuguese.

Lexical density. The proportion of content words (verbs, nouns, adjectives and adverbs), computed on a per-token basis. Grammatical features were shown to be useful in readability prediction (Heilman et al., 2007).

4 Results Analysis

Our main purpose is to investigate the variability of the feature values from the original texts to their translations. In Table 1 we report the values

[2]http://dexonline.ro

[3]http://nlp.lsi.upc.edu/freeling

obtained for 10 readability metrics computed for the *Europarl* subcorpora for Romanian, French, Italian, Spanish and Portuguese. The readability metrics we computed lead to several immediate remarks. We notice that, generally, when representing the values for a feature *F* on the real axis, the values corresponding to the translations are not placed on the same side of the value corresponding to the original text. For example, considering feature *F3* (the percentage of words from the basic lexicon), and taking Romanian as the source language, we observe that the value for the original text is between Italian (on the left side) and the other languages (on the right side).

In the absence of a widely-accepted readability metric, such as the Flesch-Kincaid formula or the Automated Readability Index, for all 5 Romance languages, we choose two other ways to evaluate the results obtained after applying the 10 readability features: a distance-based evaluation and a multi-criteria approach.

In order to compute distance measures reliably, we normalize feature values using the following formula:

$$f'_i = \frac{f_i - f_{min}}{f_{max} - f_{min}},$$

where f_{min} is the minimum value for feature *F* and f_{max} is the maximum value for feature *F*. For example, if *F* = *F1* and the source language is Romanian, then f_{min} = 26.2 and f_{max} = 29.0.

4.1 Preliminaries

In this subsection we shortly describe the two techniques used. The experimented reader can skip this subsection.

4.1.1 Rank Aggregation

Rank distance (Dinu and Dinu, 2005) is a metric used for measuring the similarity between two ranked lists. A ranking of a set of n objects can be represented as a permutation of the integers $1, 2, ..., n$. S is a set of ranking results, $\sigma \in S$. $\sigma(i)$ represents the rank of object i in the ranking result σ. The rank distance is computed as:

$$\Delta(\sigma, \tau) = \sum_{i=1}^{n} |\sigma(i) - \tau(i)|$$

The ranks of the elements are given from bottom up, i.e., from n to 1, in a Borda order. The elements which do not occur in any of the rankings receive the rank 0.

In a selection process, rankings are issued for a common decision problem, therefore a ranking that "combines" all the original (base) rankings is required. One common-sense solution is finding a ranking that is as close as possible to all the particular rankings.

Formally, given m partial rankings $\mathcal{T} = \tau_1, \tau_2, ..., \tau_m$, over a universe $\mathcal{U}$, the rank aggregation problem requires a partial ranking that is as close as possible to all these rankings to be determined. In other words, it requires a means of combining the rankings. There are many ways to solve this problem, one of which is by trying to find a ranking such that the sum of rank distances between it and the given rankings is minimal. In other words, find σ such that:

$$\Delta(\sigma, \mathcal{T}) = \sum_{\tau \in \mathcal{T}} \Delta(\sigma, \tau)$$

is minimal. The set of all rankings that minimize $\Delta(\sigma, \mathcal{T})$ is called the aggregations set and is denoted by $agr(\mathcal{T})$.

Apart from many paradoxes of different aggregation methods, this problem is NP-hard for most non-trivial distances (e.g., for edit distance, see (de la Higuera and Casacuberta, 2000)). Dinu and Manea (2006) show that the rank aggregation problem using rank distance, which minimizes the sum $\Delta(\sigma, \mathcal{T})$ of the rank distances between the aggregation and each given ranking, can be reduced to solving $|\mathcal{U}|$ assignment problems, where $\mathcal{U}$ is the universe of objects. Let $n = \#\mathcal{U}$. The time complexity to obtain one such aggregation (there may be more than one) is $\mathcal{O}(n^4)$.

We then transform the aggregation problem in a categorization problem as follows (Dinu and Popescu, 2008): for a multiset *L* of rankings, we determine all the aggregations of *L* and then we apply voting on the set of *agr(L)*.

4.1.2 Cosine Distance

Cosine distance is a metric which computes the angular cosine distance between two vectors of an inner product space. Given two vectors of features, *A* and *B*, the cosine distance is represented as follows:

$$\Delta(A, B) = 1 - \frac{\sum_{i=1}^{n} A_i \times B_i}{\sqrt{\sum_{i=1}^{n} (A_i)^2} \times \sqrt{\sum_{i=1}^{n} (B_i)^2}}$$

When used in positive space, the cosine distance ranges from 0 to 1.

Source Language	Target Language	F1	F2	F3	F4	F5	F6	F7	F8	F9	F10
	RO	26.2	5.61	0.67	0.06	0.66	0.15	0.29	0.16	0.05	0.11
	FR	29.0	5.06	0.79	0.03	0.59	0.13	0.35	0.06	0.04	0.06
RO	IT	27.4	5.57	0.63	0.04	0.61	0.16	0.30	0.10	0.04	0.06
	ES	28.3	5.18	0.81	0.04	0.53	0.15	0.24	0.09	0.03	0.03
	PT	26.8	5.31	0.78	0.04	0.58	0.14	0.30	0.08	0.04	0.02
	RO	24.6	5.35	0.70	0.06	0.64	0.17	0.26	0.14	0.06	0.13
	FR	27.4	4.86	0.81	0.04	0.58	0.14	0.32	0.05	0.06	0.09
FR	IT	25.7	5.46	0.65	0.05	0.61	0.17	0.28	0.09	0.05	0.07
	ES	26.3	5.11	0.82	0.05	0.53	0.16	0.23	0.08	0.04	0.04
	PT	25.1	5.21	0.80	0.05	0.58	0.16	0.29	0.07	0.05	0.02
	RO	29.7	5.46	0.69	0.06	0.62	0.16	0.27	0.15	0.05	0.12
	FR	32.4	5.00	0.80	0.04	0.58	0.14	0.33	0.06	0.05	0.08
IT	IT	30.9	5.48	0.64	0.05	0.61	0.16	0.28	0.10	0.05	0.07
	ES	31.8	5.15	0.82	0.04	0.53	0.16	0.23	0.09	0.04	0.03
	PT	30.5	5.28	0.79	0.04	0.58	0.15	0.29	0.07	0.05	0.02
	RO	27.6	5.33	0.70	0.06	0.64	0.17	0.26	0.14	0.06	0.13
	FR	29.9	4.91	0.81	0.04	0.58	0.14	0.32	0.05	0.05	0.09
ES	IT	27.9	5.45	0.66	0.05	0.60	0.17	0.28	0.09	0.05	0.08
	ES	31.1	5.02	0.83	0.05	0.52	0.16	0.22	0.08	0.05	0.04
	PT	28.2	5.17	0.81	0.05	0.57	0.16	0.28	0.07	0.05	0.02
	RO	29.3	5.58	0.67	0.05	0.65	0.15	0.28	0.16	0.05	0.12
	FR	32.8	5.04	0.80	0.03	0.58	0.13	0.34	0.06	0.04	0.07
PT	IT	30.9	5.56	0.62	0.04	0.60	0.15	0.29	0.10	0.04	0.06
	ES	32.5	5.15	0.81	0.03	0.53	0.15	0.24	0.09	0.03	0.03
	PT	30.9	5.28	0.79	0.04	0.57	0.14	0.30	0.08	0.04	0.02

Table 1: Values for readability metrics applied on *Europarl*. The first column represents the source language (the language of the speaker). The second column represents the target language (the language in which the text is written / translated). The features F1 - F10 are as follows:

- F1 - average number of words per sentence
- F2 - average number of characters per word
- F3 - percentage of words from the basic lexicon
- F4 - type / token ratio
- F5 - lexical density
- F6 - relative frequency of POS unigrams: verbs
- F7 - relative frequency of POS unigrams: nouns
- P8 - relative frequency of POS unigrams: adjectives
- F9 - relative frequency of POS unigrams: adverbs
- F10 - relative frequency of POS unigrams: pronouns

	RO	FR	IT	ES	PT
RO	–	0.571	0.138	0.582	0.292
FR	0.513	–	0.505	0.491	0.328
IT	0.075	0.416	–	0.502	0.212
ES	0.531	0.423	0.545	–	0.256
PT	0.300	0.227	0.252	0.275	–

Table 2: Cosine distance between feature vectors. The first column represents the source language and the first line represents the target language.

4.2 Experiment Analysis: Original vs. Translation

Our main goal is to determine a robust way to evaluate the variation in readability from the original texts to their translations, after applying the 10 readability features described in Section 3.2.

A natural approach is to use an evaluation methodology based on a distance metric between feature vectors to observe how close translations are in various languages, with respect to readability. The closer the distance is to 0, the more easily can one language be translated into the other, in terms of readability. Briefly, our first approach is as follows: for each source language L in column 1 of Table 1, we consider the feature vector corresponding to this language from column 2 and we compute the cosine distance between this vector and all the other 4 vectors remaining in column 2, one for each target language. The obtained values are reported in Table 2, on the line corresponding to language L.

Table 2 provides not only information regarding the closest language, but also the hierarchy of languages in terms of readability. For example, the closest language to Romanian is Italian, followed by Portuguese, French and Spanish. Overall, the lowest distance between an original text and its translation occurs when Italian is the source language and Romanian the target language. The highest distance is reported for translations from Romanian into Spanish.

The second approach we use for investigating the readability of translation is multi-criteria aggregation: since the 10 monitored features can be seen as individual classifiers for readability (and in various papers they were used either individually or combined as representative features for predicting readability), we experiment with a multi-criteria aggregation of these metrics in order to predict which language is closest to the source language in terms of readability.

For segments of text having the source language L, we consider each feature F_i, one at a time, and we compute the absolute value of the difference between the F_i value for the original text and the F_i values for its translations. Then, we sort the values in ascending order, thus obtaining for each language L and feature F_i a ranking with 4 elements (one for each translation) determined as follows: the language having the lowest computed absolute value is placed on the first position, the language having the second to lowest computed absolute value is placed on the second position, and so on. Finally, we have, for each language L, 10 rankings (one for each feature) with 4 elements (one for each translation), each ranking indicating on the first position the target language which is closest to the source language with regard to readability measured by feature F_i. In case of equal values for the computed absolute distance, we consider all possible rankings.

Given these rankings, the task we propose is to determine which target language is closest to the source language in terms of readability. To solve this requirement, we apply multi-criteria aggregation based on rank distance. For each language, we aggregate the 10 corresponding rankings and determine the closest language with respect to readability across translation. The results we obtain for Romance languages after the rank aggregation are as follows: the closest translation language for Romanian is Italian (followed by Portuguese, Spanish and French). Conversely, for Italian the closest language is Romanian (followed by Portuguese, French and Spanish). For French, Portuguese occupies the first position in the ranking (followed by Spanish, Italian and Romanian). For Spanish, Portuguese ranks first (followed by Italian, French and Romanian), while for Portuguese, Italian is the closest language (followed by French, Spanish and Romanian).

The obtained results are very similar to those computed by the cosine distance and reported in Table 2. The only difference regarding the closest language in terms of readability is that rank aggregation reports Italian as being closest to Portuguese, while the cosine distance reports French instead. However, the differences between the first two ranked languages for Portuguese, namely French and Italian, are insignificant.

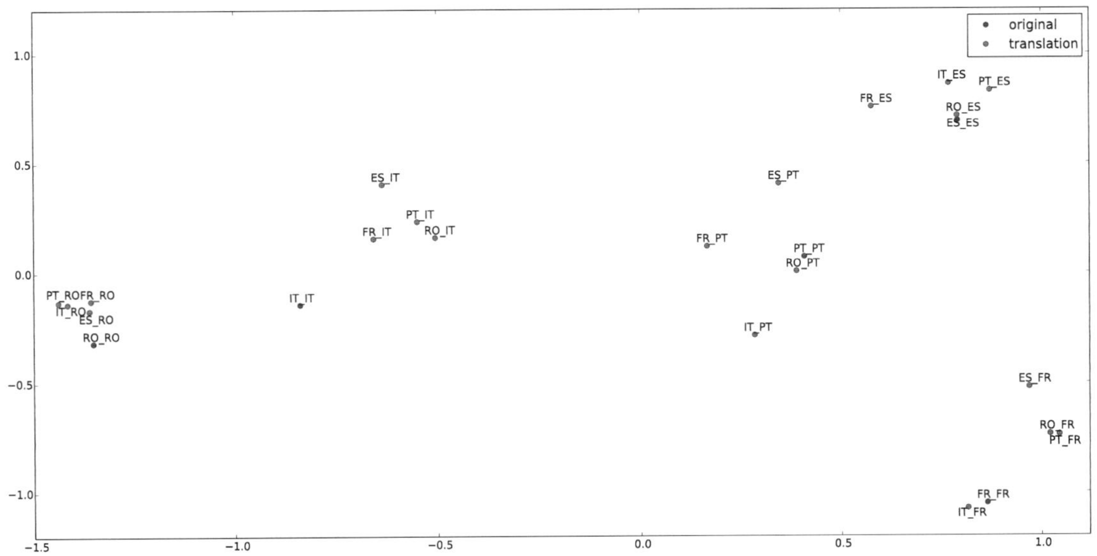

Figure 1: PCA. Languages are annotated in the figure as follows: $L_1\_L_2$, where L_1 is the source language and L_2 is the target language.

4.3 PCA: Original vs. Translation

In Figure 1 we employ Principal Component Analysis (PCA) to perform linear data reduction in order to obtain a better representation of the readability feature vectors without losing much information. We use the Modular toolkit for Data Processing (MDP), a Python data processing framework (Zito et al., 2008). We observe that clusters tend to be formed based on the target language. rather than based on the source language. While for Romanian and Italian the original texts are to some extent isolated from their translations, for French, Spanish and Portuguese the original texts are more integrated within the groups of translations. The most compact cluster corresponds to Romanian as a target language.

5 Conclusions

In this paper we investigate the behaviour of various readability metrics across parallel translations of texts from a source language to target languages. We focus on Romance languages and we propose two methods for the analysis of the closest translation, in terms of readability. Given a text in a source language, we determine which of its translations in various target languages is closest to the original text with regard to readability. In our future works, we plan to extend our analysis to more languages, in order to cover a wider variety of linguistic families. We are mainly interested in the 21 languages covered by *Europarl*. Moreover, we intend to enrich the variety of the texts, beginning with an analysis of translations of literary works. As far as resources are available, we plan to investigate other readability metrics as well and to combine our findings with the views of human experts. We believe our method can provide valuable information regarding the difficulty of translation from one language into another in terms of readability.

Acknowledgements

The authors thank the anonymous reviewers for their helpful and constructive comments. The contribution of the authors to this paper is equal. Research supported by a grant of the Romanian National Authority for Scientific Research, CNCS UEFISCDI, project number PN-II-ID-PCE-2011-3-0959.

References

Sandra Aluisio, Lucia Specia, Caroline Gasperin, and Carolina Scarton. 2010. Readability Assessment for Text Simplification. In *Proceedings of the NAACL HLT 2010 Fifth Workshop on Innovative Use of NLP for Building Educational Applications, IUNLPBEA 2010*, pages 1–9.

Jordi Atserias, Bernardino Casas, Elisabet Comelles, Meritxell González, Lluís Padró, and Muntsa Padró. 2006. FreeLing 1.3: Syntactic and semantic services in an open-source NLP library. In *Proceedings of the 5th International Conference on Language Resources and Evaluation, LREC 2006*, pages 2281–2286.

Xavier Carreras, Isaac Chao, Lluís Padró, and Muntsa Padró. 2004. FreeLing: An Open-Source Suite of Language Analyzers. In *Proceedings of the 4th International Conference on Language Resources and Evaluation, LREC 2004*, pages 239–242.

Meri Coleman and T. L. Liau. 1975. A computer readability formula designed for machine scoring. *Journal of Applied Psychology*, 60(2):283–284.

Kevyn Collins-Thompson and James P. Callan. 2004. A Language Modeling Approach to Predicting Reading Difficulty. In *Proceedings of the Human Language Technology Conference of the North American Chapter of the Association of Computational Linguistics, HLT-NAACL 2004*, pages 193–200.

Kevyn Collins-Thompson. 2011. Enriching Information Retrieval with Reading Level Prediction. In *SIGIR 2011 Workshop on Enriching Information Retrieval*.

Edgar Dale and Jeanne Chall. 1995. *Readability Revisited: The New Dale-Chall Readability Formula*. Brookline Books, Cambridge.

C. de la Higuera and F. Casacuberta. 2000. Topology of Strings: Median String is NP-complete. *Theoretical Computer Science*, 230(1-2):39–48.

Felice Dell'Orletta, Simonetta Montemagni, and Giulia Venturi. 2011. READ–IT: Assessing Readability of Italian Texts with a View to Text Simplification. In *Proceedings of the 2nd Workshop on Speech and Language Processing for Assistive Technologies, SLPAT 2011*, pages 73–83.

Anca Dinu and Liviu P. Dinu. 2005. On the Syllabic Similarities of Romance Languages. In *Proceedings of the 6th International Conference on Computational Linguistics and Intelligent Text Processing, CICLing 2005*, pages 785–788.

Liviu P. Dinu and Florin Manea. 2006. An Efficient Approach for the Rank Aggregation Problem. *Theoretical Computer Science*, 359(1):455–461.

Liviu P. Dinu and Marius Popescu. 2008. A Multi-Criteria Decision Method Based on Rank Distance. *Fundamenta Informaticae*, 86(1-2):79–91.

Noemie Elhadad and Komal Sutaria. 2007. Mining a Lexicon of Technical Terms and Lay Equivalents. In *Proceedings of the Workshop on BioNLP 2007: Biological, Translational, and Clinical Language Processing, BioNLP 2007*, pages 49–56.

Lijun Feng, Martin Jansche, Matt Huenerfauth, and Noémie Elhadad. 2010. A Comparison of Features for Automatic Readability Assessment. In *Proceedings of the 23rd International Conference on Computational Linguistics: Posters, COLING 2010*, pages 276–284.

Lijun Feng. 2009. Automatic Readability Assessment for People with Intellectual Disabilities. *SIGACCESS Access. Comput.*, (93):84–91.

Rudolf Flesch. 1946. *The Art of plain talk*. T. Harper.

Thomas François and Eleni Miltsakaki. 2012. Do NLP and Machine Learning Improve Traditional Readability Formulas? In *Proceedings of the First Workshop on Predicting and Improving Text Readability for Target Reader Populations, PITR 2012*, pages 49–57.

Valerio Franchina and Roberto Vacca. 1986. Adaptation of Flesch readability index on a bilingual text written by the same author both in Italian and English languages. *Linguaggi*, 3:47–49.

Arthur C. Graesser, Danielle S. McNamara, Max M. Louwerse, and Zhiqiang Cai. 2004. Coh-Metrix: Analysis of text on cohesion and language. *Behavior Research Methods, Instruments, and Computers*, 36(2):193–202.

Robert Gunning. 1952. *The technique of clear writing*. McGraw-Hill; Fouth Printing edition.

Michael Heilman, Kevyn Collins-Thompson, Jamie Callan, and Maxine Eskenazi. 2007. Combining Lexical and Grammatical Features to Improve Readability Measures for First and Second Language Texts. In *Proceedings of the Human Language Technology Conference of the North American Chapter of the Association of Computational Linguistics, HLT-NAACL 2007*, pages 460–467.

F. Huerta. 1959. Medida sencillas de lecturabilidad. *Consigna*, 214:29–32.

Zahurul Islam and Alexander Mehler. 2012. Customization of the Europarl Corpus for Translation Studies. In *Proceedings of the 8th International Conference on Language Resources and Evaluation, LREC 2012*, pages 2505–2510.

Douglas Jones, Edward Gibson, Wade Shen, Neil Granoien, Martha Herzog, Douglas Reynolds, and Clifford Weinstein. 2005. Measuring Human Readability of Machine Generated Text: Three Case Studies in Speech Recognition and Machine Translation. In *Proceedings of the IEEE International Conference on Acoustics, Speech, and Signal Processing, ICASSP 2005*, pages 1009–1012.

L. Kandel and A. Moles. 1958. Application de l'indice de Flesch a la langue française. *Cahiers Etudes de Radio-Television*, 19:253–274.

J. Peter Kincaid, Lieutenant Robert P. Fishburne Jr., Richard L. Rogers, and Brad S. Chissom. 1975. *Derivation of new readability formulas (Automated Readability Index, Fog Count and Flesch Reading*

Ease formula) for Navy enlisted personnel. Research Branch Report, Millington, TN: Chief of Naval Training.

Philipp Koehn. 2005. Europarl: A Parallel Corpus for Statistical Machine Translation. In *Proceedings of the 10th Machine Translation Summit*, pages 79–86.

Pietro Lucisano and Maria Emanuela Piemontese. 1988. Gulpease. una formula per la predizione della difficoltà dei testi in lingua italiana. *Scuola e Città*, 39:110–124.

G. Harry McLaughlin. 1969. Smog grading: A new readability formula. *Journal of Reading*, 12(8):639–646.

Eugene A. Nida and Charles R. Taber. 1969. *The Theory and Practice of Translation.* Leiden: E.J. Brill.

Lluís Padró and Evgeny Stanilovsky. 2012. FreeLing 3.0: Towards Wider Multilinguality. In *Proceedings of the 8th International Conference on Language Resources and Evaluation, LREC 2012*, pages 2473–2479.

Lluís Padró, Miquel Collado, Samuel Reese, Marina Lloberes, and Irene Castellón. 2010. FreeLing 2.1: Five Years of Open-source Language Processing Tools. In *Proceedings of the 7th International Conference on Language Resources and Evaluation, LREC 2010*, pages 931–936.

Lluís Padró. 2011. Analizadores Multilingües en FreeLing. *Linguamatica*, 3(2):13–20.

Sarah E. Petersen and Mari Ostendorf. 2009. A Machine Learning Approach to Reading Level Assessment. *Computer Speech and Language*, 23(1):89–106.

Emily Pitler and Ani Nenkova. 2008. Revisiting Readability: A Unified Framework for Predicting Text Quality. In *Proceedings of the Conference on Empirical Methods in Natural Language Processing, EMNLP 2008*, pages 186–195.

Dragomir R. Radev and Weiguo Fan. 2000. Automatic Summarization of Search Engine Hit Lists. In *Proceedings of the ACL-2000 Workshop on Recent Advances in Natural Language Processing and Information Retrieval: Held in Conjunction with the 38th Annual Meeting of the Association for Computational Linguistics, RANLPIR 2000*, pages 99–109.

Gary A. Richwald, Margarita Schneider-Mufnoz, and R. Burciaga Valdez. 1989. Are Condom Instructions in Spanish Readable? Implications for AIDS Prevention Activities for Hispanics. *Hispanic Journal of Behavioral Sciences*, 11(1):70–82.

Marius Sala. 1988. *Vocabularul Reprezentativ al Limbilor Romanice.* Editura Academiei, Bucureşti.

Christina Schäffner and Susan Bassnett. 2010. Politics, Media and Translation - Exploring Synergies. In *Political Discourse, Media and Translation*, pages 1–29. Newcastle upon Tyne: Cambridge Scholars Publishing.

Luo Si and Jamie Callan. 2001. A Statistical Model for Scientific Readability. In *Proceedings of the 10th International Conference on Information and Knowledge Management, CIKM 2001*, pages 574–576.

E.A. Smith and R.J. Senter. 1967. Automated readability index. *Wright-Patterson Air Force Base. AMRL-TR-6620.*

Sara Stymne, Jörg Tiedemann, Christian Hardmeier, and Joakim Nivre. 2013. Statistical Machine Translation with Readability Constraints. In *Proceedings of the 19th Nordic Conference on Computational Linguistics, NODALIDA 2013*, pages 375–386.

Yifeng Sun. 2012. Translation and strategies for cross-cultural communication. *Chinese Translators Journal*, 33(1):16–23.

Jörg Tiedemann. 2012. Parallel Data, Tools and Interfaces in OPUS. In *Proceedings of the 8th International Conference on Language Resources and Evaluation, LREC 2012*, pages 2214–2218.

Sara Tonelli, Ke Tran Manh, and Emanuele Pianta. 2012. Making Readability Indices Readable. In *Proceedings of the 1st Workshop on Predicting and Improving Text Readability for Target Reader Populations, PITR 2012*, pages 40–48.

Anna Trosborg, editor. 1997. *Text Typology and Translation.* Benjamins Translation Library.

Sowmya Vajjala and Detmar Meurers. 2012. On Improving the Accuracy of Readability Classification Using Insights from Second Language Acquisition. In *Proceedings of the 7th Workshop on Building Educational Applications Using NLP*, pages 163–173.

Hans van Halteren. 2008. Source Language Markers in EUROPARL Translations. In *Proceedings of the 22nd International Conference on Computational Linguistics, COLING 2008*, pages 937–944.

Tiziano Zito, Niko Wilbert, Laurenz Wiskott, and Pietro Berkes. 2008. Modular toolkit for Data Processing (MDP): a Python data processing frame work. *Front. Neuroinform.*, 2(8).

Classifying easy-to-read texts without parsing

Johan Falkenjack, Arne Jönsson
Department of Information and Computer Science
Linköping University
581 83, Linköping, Sweden
johan.falkenjack@liu.se, arne.jonsson@liu.se

Abstract

Document classification using automated linguistic analysis and machine learning (ML) has been shown to be a viable road forward for readability assessment. The best models can be trained to decide if a text is easy to read or not with very high accuracy, e.g. a model using 117 parameters from shallow, lexical, morphological and syntactic analyses achieves 98,9% accuracy.

In this paper we compare models created by parameter optimization over subsets of that total model to find out to which extent different high-performing models tend to consist of the same parameters and if it is possible to find models that only use features not requiring parsing. We used a genetic algorithm to systematically optimize parameter sets of fixed sizes using accuracy of a Support Vector Machine classifier as fitness function.

Our results show that it is possible to find models almost as good as the currently best models while omitting parsing based features.

1 Introduction

The problem of readability assessment is the problem of mapping from a text to some unit representing the text's degree of readability. Measures of readability are mostly used to inform a reader how difficult a text is to read, either to give them a hint that they may try to find an easier to read text on the same topic or simply to inform them that a text may take some time to comprehend. Readability measures are mainly used to inform persons with reading disabilities on the complexity of a text, but can also be used to, for instance, assist teachers with assessing the reading ability of a student. By measuring the reading abilities of a person, it might also be possible to automatically find texts that fits that persons reading ability.

Since the early 2000s the speed and accuracy of text analysis tools such as lemmatizers, part-of-speech taggers and syntax parsers have made new text features available for readability assessment. By using machine learning a number of researchers have devised innovative ways of assessing readability. For instance, phrase grammar parsing has been used to find the average number of sub-clauses, verb phrases, noun phrases and average tree depth (Schwarm and Ostendorf, 2005).

The use of language models to assess the degree of readability was also introduced in the early 2000s (Collins-Thompson and Callan, 2004) and later combined with classification algorithms such as support vector machines to further increase accuracy (Petersen, 2007; Feng, 2010).

In this paper we investigate if it is possible to find a set of parameters for easy-to-read classification, on par with the best models used today, without using parsing based features. Finding such a set would facilitate portability and provide faster assessment of readability.

2 Method

To train and test our classifier we used one easy-to-read corpus and five corpora representing ordinary language in different text genres. The latter corpora is referred to as non-easy-to-read in this paper. For each category we used 700 texts.

Our source of easy-to-read material was the LäSBarT corpus (Mühlenbock, 2008). LäSBarT consists of manually created easy-to-read texts from a variety of sources and genres.

The non-easy-to-read material comprised texts from a variety of corpora. This material consisted of 215 news text articles from GP2007 (The Swedish news paper Göteborgs Posten), 34 whole issues of the Swedish popular science magazine Forskning och Framsteg, 214 articles from the professional news magazine Läkartidningen 05 (physician news articles), 214 public information notices from The Public Health Agency of Sweden (Smittskyddsinstitutet) and 23 full fiction novels from a Swedish book publisher (the Norstedts publishing house).

By using a corpus with such a variety of documents we got non-easy-to-read documents from different genres which is important as we want to be able to use the same model on all types of text. We also lowered the risk of genre classification rather than degree of readability classification.

The texts were preprocessed using the Korp corpus import tool (Borin et al., 2012). Steps in the preprocessing chain relevant for this study were tokenization, lemmatisation, part-of-speech tagging and dependency grammar parsing.

We used a large number of different text features proposed for readability assessment for both Swedish and English. We use both the term's feature (property of the text) and parameter (input to the ML-system). Some features consist of more than one parameter. In the paper we use the terms features and parameters somewhat interchangeably. However, technically, a feature is a property of the text, a parameter is input to the machine learning system. A few of the text features we use are represented as a combination of parameters and in these cases we select single parameters, not full features.

2.1 Non-parsing features

The three most used traditional text quality metrics used to measure readability for Swedish are:

LIX Läsbarhetsindex, readability index. Ratio of words longer than 6 characters coupled with average sentence length, Equation 1. This is the standard readability measure used for Swedish and can be considered baseline similar to the Flesch-Kincaid formula (Kincaid et al., 1975).

$$lix = \frac{n(w)}{n(s)} + (\frac{n(words > 6\,chars)}{n(w)} \times 100) \tag{1}$$

where $n(s)$ denotes the number of sentences and $n(w)$ the number of words.

OVIX Ordvariationsindex, word variation index, related to type-token ratio. Logarithms are used to cancel out type-token ratio problems with variable text length, Equation 2.

$$ovix = \frac{log(n(w))}{log(2 - \frac{log(n(uw))}{log(n(w))})} \tag{2}$$

where $n(w)$ denotes the number of words and $n(uw)$ the number of unique words.

NR Nominal ratio, the ratio of nominal word, used to measure formality of text rather than readability, however, this is traditionally assumed to correlate to readability, Equation 3.

$$Nr = \frac{n(noun) + n(prep) + n(part)}{n(pro) + n(adv) + n(v)} \tag{3}$$

where $n(noun)$ denotes the number of nouns, $n(prep)$ the number of prepositions, $n(part)$ the number of participles, $n(pro)$ the number of pronouns, $n(adv)$ the number of adverbs, and $n(v)$ the number of verbs.

2.1.1 Shallow features

The shallow text features are the main features traditionally used for simple readability metrics. They occur in the "shallow" surface structure of the text and can be extracted after tokenization by simply counting words and characters. They include:

AWLC Average word length calculated as the average number of characters per word.

AWLS Average word length calculated as the average number of syllables per word. The number of syllables is approximated by counting the number of vowels.

ASL Average sentence length calculated as the average number of words per sentence.

Longer sentences, as well as longer words, tend to predict a more difficult text as exemplified by the performance of the LIX metric and related metrics for English. These types of features have been used in a number of readability studies based on machine learning (Feng, 2010) and as baseline when evaluating new features (Pitler and Nenkova, 2008).

2.1.2 Lexical features

Our lexical features are based on categorical word frequencies. The word frequencies are extracted after lemmatization and are calculated using the basic Swedish vocabulary SweVoc (Heimann Mühlenbock, 2013). SweVoc is comparable to the list used in the classic Dale-Chall formula for English (Dale and Chall, 1949). Though developed for similar purposes, special sub-categories have been added (of which three are specifically considered). The following frequencies are calculated, based on different categories in SweVoc:

SweVocC SweVoc lemmas fundamental for communication (category C).

SweVocD SweVoc lemmas for everyday use (category D).

SweVocH SweVoc other highly frequent lemmas (category H).

SweVocT Unique, per lemma, SweVoc words (all categories, including some not mentioned above) per sentence.

A high ratio of SweVoc words should indicate a more easy-to-read text. The Dale-Chall metric (Chall and Dale, 1995) has been used as a similar feature in a number of machine learning based studies of text readability for English (Feng, 2010; Pitler and Nenkova, 2008). The SweVoc metrics are also related to the language model features used in a number of studies (Schwarm and Ostendorf, 2005; Heilman et al., 2008).

2.1.3 The morpho-syntactic features

The morpho-syntactic features concern a morphology based analysis of text. For the purposes of this study the analysis relies on previously part-of-speech annotated text, which is investigated with regard to the following features:

Part-of-speech tag ratio Unigram probabilities for the different parts-of-speech tags in the document, that is, the ratio of each part-of-speech, on a per token basis, as individual parameters. This is viewed as a single feature but is represented by 26 parameters, see Table 2. Such a language model based on part-of-speech, and similar metrics, has shown to be a relevant feature for readability assessment for English (Heilman et al., 2007; Petersen, 2007; Dell'Orletta et al., 2011) and for Swedish (Falkenjack et al., 2013).

RC The ratio of content words (nouns, verbs, adjectives and adverbs), on a per token basis, in the text. Such a metric has been used in a number of related studies (Alusio et al., 2010).

2.2 Parsing based features

These features are estimable after syntactic parsing of the text. The syntactic feature set is extracted after dependency parsing using the Maltparser (Nivre et al., 2006). Such parsers have been used for preprocessing texts for readability assessment for Italian (Dell'Orletta et al., 2011). The dependency based features consist of:

ADDD The average dependency distance in the document on a per dependent basis. A longer average dependency distance could indicate a more complex text (Liu, 2008).

ADDS The average dependency distance in the document on a per sentence basis. A longer average total dependency distance per sentence could indicate a more complex text (Liu, 2008).

RD The ratio of right dependencies to total number of dependencies in the document. A high ratio of right dependencies could indicate a more complex text.

SD The average sentence depth. Sentences with deeper dependency trees could be indicative of a more complex text in the same way as phrase grammar trees has been shown to be (Petersen and Ostendorf, 2009).

Dependency type tag ratio Unigram probabilities for the dependency type tags resulting from the dependency parsing, on a per token basis, as individual parameters. This is viewed as a single feature but is represented by 63 parameters, see Tables 4 and 5.

These parameters make up a unigram language model and is comparable to the phrase type rate based on phrase grammar parsing used in earlier research (Nenkova et al., 2010). Such a language model was shown to be a good predictor for degree of readability in Swedish text (Falkenjack et al., 2013).

VR The ratio of sentences with a verbal root, that is, the ratio of sentences where the root word is a verb to the total number of sentences (Dell'Orletta et al., 2011).

AVA The average arity of verbs in the document, calculated as the average number of dependents per verb (Dell'Orletta et al., 2011).

UVA The ratio of verbs with an arity of 0-7 as distinct features (Dell'Orletta et al., 2011). This is viewed as a single feature but is represented by 8 parameters.

TPC The average number of tokens per clause in the document. This is related to the shallow feature average number of tokens per sentence.

PreM The average number of nominal premodifiers per sentence.

PostM The average number of nominal postmodifiers per sentence.

PC The average number of prepositional complements per sentence in the document.

Compound models We have also created a number of compound models, comprising metrics from sets of features; all traditional measures, all shallow features, all lexical features, all morpho-syntactic features, all syntactic features, and all features (Total), see Table 3. Falkenjack et al. (2013) also looked at incremental combinations of these same models.

2.3 Parameter optimization

The models for parameter optimization are created from various subsets of the text features using a genetic algorithm. Lau (2006) performed experiments on using genetic algorithms to select significant features that are useful when assessing readability for Chinese. Starting with 64 features, mainly various stroke features but also more traditional features, such as, measuring amount of familiar and common words, a genetic algorithm was used to find optimal feature subsets. Based on investigations of using three different fitness functions it was shown that a set of 15 features is sufficient and the best feature set for each fitness function is selected for further studies. These feature sets are then evaluated using SVR (Support Vector Regression) to train readability models and finally test them on the texts.

In our work we do not first select feature sets and then train the model on them. Instead feature sets, generated by genetic search, are used to train the readability model, using SVM, and then the models are tested.

We performed a number of trials based on different base sets of parameters. In each case the space we searched through had the size $\binom{|b|}{s}$, where b is the base set of parameters and s is the size of the model we were searching for.

We performed genetic searches through model spaces for 1000 generations. Each generation contained 10 chromosomes, i.e. models, 7 created by crossover and 3 randomly generated to avoid getting stuck in local maxima.

The crossover worked by randomly selecting parameters from the locally optimal parameter set of the prior generation. This locally optimal parameter set was created by taking the union of the best performing chromosomes until the size of the set exceeded the size of the target selection plus 4.

In the rare cases where the parameters in the total parent generation did not exceed this number all parameters from the parent generation were used.

The fitness function consisted of a 7-fold cross-validation test run of a Support Vector Machine trained by Sequential Minimal Optimization (Platt, 1998). For this we used the Waikato Environment for Knowledge Analysis, or Weka. The accuracy of a model was used as its fitness and used to order each generation from best to worst performing.

3 Results

We first present results from using only the single features and the compound models. We then present the results from the various models generated by our method.

We provide performance measures for single features for comparison in Tables 1 and 2. The performance for the 63 dependency types are presented in Tables 4 and 5.

Model	Accuracy	LäSBarT Prec.	LäSBarT Rec.	Other Prec.	Other Rec.
LIX	84.6 (1.9)	87.9	80.4	82.0	88.9
OVIX	85.6 (2.3)	86.8	84.4	84.9	86.9
NR	55.3 (9.1)	53.5	99.1	96.0	11.4
AWLC	79.6 (2.6)	82.3	75.7	77.4	83.4
AWLS	75.6 (2.6)	78.7	70.3	73.1	80.9
ASL	62.4 (8.1)	58.0	98.7	97.8	26.1
SweVocC	79.3 (0.8)	84.3	72.0	75.6	86.6
SweVocD	57.6 (3.8)	63.1	37.9	55.5	77.4
SweVocH	63.1 (4.5)	63.1	63.4	63.2	62.9
SweVocT	75.2 (1.4)	80.6	66.7	71.6	83.7
POS-tags	*96.8 (1.6)*	*96.9*	*96.7*	*96.7*	*96.9*
RC	50.4 (1.8)	50.4	52.7	50.4	48.1
ADDD	88.5 (2.0)	88.5	88.6	88.6	88.4
ADDS	53.9 (10.2)	52.8	99.7	28.1	8.1
RD	68.9 (2.1)	70.6	65.1	67.7	72.7
SD	75.1 (3.5)	79.1	68.4	72.2	81.9
Dep-tags	*97.9 (0.8)*	*97.7*	*98.0*	*98.0*	*97.7*
VR	72.6 (2.0)	77.0	64.6	69.5	80.6
AVA	63.4 (3.0)	64.9	58.4	62.3	68.4
UVA	*68.6 (1.7)*	*70.2*	*65.0*	*67.4*	*72.3*
TPC	71.4 (4.7)	64.2	98.6	97.0	44.3
PreM	83.4 (2.9)	78.1	93.0	91.3	73.9
PostM	57.4 (4.3)	54.1	99.9	98.4	15.0
PC	83.5 (3.5)	80.1	89.1	88.1	77.9

Table 1: Performance of the single feature models. The accuracy represents the average percentage of texts classified correctly, with the standard deviation within parentheses. Precision and Recall are also provided for both easy-to-read (LäSBarT) and non-easy-to-read (Other) sets. Italicized features consist of more than one parameter.

Model	Accuracy	LäSBarT Prec.	LäSBarT Rec.	Other Prec.	Other Rec.
VB	87.6 (1.7)	89.2	85.9	86.5	89.4
MAD	87.1 (0.9)	91.1	82.3	83.9	91.9
PAD	79.5 (1.6)	71.8	97.4	96.0	61.6
MID	76.6 (2.9)	78.6	73.3	74.9	79.9
PP	72.4 (3.8)	73.7	69.7	71.4	75.0
PN	72.1 (2.7)	79.2	60.4	67.9	83.9
NN	70.4 (2.6)	75.4	61.4	67.3	79.4
DT	67.7 (3.3)	67.9	67.6	67.6	67.9
PL	65.6 (2.5)	70.4	53.9	62.8	77.4
JJ	64.1 (4.3)	63.6	65.7	64.7	62.4
HA	62.4 (1.1)	66.5	49.9	59.9	74.9
SN	59.4 (3.7)	64.7	42.1	57.0	76.7
UO	58.2 (8.2)	55.1	98.4	94.6	18.0
KN	56.6 (3.0)	57.9	48.9	55.7	64.4
AB	56.0 (3.2)	58.4	43.0	54.7	69.0
IN	53.0 (5.1)	60.0	78.7	16.1	27.3
IE	52.6 (2.4)	61.5	19.0	51.5	86.1
PS	52.6 (1.4)	59.4	17.7	51.5	87.4
HP	52.5 (5.4)	69.9	24.0	47.2	81.0
HS	52.4 (2.0)	51.2	99.7	89.3	5.0
RG	51.6 (3.5)	51.1	96.9	69.6	6.4
HD	50.4 (0.7)	50.2	31.7	35.9	69.1
PLQS	50.0 (0.0)	50.0	100.0	0.0	0.0
RO	49.7 (0.9)	49.8	89.3	48.8	10.1
PM	49.7 (1.3)	49.8	95.0	54.9	4.4

Table 2: Performance of the POS-tag ratio parameters ordered by performance. The various models are tags used in the SUC corpus (Ejerhed et al., 2006), normally part of speech tags, e.g. VB is verb, with some extensions, but the tags comprise other features as well e.g. MAD comprises sentence terminating delimiters, PAD pair-wise delimiters such as parentheses and MID other delimiters such as comma and semicolon. Measures as described in Table 1.

Model	Acc.	LäSBarT Pre.	LäSBarT Rec.	Other Pre.	Other Rec.
TradComb	91.4 (3.0)	92.0	91.0	91.1	91.9
Shallow	81.6 (2.7)	83.3	79.4	80.3	83.9
Lexical	78.4 (2.2)	81.8	73.0	75.6	83.7
Morpho	96.7 (1.6)	96.8	96.7	96.7	96.7
Syntactic	98.0 (1.1)	97.9	98.1	98.1	97.9
Total	98.9 (1.0)	98.9	98.9	98.9	98.9

Table 3: Performance of the full feature sets. Measures as described in Table 1.

The results from using the full sets before parameter optimization are listed in Table 3. Using all features provides the best model with 98.9% accuracy which could be considered the target accuracy of our parameter optimization.

3.1 POS-ratio features

The first trial we performed was a search through the parameter space containing ratios of part-of-speech unigrams. As our data contained 26 different POS-tags (additional morphological data was ignored in this search) the size of the spaces were $\binom{26}{s}$ where s is the size of the model we were optimizing. For 3-parameter models this is no larger than $\binom{26}{3} = 2600$ while the maximum size is $\binom{26}{13} = 10400600$. We searched for optimal subsets of sizes from 1 to 25. The best models are presented in Table 6 and the performance results in Table 8. Models comprising more than 10 features are omitted as no significant performance improvement is measured beyond this point. See Table 7 for sizes.

#	Accuracy	LäSBarT		Other	
		Prec.	Rec.	Prec.	Rec.
IP	89.4 (1.7)	92.9	85.3	86.5	93.4
SS	87.4 (2.9)	88.2	86.4	86.7	88.3
ROOT	83.0 (2.4)	88.0	76.4	79.2	89.6
AT	78.1 (4.0)	75.9	82.9	81.0	73.3
ET	77.7 (2.4)	79.6	74.7	76.3	80.7
JR	76.4 (6.4)	69.0	97.7	96.0	55.0
AN	76.2 (2.5)	72.3	85.6	82.4	66.9
IQ	73.1 (2.1)	67.0	90.7	85.9	55.4
IK	72.5 (2.5)	75.0	67.9	70.6	77.1
OO	72.2 (5.3)	74.4	67.4	70.4	77.0
IR	72.1 (3.4)	64.7	97.9	95.6	46.3
DT	70.4 (1.4)	73.4	64.4	68.3	76.4
VG	70.0 (2.4)	81.1	52.1	64.8	87.9
PL	66.8 (2.7)	70.8	57.7	64.3	75.9
JC	64.8 (4.3)	59.1	97.4	92.4	32.1
CJ	64.0 (3.6)	62.2	71.7	66.6	56.3
HD	62.5 (2.7)	59.0	84.7	73.2	40.3
IC	61.3 (4.3)	56.8	97.1	90.8	25.4
OA	61.0 (3.4)	66.9	43.3	58.2	78.7
SP	60.7 (2.0)	67.4	42.4	57.9	79.0
I?	60.6 (1.3)	78.4	29.3	56.5	91.9
+A	60.1 (2.3)	58.6	68.9	62.4	51.4
TA	59.8 (2.5)	63.9	46.0	57.7	73.6
AG	59.7 (2.2)	57.0	81.6	68.4	37.9
NA	59.5 (3.5)	63.3	45.0	57.5	74.0
+F	59.0 (3.3)	64.4	40.4	56.6	77.6
UA	58.6 (3.9)	63.7	41.1	56.3	76.1
VA	58.2 (6.1)	56.2	85.3	67.1	31.1
MS	57.5 (1.8)	62.5	38.3	55.4	76.7
KA	57.5 (3.6)	75.6	35.4	47.3	79.6

Table 4: Performance of the Dependency type ratio attributes ordered by performance. Measures as described in Table 1 Continued in table 5.

3.2 Non-syntactic features

The second trial we performed was a search through the parameter space of all non-syntactic features. As our data contained 37 such parameters the size of the spaces were $\binom{37}{s}$ where s is the size of the model we were optimizing. For 3-parameter models this is no larger than $\binom{37}{3} = 7770$ while the maximum size is $\binom{37}{19} = 17672631900$. We searched for optimal subsets of sizes from 1 to 25. The best models are presented in Table 9 and the performance results in Table 10. Models larger than 8 are omitted as no significant performance improvement is measured beyond this point.

#	Accuracy	LäSBarT		Other	
		Prec.	Rec.	Prec.	Rec.
IT	56.5 (1.8)	54.1	86.7	66.6	26.3
PT	55.7 (2.9)	53.6	85.0	63.7	26.4
IS	55.6 (5.9)	53.1	99.9	85.0	11.3
JT	55.5 (3.8)	53.0	99.6	94.0	11.4
AA	55.4 (3.1)	57.4	42.1	54.3	68.7
IG	55.4 (2.8)	52.9	99.4	97.0	11.3
IU	55.1 (2.4)	82.4	26.1	45.6	84.0
RA	54.8 (2.5)	65.7	31.4	53.8	78.1
IO	54.4 (2.3)	63.6	33.4	45.5	75.4
MA	54.3 (3.3)	68.4	18.0	52.4	90.6
FS	53.8 (2.3)	72.9	12.0	52.1	95.6
CA	53.6 (3.9)	53.2	60.3	54.1	46.9
XX	53.0 (1.6)	69.4	24.7	44.5	81.3
ES	52.9 (1.7)	77.0	22.1	44.4	83.7
EF	52.4 (4.4)	52.4	75.4	41.4	29.4
++	52.3 (1.7)	51.3	93.6	65.0	11.0
XA	52.1 (1.7)	51.1	97.6	65.4	6.7
XT	52.1 (2.2)	51.2	97.0	50.9	7.3
EO	51.8 (2.4)	36.7	70.4	60.4	33.1
IF	51.2 (2.3)	55.4	39.7	48.1	62.7
FP	51.0 (1.3)	61.3	60.1	22.0	41.9
JG	51.0 (1.7)	29.1	57.0	48.6	45.0
DB	50.6 (0.9)	63.5	48.7	28.9	52.6
IV	50.5 (0.5)	75.0	44.0	28.8	57.0
OP	50.4 (0.9)	36.0	65.3	21.8	35.4
FO	50.2 (0.3)	57.1	29.0	35.8	71.4
VS	50.1 (0.4)	43.8	72.7	14.4	27.6
YY	50.0 (0.0)	50.0	100.0	0.0	0.0
XF	49.9 (0.2)	50.0	85.1	14.1	14.7
FV	49.8 (1.0)	55.6	57.9	21.3	41.7
VO	49.8 (3.3)	52.9	73.3	15.6	26.3

Table 5: Performance of the Dependency type ratio attributes ordered by performance. Measures as described in Table 1. Continued from table 4.

#	Set
2	VB, MAD
3	MAD, VB, MID
4	VB, PAD, MID, MAD
5	MAD, VB, MID, PAD, PM
6	MID, VB, HA, PAD, AB, MAD
7	PAD, JJ, PN, VB, MAD, KN, MID
8	PAD, HD, PM, MID, PN, VB, PL, MAD
9	PAD, SN, PLQS, MAD, DT, VB, RG, PM, MID
10	MAD, PM, PAD, KN, MID, PLQS, IE, VB, HA, DT

Table 6: Features in the best performing sets found for each size by the genetic search through the POS-ratio space.

4 Discussion

From the models using POS-ratio features, Tables 6 and 8, we see that it is possible to find models

#	Size
1 and 25	26
2 and 24	325
3 and 23	2 600
4 and 22	14 950
5 and 21	65 780
6 and 20	230 230
7 and 19	657 800
8 and 18	1 562 275
9 and 17	3 124 550
10 and 16	5 311 735
11 and 15	7 726 160
12 and 14	9 657 700
13	10 400 600

Table 7: Sizes of model space based on number of attributes in the target model.

		LäSBarT		Other	
Model	Accuracy	Prec.	Rec.	Prec.	Rec.
2	95.4 (1.5)	94.7	96.3	96.2	94.6
3	96.4 (0.9)	96.2	96.7	96.7	96.1
4	96.9 (1.0)	97.0	96.9	96.9	97.0
5	97.0 (1.1)	97.0	97.0	97.0	97.0
6	97.0 (1.2)	97.6	96.4	96.5	97.6
7	97.0 (1.1)	96.8	97.3	97.3	96.7
8	96.9 (1.1)	96.9	97.0	97.0	96.9
9	96.9 (1.3)	96.8	97.1	97.1	96.7
10	97.4 (1.1)	97.6	97.1	97.2	97.6
All(26)	96.8 (1.6)	96.9	96.7	96.7	96.9

Table 8: Performance of the feature sets selected from the set of POS-tag ratio features ordered by number of parameters. Measures as described in Table 1.

#	Set
2	OVIX, MAD
3	OVIX, MAD, MID
4	MID, PAD, MAD, OVIX
5	MAD, OVIX, VB, SN, SweVocT
6	MAD, HD, MID, PL, OVIX, SweVocC
7	MAD, AB, PP, HD, MID, OVIX, DT
8	MID, AB, PAD, OVIX, MAD, SweVocH, HS, RG

Table 9: Features in the best performing sets found for each size by the genetic search through the non-syntactic space.

that outperform most single feature models. We have in Table 8 included the performance of the full, 26 feature, model which shows that performance might be increased slightly by filtering out confusing features.

		LäSBarT		Other	
Model	Accuracy	Prec.	Rec.	Prec.	Rec.
2	96.6 (1.0)	95.5	98.0	98.0	95.3
3	97.4 (1.3)	97.3	97.4	97.5	97.3
4	98.2 (1.3)	97.8	98.7	98.7	97.7
5	97.9 (1.2)	97.1	98.9	98.8	97.0
6	98.0 (1.0)	97.2	98.9	98.8	97.1
7	97.8 (1.3)	97.1	98.6	98.6	97.0
8	98.5 (1.0)	97.9	99.1	99.1	97.9
All (37)	98.3 (1.0)	97.4	99.3	99.3	97.3

Table 10: Performance of the feature sets selected from the set of all non- syntactic features ordered by number of parameters. Measures as described in Table 1.

We can also see that the sets beyond 4 parameters do not fully correlate to the best performing single parameters in the parameter space. This implies that combinations of some features may be better predictors than the individual features.

When we search through all non-syntactic features we get results similar to the POS-ratio space search. While the first generated sets seem to consist of the best performing single parameters, larger models seem to be more "exotic" using low performing single parameters to create stronger combination effects, see Table 9.

The most interesting result here is that a model with 8 non-syntactic parameters, model 8 in Table 10, performs almost as well (-0.4 pp) as the 117 parameter total model, see Table 3.

Another interesting result is that the ratio of verbs (VB in Table 2) has an accuracy of 87.6%, only outperformed by the syntactic feature ADDD.

Even more interesting is the fact that the ratio of sentence terminating delimiters (MAD in Table 2) has such high performance. Especially as the average sentence length (ASL) is not a very good predictor of readability, see Table 3 and Falkenjack et al. (2013).

Theoretically, the ratio of MADs is the inverse of the ASL and as such their performance should align. However, the two metrics are calculated differently, sentence length is based on parsing data and MAD ratio is based on POS-tagging data. While a sentence should contain exactly one MAD there are instances where more than one (informal language, transcribed spoken language, misidentified ellipsis, quotations etc.) or less than one (bullet points, tables etc.) might occur in the actual text. It should be noted that if the aforementioned is true MAD might rather be a style predictor than a direct readability predictor. However, in that case style and readability appears to correlate which is not surprising.

We further note how much accuracy can be improved by combining very few measures. For instance, OVIX gives an accuracy of only 85.6% and MAD gives 87.1%, but combined they give 96.6%, set 2 in Table 10

5 Conclusion

In this paper we introduced and evaluated a method for finding optimal subsets of text features for readability based document classification. The method uses genetic search to systematically generate models using various sets of text features. As fitness function for the genetic algorithm we used SVM created models that were 7-fold cross validated on one easy-to-read corpus and one corpus of regular texts.

Our results show that, at least for Swedish, it is possible to find models almost as good the currently best models while omitting parsing based features. Our algorithm found a model of 8 non-syntactic parameters which predicted readability with an accuracy of 98.5%. This is almost as accurate as a 117 parameter model, including parsing based features, with an accuracy of 98.9%

Our study was conducted for Swedish texts but only a few of the metrics used are specific to Swedish and the optimization method itself is language independent, thus, the method can easily be applied to other languages. The method can be used for optimization of readability assessment systems as well as for basic linguistic research into readability.

Acknowledgments

We would like to thank Stiftelsen Marcus och Amalia Wallenbergs Minnesfond and SICS East Swedish ICT AB for funding this research as well as the staff members at Språkbanken who created and let us use the Korp corpus import tool.

References

Sandra Alusio, Lucia Specia, Caroline Gasperin, and Carolina Scarton. 2010. Readability assessment for text simplification. In *Proceedings of the NAACL HLT 2010 Fifth Workshop on Innovative Use of NLP for Building Educational Applications*, pages 1–9.

Lars Borin, Markus Forsberg, and Johan Roxendal. 2012. Korp – the corpus infrastructure of Språkbanken. In *Proceedings of the Eighth International Conference on Language Resources and Evaluation (LREC'12)*.

Jeanne S. Chall and Edgar Dale. 1995. *Readability revisited: The new Dale–Chall readability formula*. Brookline Books, Cambride, MA.

Kevyn Collins-Thompson and Jamie Callan. 2004. A Language Modeling Approach to Predicting Reading Difficulty. In *Proceedings of the Human Language Technology Conference of the North American Chapter of the Association for Computational Linguistics*.

Edgar Dale and Jeanne S. Chall. 1949. The concept of readability. *Elementary English*, 26(23).

Felice Dell'Orletta, Simonetta Montemagni, and Giulia Venturi. 2011. READ-IT: Assessing Readability of Italian Texts with a View to Text Simplification. In *Proceedings of the 2nd Workshop on Speech and Language Processing for Assistive Technologies*, pages 73–83, July.

Eva Ejerhed, Gunnel Källgren, and Benny Brodda. 2006. Stockholm Umeå Corpus version 2.0.

Johan Falkenjack, Katarina Heimann Mühlenbock, and Arne Jönsson. 2013. Features indicating readability in Swedish text. In *Proceedings of the 19th Nordic Conference of Computational Linguistics (NoDaLiDa-2013), Oslo, Norway*, NEALT Proceedings Series 16.

Lijun Feng. 2010. *Automatic Readability Assessment*. Ph.D. thesis, City University of New York.

Michael J. Heilman, Kevyn Collins-Thompson, Jamie Callan, and Maxine Eskenazi. 2007. Combining Lexical and Grammatical Features to Improve Readability Measures for First and Second Language Texts. In *Proceedings of NAACL HLT 2007*, pages 460–467.

Michael J. Heilman, Kevyn Collins-Thompson, and Maxine Eskenazi. 2008. An Analysis of Statistical Models and Features for Reading Difficulty Prediction. In *Proceedings of the Third ACL Workshop on Innovative Use of NLP for Building Educational Applications*, pages 71–79, June.

Katarina Heimann Mühlenbock. 2013. *I see what you mean. Assessing readability for specific target groups*. Dissertation, Språkbanken, Dept of Swedish, University of Gothenburg.

J. P. Kincaid, R. P. Fishburne, R. L. Rogers, and B. S. Chissom. 1975. Derivation of new readability formulas (Automated Readability Index, Fog Count, and Flesch Reading Ease Formula) for Navy enlisted personnel. Technical report, U.S. Naval Air Station, Millington, TN.

Tak Pang Lau. 2006. Chinese readability analysis and its applications on the internet. Master's thesis, The Chinese University of Hong Kong.

Haitao Liu. 2008. Dependency distance as a metric of language comprehension difficulty. *Journal of Cognitive Science*, 9(2):169–191.

Katarina Mühlenbock. 2008. Readable, Legible or Plain Words – Presentation of an easy-to-read Swedish corpus. In Anju Saxena and Åke Viberg, editors, *Multilingualism: Proceedings of the 23rd Scandinavian Conference of Linguistics*, volume 8 of *Acta Universitatis Upsaliensis*, pages 327–329, Uppsala, Sweden. Acta Universitatis Upsaliensis.

Ani Nenkova, Jieun Chae, Annie Louis, and Emily Pitler. 2010. Structural Features for Predicting the Linguistic Quality of Text Applications to Machine Translation, Automatic Summarization and Human–Authored Text. In E. Krahmer and M. Theune, editors, *Empirical Methods in NLG*, pages 222–241. Springer-Verlag.

Joakim Nivre, Johan Hall, and Jens Nilsson. 2006. MaltParser: A Data-Driven Parser-Generator for Dependency Parsing. In *Proceedings of the fifth international conference on Language Resources and Evaluation (LREC2006)*, pages 2216–2219, May.

Sarah Petersen and Mari Ostendorf. 2009. A machine learning approach toreading level assessment. *Computer Speech and Language*, 23:89–106.

Sarah Petersen. 2007. *Natural language processing tools for reading level assessment and text simplification for bilingual education*. Ph.D. thesis, University of Washington, Seattle, WA.

Emily Pitler and Ani Nenkova. 2008. Revisiting Readability: A Unified Framework for Predicting Text Quality. In *Proceedings of the 2008 Conference on Empirical Methods in Natural Language Processing*, pages 186–195, Honolulu, HI, October.

John C. Platt. 1998. Sequential Minimal Optimization: A Fast Algorithm for Training Support Vector Machines. Technical Report MSR-TR-98-14, Microsoft Research, April.

Sarah E. Schwarm and Mari Ostendorf. 2005. Reading level assessment using support vector machines and statistical language models. In *Proceedings of the 43rd Annual Meeting of the Association for Computational Linguistics*.

Johan Sjöholm. 2012. Probability as readability: A new machine learning approach to readability assessment for written Swedish. Master's thesis, Linköping University.

An Analysis of Crowdsourced Text Simplifications

Marcelo Adriano Amancio
Department of Computer Science
University of Sheffield
Sheffield, UK
acp12maa@sheffield.ac.uk

Lucia Specia
Department of Computer Science
University of Sheffield
Sheffield, UK
l.specia@sheffield.ac.uk

Abstract

We present a study on the text simplification operations undertaken collaboratively by Simple English Wikipedia contributors. The aim is to understand whether a complex-simple parallel corpus involving this version of Wikipedia is appropriate as data source to induce simplification rules, and whether we can automatically categorise the different operations performed by humans. A subset of the corpus was first manually analysed to identify its transformation operations. We then built machine learning models to attempt to automatically classify segments based on such transformations. This classification could be used, e.g., to filter out potentially noisy transformations. Our results show that the most common transformation operations performed by humans are paraphrasing (39.80%) and drop of information (26.76%), which are some of the most difficult operations to generalise from data. They are also the most difficult operations to identify automatically, with the lowest overall classifier accuracy among all operations (73% and 59%, respectively).

1 Introduction

Understanding written texts in a variety of forms (newspapers, educational books, etc.) can be a challenge for certain groups of readers (Paciello, 2000). Among these readers we can cite second language learners, language-impaired people (e.g. aphasic and dyslexic), and the elderly. Sentences with multiple clauses, unusual word order and rare vocabulary are some of the linguistic phenomena that should be avoided in texts written for these audiences. Although initiatives like the Plain English (Flesch, 1979) have long advocated for the use of clear and concise language, these have only been adopted in limited cases (UK government bodies, for example). The vast majority of texts which are aimed at the broad population, such as news, are often too complex to be processed by a large proportion of the population.

Adapting texts into their simpler variants is an expensive task. Work on automating this process only started in recent years. However, already in the 1920's Lively and Pressey (1923) created a method to distinguish simple from complex texts based on readability measures. Using such measures, publishers were able to grade texts according to reading levels (Klare and Buck, 1954) so that readers could focus on texts that were appropriate to them. The first attempt to automate the process of simplification of texts was devised by Chandrasekar et al. (1996). This pioneer work has shown that it was possible to simplify texts automatically through hand-crafted linguistic rules. In further work, Chandrasekar et al. (1997) developed a method to extract these rules from data.

Siddharthan (2002) defines Text Simplification as any method or process that simplifies text while maintaining its information. Instead of hand-crafted rules, recent methodologies are mostly data-driven, i.e., based on the induction of simplification rules from parallel corpora of complex segments and their corresponding simpler variants. Specia (2010) and Zhu et al. (2010) model the task using the Statistical Machine Translation framework, where simplified sentences are considered the "target language". Yatskar et al. (2010) construct a simplification model based on edits in the Simple English Wikipedia. Woodsend and Lapata (2011) adopt a quasi-synchronous grammar with optimisation via integer linear programming. This research focuses the corpus used by most of previous data-driven Text Simplification work: the parallel corpus of the main and simple English Wikipedia.

Following the collaborative nature of Wikipedia, a subset of the Main English Wikipedia (*MainEW*) has been edited by volunteers to make the texts more readable to a broader audience. This resulted in the Simple English Wikipedia (*SimpleEW*)[1], which we consider a crowdsourced text simplification corpus. Coster and Kauchak (2011) paired articles from these two versions and automatically extracted parallel paragraphs and sentences from them (*ParallelSEW*). The first task was accomplished in a straightforward way, given that corresponding articles have the same title as unique identification. The paragraph alignment was performed selecting paragraphs when their normalised TF-IDF weighted cosine distance reached a minimum threshold. Sentence alignment was performed using monolingual alignment techniques (Barzilay and Elhadad, 2003) based on a dynamic programming algorithm. In total, $137,000$ sentences were found to be parallel. The resulting parallel corpora contains transformation operations of various types, including rewording, reordering, insertion and deletion. In our experiments we analyse the distribution of these operations and perform some further analysis on their nature.

Most studies on data-driven Text Simplification have focused on the learning of the operations, with no or little qualitative analysis of the Text Simplification corpora used (Yasseri et al., 2012). As in any other area, the quality of machine learning models for Text Simplification will depend on the size and quality of the training dataset. Our study takes a step back to carefully look at the most common simplification corpus and: (i) understand the most common transformation operations performed by humans and judge whether this corpus is adequate to induce simplification rules from, and (ii) automatically categorise transformation operations such as to further process and "clean" the corpus, for example to allow the modelling of specific simplification phenomena or groups of phenomena individually. After reviewing some of the relevant related work (Section 2), in Section 3, we present the manual analysis of a subset of the *ParallelSEW* corpus. In Section 4 we present a classification experiments to label this corpus according to different simplification operations. Finally, we present a discussion of the results in section 5.

2 Literature Review

The closest work to ours is that of Yasseri et al. (2012). They present a statistical analysis of linguistic features that can indicate language complexity in both *MainEW* and *SimpleEW*. Different from our work, their analysis was automatic, and therefore more superficial by nature (mostly counts based on pattern matching and simple readability metrics). They have found equivalent vocabulary complexity in both versions of *Wikipedia*, although one could expect simpler vocabulary in *SimpleEW*. They have also demonstrated that *SimpleEW* is considered simpler mainly because it presents shorter sentences, as opposed to simpler grammar. Additionally, they found a high interdependence between topicality and language complexity. Conceptual wikipages were found to be linguistically more complex than biographical ones, for example. For measuring language complexity, the Gunning readability index (Gunning, 1969) was used. As in Besten and Dalle (2008), additional complexity metrics are said to be necessary to better assess readability issues in *SimpleEW*.

(Petersen and Ostendorf, 2007)'s work is in the context of bilingual education. A corpus of 104 news parallel texts, original and simplified versions of the *Literacyworks* corpus (Petersen and Ostendorf, 2007), was used. The goal was to identify which simplification operations were more frequent and provide a classifier (using machine learning) as an aiding tool for teachers to determine which sentences should be (manually) simplified. For the classification of sentences that should be split, attributes such as sentence length, POS tags, average length of specific phrases (e.g. S, SBAR, NP) were used. For the classification of sentences that should be dropped, the features used included the position of the sentence in the document, its paragraph position, the presence of quotation marks, rate of stop words in the sentence, and percentage of content words. It was reported that the simplified versions of texts had 30% fewer words, and that sentences were 27% shorter, with the elimination of adjectives, adverbs and coordinating conjunctions, and the increase of

[1] http://simple.wikipedia.org/wiki/Main_Page

nouns (22%) and pronouns (33%). In the experiments in this paper, we use similar features to classify a broader set of text simplification operations.

With similar goal and methodology, (Gasperin et al., 2009) use a parallel corpus containing original and simple news sentences in Portuguese. A binary classifier was built to decide which sentences to split, reaching precision of above 73%. The feature set used was rich, including surface sentence cues (e.g. number of words, number of verbs, numbers of coordinative conjunctions), lexicalized cue phrases and rhetoric relations (e.g. conclusions, contrast), among others.

Medero and Ostendorf (2011) work was motivated by language-learning contexts, where teachers often find themselves editing texts such that they are adequate to readers with certain native languages. In order to develop aiding tools for this task, a number of attributes that lead to different operations were identified. Attributes leading to sentences splitting include sentence length and POS tags frequency. Attributed that lead to sentences being dropped include position of a sentence in a document, paragraph number, presence of a direct quotation, percentage of stop words, etc. Based on these attributes, a classifier was built to make splitting and dropping decisions automatically, reaching average error rates of 29% and 15%, respectively.

Stajner et al. (2013) focus on selecting candidates for simplification in a parallel corpus of original and simplified Spanish sentences. A classifier is built to decide over the following operations: sentence splitting, deletion and reduction. The features are similar to those in (Petersen and Ostendorf, 2007; Gasperin et al., 2009), with additional complexity features, such as sentence complexity index, lexical density, and lexical richness. They achieve an F-measure of 92%.

3 Corpus Annotation and Statistics

Our first study was exploratory. We randomly extracted 143 sentence pairs from the *ParallelSWE* corpus. We then annotated each sentence in the simplified version for the transformation operations (TOs) undertaken by *Simple Wikipedia* contributors on the *Main English Wikipedia* to generate this version. We refer to this corpus as *Parallel143*. These annotations will be used as labels for the classification experiments in Section 4.

We start our analysis by looking at the number of transformations that have been applied to each sentence: on average, 2.1. More detailed statistics are shown in Table 1 .

# Sentences	143
# TOs	299
Avg. TOs/sentence	2.10

Table 1: Counts of transformation operations in the *Parallel143* corpus

A more interesting way to look at these numbers is the mode of the operations, as shown in Table 2. From this table we can notice that most sentences had only one transformation operation (about 48.2% of the corpus). Two to three operations together were found in 36.4% of the corpus. Four or more operations in only about 11.8%.

N. of TOs.	N. of sent.	% of sent.
1	69	0.48
2	30	0.21
3	22	0.15
4	12	0.08
5	6	0.03
6	3	0.02
7	0	0.00
8	1	0.01

Table 2: Mode of transformation operations in the *Parallel143* corpus

The 299 operations found in the corpus were classified into five main transformation operations, which are also common in the previous work mentioned in Section 2: Sentence Splitting (SS); Paraphrasing (PR); Drop of Information (DI); Sentence Reordering (SR); Information Insertion (II); and a label for "Not a Parallel Sentence" (NPS). Paraphrasing is often not considered as an operation on itself. Here we use it to refer to transformations that involve rewriting the sentence, be it of a single word or of the entire sentence. In Table 3 we show the distribution these operations in the corpus. We can observe that the most common operations were paraphrasing and drop of information. Also, it is interesting to notice that more than 7% of the corpus contains sentences that are not actually parallel (NPS), that is, where the simplified version does not correspond, in meaning, to the original version.

TO	Frequency of TO	% of TO
PR	119	39.80
DI	80	26.76
II	38	12.71
NPS	23	7.69
SS	21	7.02
SR	18	6.02

Table 3: Main transformation operations found in the *Parallel143* corpus

Different from previous work, we further categorise each of these five main transformation operations into more specific operations. These subcategorisation allowed us to further study the transformation phenomena that can occur in the *ParallelSWE* corpus. In the following sections we describe the main operations and their subcategories in detail and provide examples.

3.1 Sentence Splitting (SS)

Sentence Splitting (SS) is the rewriting of a sentence by breaking it into two or more sentences, mostly in order avoid to embedded sentences. This is overall the most common operation modelled in automatic Text Simplification systems, as it is relatively simple if a good syntactic parser is available. It has been found to be the most common operation in other corpora. For example, in the study in (Caseli et al., 2009) it accounts for 34% of the operations. Nevertheless, it was found to be relatively rare in the *Parallel143* corpus, accounting for only 7% of the operations. One possible reason for this low number is the automatic alignment of our corpus according to similarity metrics. This matching algorithm could occasionally fail in matching sentences that have been split. Within the SS categories, we have identified three subcategories: (1) simple sentence splitting (59.01%), where the splitting does not alter the discourse structure considerably; (2) complex sentence splitting (36.36%), where sentence splitting is associated with strong paraphrasing, and (3) inverse sentence splitting (4.63%), i.e., the joining of two or more sentences into one.

Sentences 1 and 2 show an example of complex sentence splitting. In this case, the splitting separates the information about the **Birmingham Symphony Orchestra**'s origin from where it is located into two different sentences. The operation also includes paraphrasing and adding information to complement the original sentence.

> **Sentence 1** — `MainEW`:
> "The City of Birmingham Symphony Orchestra is a British orchestra based in Birmingham, England."

> **Sentence 2** — `SimpleEW`:
> "The City of Birmingham Symphony Orchestra is one of the **leading** British orchestras. It is based **in the Symphony Hall**, Birmingham, England."

3.2 Drop of Information (DI)

In the *Parallel143* corpus we have observed that the second most frequent operation is dropping parts of the segment. We have sub-classified the information removal into three classes: (1) drop of redundant words (11.25%), for cases when dropped words have not altered the sentence meaning, (2) drop of auxiliary information (12.50%), where the auxiliary information in the original sentence adds extra information that can elicit and reinforce its meaning, and (3) drop of phrases (76.25 %), when phrases with important nuclear information are dropped, incurring in information loss.

Sentences 3 and 4 show an example of parallel sentence with two occurrences of DI cases. The phrases **At an elevation of 887m** and **in the Kingdom of** are dropped, with the first phrase representing a loss of information, which the second could be considered redundant.

> **Sentence 3** — `MainEW`:
> "**At an elevation of 877m**, it is the highest point **in the Kingdom of the Netherlands**."

> **Sentence 4** — `SimpleEW`:
> "It is the highest point in the Netherlands."

3.3 Information Insertion (II)

Information Insertion represents the adding of information to the text. During the corpus analysis we have found different sub-categories of this operation: (1) eliciting information (78.95%), in cases when some grammatical construct or auxiliary phrase is inserted enriching the main information already in the text, or making it more explicit, (2) complementary external information (18.42%), for cases when external information is inserted to complement the existing information, and (3) spurious information (2.63%), for when new information is inserted but it does not relate with the original text. We assume that latter case happens due to errors in the sentence alignment algorithm used to build the corpus.

In sentences 5 and 6, we show an example of external information insertion. In this case, the operation made the information more specific.

> **Sentence 5** — `MainEW`:
> "The 14 generators in the north side of the dam have already been installed."

> **Sentence 6** — `SimpleEW`:
> "The 14 **main** generators in the north side were installed **from 2003 to 2005**."

3.4 Sentence Reordering (RE)

Some of the transformation operations results in the reordering of parts of the sentence. We have classified reordering as (1) reorder individual phrases (33.33%), when a phrase is moved within the sentence; and (2) invert pairs of phrases (66.67%), when two phrases have their position swapped in the sentence. In sentences 7 and 8 we can see an example moving the phrase **June 20, 2003** to the end of the *SimpleEW* sentence.

> **Sentence 7** — `MainEW`:
> "The creation of the foundation was officially announced on **June 20, 2003** by Wikipedia co-founder Jimmy Wales , who had been operating Wikipedia under the aegis of his company Bomis."

> **Sentence 8** — `SimpleEW`:
> "The foundations creation was officially announced by Wikipedia co-founder Jimmy Wales, who was running Wikipedia within his company Bomis, on **June 20, 2003**."

3.5 Paraphrasing (PR)

Paraphrase operations are the most common modification found in the *Parallel143* corpus. We further classified it into 12 types:

- Specific to generic (21.01%): some specific information is substituted by a broader and more generic concept;
- Generic to specific (5.88%): the opposite of the above operation;
- Noun to pronoun (3.36%): a noun is substituted by a pronoun;
- Pronoun instantiation (2.52%): a pronoun is substituted by its referring noun;
- Word synonym (14.29%): a word is substituted by a synonym;
- Discourse marker (0.84%): a discourse marker is altered;
- Word definition (0.84%): a word is substituted by its dictionary description;
- Writing style (7.56%): the writing style of the word, e.g. hyphenation, changes;
- Preposition (3.36%): a proposition is substituted;
- Verb substitution (5.04%): a verb is replaced by another verb;
- Verb tense (2.52%): the verb tense is changed; and
- Abstract change (32.78%): paraphrase substitution that contains abstract, non-systematic changes, usually depending on external information and human reasoning, resulting in considerable modifications in the content of the simplified sentence.

In sentences 9 and 10 we can observe a case of *abstract change*. The *MainEW* sentence has descriptive historical details of the city of Prague. The *SimpleEW* version is shorter, containing less factual information when compared to the first sentence.

> **Sentence 9** — `MainEW`:
> "In 1993, after the split of Czechoslovakia, Prague became the capital city of the new Czech Republic."

> **Sentence 10** — `SimpleEW`:
> "Prague is the capital and the biggest city of the Czech Republic."

Another common operation is shown in Sentences 11 and 12. The substitution of the word **hidden** by **put** represents a change of *specific to generic*.

Sentence 11 — `MainEW`:
"The bells were transported north to Northampton-Towne, and **hidden** in the basement of the Old Zion Reformed Church, in what is now center city Allentown."

Sentence 12 — `SimpleEW`:
"The bells were moved north to Northampton-Towne, and **put** in the basement of the Old Zion Reformed Church, in what is now center of Allentown."

The outcome of this study that is of most relevance to our work is the high percentage of sentences that have undergone paraphrasing/rewriting, and in special the ones that suffered abstract changes. These cases are very hard to generalise, and any learning method applied to a corpus with a high percentage of these cases is likely to fail or to induce noisy or spurious operations.

4 Classification Experiments

Our ultimate goal of this experiment is to select parts of the *ParallelSWE* corpus that are more adequate for the learning of certain simplification rules. While it may seem that simplification operations comprise a small set which is already known based on previous work, we would like to focus on the learning of fine-grained, lexicalized rules. In other words, we are interested in the learning of more specific rules based on lexical items in addition to more general information such as POS tags and syntactic structures. The learning of such rules could benefit from a high quality corpus that is not only noise-free, but also for which one already has some information about the general operation(s) covered. In an ideal scenario, one could for example use a subset of the corpus that contains only sentence splitting operations to learn very specific and accurate rules to perform different types of sentence splitting in unseen data. Selecting a subset of the corpus that contain only one transformation operation per segment is also appealing as it would facilitate the learning. The process of manually annotating the corpus with the corresponding transformation operations is however a laborious task. For this reason, we have trained classifiers on the labelled data described in the previous section with two purposes:

- Decide over the six main transformation operations presented in the previous section; and
- Decide whether a sentence was simplified by one operation only, or by more than one operation.

The features used in both experiments are described in Section 4.1 and the algorithms and results are presented in Section 4.2.

4.1 Features

We extract simple features from the *source* (original, complex) and *target* (simplified) sentences. These were inspired by previous work, including (Medero and Ostendorf, 2011; Petersen and Ostendorf, 2007; Gasperin et al., 2009; Štajner et al., 2013):

- Size of the source sentence: how many words there are in the source sentence;
- Size of the target sentence: how many words there are in the target sentence;
- Target/source size ratio: the number of words in the target sentence divided by the number of words in the source sentence;
- Number of sequences of words dropped in the target sentence;
- Number of sequences of words inserted in the target sentence; and
- Occurrence of lexical substitution (true or false).

4.2 Machine Learning Models

Our experiments are divided in two parts. In the first part, we train six binary classifiers to test the presence of the following transformation operations: Information Insertion (II); Drop of Information (DI); Paraphrasing (PR); Sentence Reordering (SR); Sentence Splitting (SS); Not a Parallel Sentence (NPS).

The second experiment evaluated whether the simplification operation performed in the segment was simple or complex (S/C). We consider simple a transformation that has only one operation, and complex when it has two or more operations.

A few popular classifiers from the *Weka* package (Hall et al., 2009) with default parameters were selected. The experiments were devised using the 10-fold cross validation. The results – measured in terms of accuracy – for each of these classifiers with the best machine learning algorithm are shown in Table 4. These are compared to the accuracy of the majority class baseline (i.e., the class with the highest frequency in the training set). Table 5 shows the best machine learning algorithm for each classification problem.

TO	Baseline (%)	Model (%)
NPS	83.3	90.2
SR	89	90
SS	86	87
II	79	86
PR	61	73
DI	59	69
S/C	51	81

Table 4: Baselines and classifiers accuracy of the transformation operations

According to Table 4, the identification of non-parallel sentences (NPS) and sentence reordering (SR) achieved the highest accuracies of 90.2% and 90%, followed by syntactic simplification (SS) and Information Insertion (II) with values of 87% and 86%, respectively. Paraphrases (PR) and drop information (DI) have scored last, although they yielded a significant gain of 12% and 10% absolute points, respectively, when compared with baseline. The decision between simple and complex transformations was the task with best relative gain in accuracy compared to the baseline (30%).

TO	Best algorithm
NPS	Bayesian Logistic
SR	SMO
SS	Simple Logistic
II	Simple Logistic
PR	Logistic
DI	Simple Logistic
S/C	Bayes Net

Table 5: Best machine learning algorithm for each operation/task

The difference in the performance of different algorithms for each operation requires further examination. For different classifiers on the same dataset, the accuracy figures varied from 2 to 10 points, which is quite significant.

We found the results of these experiments promising, particularly for the classifiers NPS and S/C. The outcome of the classifier for NPS, for example, means that with an accuracy of over 90% we can filter out sentences from the Simple Wikipedia Corpus which are not entirely parallel, and therefore would only add noisy to any rule induction algorithm. The positive outcome of S/C means that with 80% accuracy one could select parallel sentences where the target contain only one operation to simplify the rule induction process.

Overall, these results are even more promising given two factors: the very small size of our labelled corpus (143 sentences) and the very simple set of features used. Improvements on both fronts are likely to lead to better results.

5 Conclusion

This research has focused on studying the parallel corpus of the Main English Wikipedia and its Simple English Wikipedia corresponding version. Most current data-driven methods for text simplification are based on this resource. Our experiments include the identification and quantification of the transformation operations undertaken by contributors generating the simplified version of the corpus, and the construction of classifiers to categorise these automatically.

Particularly interesting outcomes of our experiments include: (i) the high proportion of complex paraphrasing cases observed in the corpus ($\sim$40% of the operations), which is important since paraphrase generation is a difficult task to automate, particularly via machine learning algorithms; and (ii) the relatively high accuracy of our classifiers on the categorisation of certain phenomena, namely the identification of segment pairs which are not parallel in meaning, and the filtering of the corpus to select sentences that have undergone a single transformation operation. These classifiers can be used as filtering steps to improve the quality of text simplification corpora, which we believe can in turn lead to better performance of learning algorithms inducing rules from such corpora.

Acknowledgements

This research was supported by the CAPES PhD research grant n. 31983594814, process n. 5475/10-4.

References

Regina Barzilay and Noemie Elhadad. 2003. Sentence alignment for monolingual comparable corpora. In *Proceedings of the 2003 conference on Empirical methods in natural language processing*, pages 25–32. Association for Computational Linguistics.

Matthijs Den Besten and Jean-Michel Dalle. 2008. Keep it simple: A companion for simple wikipedia? *Industry and Innovation*, 15(2):169–178.

Helena M. Caseli, Tiago F. Pereira, Lucia Specia, Thiago A.S. Pardo, Caroline Gasperin, and Sandra M. Aluísio. 2009. Building a brazilian portuguese parallel corpus of original and simplified texts. *Advances in Computational Linguistics, Research in Computer Science*, 41:59–70.

Raman Chandrasekar and Bangalore Srinivas. 1997. Automatic induction of rules for text simplification. *Knowledge-Based Systems*, 10(3):183–190.

Raman Chandrasekar, Christine Doran, and Bangalore Srinivas. 1996. Motivations and methods for text simplification. In *Proceedings of the 16th conference on Computational linguistics-Volume 2*, pages 1041–1044. Association for Computational Linguistics.

William Coster and David Kauchak. 2011. Simple english wikipedia: a new text simplification task. In *Proceedings of the 49th Annual Meeting of the Association for Computational Linguistics. Stroudsburg, PA: Association for Computational Linguistics*, pages 665–669.

Rudolf Flesch. 1979. How to write plain english. *URL: http://www. mang. canterbury. ac. nz/courseinfo/AcademicWriting/Flesch. htm [accessed 2003 Oct 13][WebCite Cache]*.

Caroline Gasperin, Lucia Specia, Tiago Pereira, and Sandra Aluísio. 2009. Learning when to simplify sentences for natural text simplification. *Proceedings of ENIA*, pages 809–818.

Robert Gunning. 1969. The fog index after twenty years. *Journal of Business Communication*, 6(2):3–13.

Mark Hall, Eibe Frank, Geoffrey Holmes, Bernhard Pfahringer, Peter Reutemann, and Ian H Witten. 2009. The weka data mining software: an update. *ACM SIGKDD Explorations Newsletter*, 11(1):10–18.

George Roger Klare and Byron Buck. 1954. *Know your reader: The scientific approach to readability*. Hermitage House.

Bertha A Lively and Sidney L Pressey. 1923. A method for measuring the vocabulary burden of textbooks. *Educational administration and supervision*, 9(389-398):73.

Julie Medero and Mari Ostendorf. 2011. Identifying targets for syntactic simplification. In *Proceedings of the SLaTE 2011 workshop*.

Michael Paciello. 2000. *Web accessibility for people with disabilities*. Taylor & Francis US.

Sarah E Petersen and Mari Ostendorf. 2007. Text simplification for language learners: a corpus analysis. In *In Proc. of Workshop on Speech and Language Technology for Education*.

Advaith Siddharthan. 2002. An architecture for a text simplification system. In *Language Engineering Conference, 2002. Proceedings*, pages 64–71. IEEE.

Lucia Specia. 2010. Translating from complex to simplified sentences. In *Computational Processing of the Portuguese Language*, pages 30–39. Springer.

Sanja Štajner, Biljana Drndarevic, and Horacio Saggion. 2013. Corpus-based sentence deletion and split decisions for spanish text simplification.

Kristian Woodsend and Mirella Lapata. 2011. Learning to simplify sentences with quasi-synchronous grammar and integer programming. In *Proceedings of the Conference on Empirical Methods in Natural Language Processing*, pages 409–420. Association for Computational Linguistics.

Taha Yasseri, András Kornai, and János Kertész. 2012. A practical approach to language complexity: a wikipedia case study. *PloS one*, 7(11):e48386.

Mark Yatskar, Bo Pang, Cristian Danescu-Niculescu-Mizil, and Lillian Lee. 2010. For the sake of simplicity: Unsupervised extraction of lexical simplifications from wikipedia. In *Human Language Technologies: The 2010 Annual Conference of the North American Chapter of the Association for Computational Linguistics*, pages 365–368. Association for Computational Linguistics.

Zhemin Zhu, Delphine Bernhard, and Iryna Gurevych. 2010. A monolingual tree-based translation model for sentence simplification. In *Proceedings of the 23rd international conference on computational linguistics*, pages 1353–1361. Association for Computational Linguistics.

An evaluation of syntactic simplification rules for people with autism

Richard Evans, Constantin Orăsan and Iustin Dornescu
Research Institute in Information and Language Processing
University of Wolverhampton
United Kingdom
{R.J.Evans, C.Orasan, I.Dornescu2}@wlv.ac.uk

Abstract

Syntactically complex sentences constitute an obstacle for some people with Autistic Spectrum Disorders. This paper evaluates a set of simplification rules specifically designed for tackling complex and compound sentences. In total, 127 different rules were developed for the rewriting of complex sentences and 56 for the rewriting of compound sentences. The evaluation assessed the accuracy of these rules individually and revealed that fully automatic conversion of these sentences into a more accessible form is not very reliable.

1 Introduction

People with Autistic Spectrum Disorders (ASD) show a diverse range of reading abilities: on the one hand, 5%-10% of users have the capacity to read words from an early age without the need for formal learning (hyperlexia), on the other hand many users demonstrate weak comprehension of what has been read (Volkmar and Wiesner, 2009). They may have difficulty inferring contextual information or may have trouble understanding mental verbs or emotional language, as well as long sentences with complex syntactic structure (Tager-Flusberg, 1981; Kover et al., 2012). To address these difficulties, the FIRST project[1] is developing a tool which makes texts more accessible for people with ASD. In order to get a better understanding of the needs of these readers, a thorough analysis was carried out to derive a list of high priority obstacles to reading comprehension. Some of these obstacles are related to syntactic complexity and constitute the focus of this paper. Even though the research in the FIRST project focuses on people with ASD, many of the obstacles identified in the project can pose difficulties for a wide range of readers such as language learners and people with other language disorders.

This paper presents and evaluates a set of rules used for simplifying English complex and compound sentences. These rules were developed as part of a syntactic simplification system which was initially developed for users with ASD, but which can also be used for other tasks that require syntactic simplification of sentences. In our research, we consider that syntactic complexity is usually indicated by the occurrence of certain markers or signs of syntactic complexity, referred to hereafter as *signs*, such as punctuation ([,] and [;]), conjunctions ([and], [but], and [or]), complementisers ([that]) or wh-words ([what], [when], [where], [which], [while], [who]). These signs may have a range of syntactic linking and bounding functions which need to be automatically identified, and which we analysed in more detail in (Evans and Orasan, 2013).

Our syntactic simplification process operates in two steps. In the first, signs of syntactic complexity are automatically classified and in the second, manually crafted rules are applied to simplify the relevant sentences. Section 3 presents more details about the method. Evaluation of automatic simplification is a difficult issue. Given that the purpose of this paper is to gain a better understanding of the performance of the rules used for simplifying compound sentences and complex sentences, Section 4 presents the methodology developed for this evaluation and discusses the results obtained. The paper finishes with conclusions.

2 Background information

Despite some findings to the contrary (Arya et al., 2011), automatic syntactic simplification has been motivated by numerous neurolinguistic and psycholinguistic studies. Brain imaging studies indicate that processing syntactically complex struc-

[1] http://first-asd.eu

tures requires more neurological activity than processing simple structures (Just et al., 1996). A study undertaken by Levy et al. (2012) showed that people with aphasia are better able to understand syntactically simple reversible sentences than syntactically complex ones.

Further motivation is brought by research in NLP, which demonstrates that performance levels in information extraction (Agarwal and Boggess, 1992; Rindflesch et al., 2000; Evans, 2011), syntactic parsing (Tomita, 1985; McDonald and Nivre, 2011), and, to some extent, machine translation (Gerber and Hovy, 1998) are somewhat determined by the length and syntactic complexity of the sentences being processed.

Numerous rule-based methods for syntactic simplification have been developed (Siddharthan, 2006) and used to facilitate NLP tasks such as biomedical information extraction (Agarwal and Boggess, 1992; Rindflesch et al., 2000; Evans, 2011). In these approaches, rules are triggered by pattern-matching applied to the output of text analysis tool such as partial parsers and POS taggers. Chandrasekar and Srinivas (1997) presented an automatic method to learn syntactic simplification rules for use in such systems. Unfortunately, that approach is only capable of learning a restricted range of rules and requires access to expensive annotated resources.

With regard to applications improving text accessibility for human readers, Max (2000) described the use of syntactic simplification for aphasic readers. In work on the PSET project, Canning (2002) implemented a system which exploits a syntactic parser in order to rewrite compound sentences as sequences of simple sentences and to convert passive sentences into active ones for readers with aphasia. The success of these systems is tied to the performance levels of the syntactic parsers that they employ.

More recently, the availability of resources such as *Simple Wikipedia* has enabled text simplification to be included in the paradigm of statistical machine translation (Yatskar et al., 2010; Coster and Kauchak, 2011). In this context, translation models are learned by aligning sentences in *Wikipedia* with their corresponding versions in *Simple Wikipedia*. Manifesting *Basic English* (Ogden, 1932), the extent to which *Simple Wikipedia* is accessible to people with autism has not yet been fully assessed.

The field of text summarisation includes numerous approaches that can be regarded as examples of syntactic simplification. For example, Cohn and Lapata (2009) present a tree-to-tree transduction method that is used to filter non-essential information from syntactically parsed sentences. This compression process often reduces the syntactic complexity of those sentences. An advantage of this approach is that it can identify elements for deletion even when such elements are not indicated by explicit signs of syntactic complexity. The difficulty is that they rely on high levels of accuracy and granularity of automatic syntactic analysis. As noted earlier, it has been observed that the accuracy of parsers is inversely proportional to the length and complexity of the sentences being analysed (Tomita, 1985; McDonald and Nivre, 2011).

The approach to syntactic simplification described in the current paper is a two step process involving detection and tagging of the bounding and linking functions of various signs of syntactic complexity followed by a rule-based sentence rewriting step. Relevant to the first step, Van Delden and Gomez (2002) developed a machine learning method to determine the syntactic roles of commas. Meier et al. (2012) describe German language resources in which the linking functions of commas and semicolons are annotated. The annotated resources exploited by the machine learning method presented in Section 3.2.1 of the current paper are presented in (Evans and Orasan, 2013). From a linguistic perspective, Nunberg et al. (2002) provide a grammatical analysis of punctuation in English.

The work described in this paper was undertaken in a project aiming to improve the accessibility of text for people with autism. It was motivated at least in part by the work of O'Connor and Klein (2004), which describes strategies to facilitate the reading comprehension of people with ASD.

The proposed method is intended to reduce complexity caused by both complex and compound sentences and differs from those described earlier in this section. Sentence compression methods are not suitable for the types of rewriting required in simplifying compound sentences. Parsers are more likely to have lower accuracy when processing these sentences, and therefore the proposed method does not use information about the syntactic structure of sentences in the process. Our method is presented in the next section.

3 The syntactic simplifier

In our research, we regard coordination and subordination as key elements of syntactic complexity. A thorough study of the potential obstacles to the reading comprehension of people with autism highlighted particular types of syntactic complexity, many of which are linked to coordination and subordination. Section 3.1 briefly presents the main obstacles linked to syntactic complexity identified by the study. It should be mentioned that most of the obstacles are problematic not only for autistic people and other types of reader can also benefit from their removal. The obstacles identified constituted the basis for developing the simplification approach briefly described in Section 3.2.

3.1 User requirements

Consultations with 94 subjects meeting the strict DSM-IV criteria for ASD and with IQ > 70 led to the derivation of user preferences and high priority user requirements related to structural processing. A comprehensive explanation of the findings can be found in (Martos et al., 2013). This section discusses briefly the two types of information of relevance to the processing of sentence complexity obtained in our study.

First, in terms of the demand for access to texts of particular genres/domains, it was found that young people (aged 12-16) seek access to documents in informative (arts/leisure) domains and they have less interest in periodicals and newspapers or imaginative texts. Adults (aged 16+) seek access to informative and scientific texts (including newspapers), imaginative text, and the language of social networking and communication. In an attempt to accommodate the interests of both young people and adults, we developed a corpus which contains newspaper articles, texts about health, and literary texts.

Second, the specific morpho-syntactic phenomena that pose obstacles to reading comprehension that are relevant to this paper are:

1. Compound sentences, which should be split into sentences containing a single clause.
2. Complex sentences: in which relative clauses should either be:
   (a) converted into adjectival pre-modifiers or
   (b) deleted from complex sentences and used to generate copular constructions linking the NP in the matrix clause with the predication of the relative clause

In addition, the analysis revealed other types of obstacles such as explicative clauses, which should be deleted, and uncommon conjunctions (including conjuncts) which should be replaced by more common ones. Conditional clauses that follow the main clause and non-initial adverbial clauses should be pre-posed, and passive sentences should be converted in the active form. Various formatting issues such as page breaks that occur within paragraphs and end-of-line hyphenation are also problematic and should be avoided.

Section 3.2 describes the method developed to address the obstacles caused by compound and complex sentences.

3.2 The approach

Processing of obstacles to reading comprehension in this research has focused on detection and reduction of syntactic complexity caused by the occurrence in text of compound sentences (1) and complex sentences (2).

(1) Elaine Trego never bonded with 16-month-old Jacob [and] he was often seen with bruises, a murder trial was told.

(2) The two other patients, who are far more fragile than me, would have been killed by the move.

In (1), the underlined phrases are the conjoins of a coordinate constituent. In (2), the underlined phrase is a subordinate constituent of the larger, superordinate phrase *the two other patients, who are far more fragile than me*.

The overall syntactic simplification pipeline consists of the following steps:

Step 1. Tagging of signs of syntactic complexity with information about their syntactic linking or bounding functions

Step 2. The complexity of sentences tagged in step 1 is assessed and used to trigger the application of two iterative simplification processes, which are applied exhaustively and sequentially to each input sentence:

a. Decomposition of compound sentences (the simplification function converts one input string into two output strings)

b. Decomposition of complex sentences (the simplification function converts one input string into two output strings)

Step 3. Personalised transformation of sentences according to user preference profiles which list obstacles to be tackled and the threshold complexity levels that specify whether simplification is necessary.

Steps 1 and 2 are applied iteratively ensuring that an input sentence can be exhaustively simplified by decomposition of the input string into pairs of progressively simpler sentences. No further simplification is applied to a sentence when the system is unable to detect any signs of syntactic complexity within it. This paper reports on steps 1 and 2. The personalisation step, which takes into consideration the needs of individual users, is not discussed.

3.2.1 Identification of signs of complexity

Signs of syntactic complexity typically indicate constituent boundaries, e.g. punctuation marks, conjunctions, and complementisers. To facilitate information extraction, a rule-based approach to simplify coordinated conjoins was proposed by Evans (2011), which relies on classifying signs based on their linking functions.

In more recent work, an extended annotation scheme was proposed in (Evans and Orasan, 2013) which enables the encoding of links and boundaries between a wider range of syntactic constituents and covers more syntactic phenomena. A corpus covering three text categories (news articles, literature, and patient healthcare information leaflets), was annotated using this extended scheme.[2]

Most sign labels contain three types of information: boundary type, syntactic projection level, and grammatical category of the constituent(s). Some labels cover signs which bound interjections, tag questions, and reported speech and a class denoting false signs of syntactic complexity, such as use of the word *that* as a specifier or anaphor. The class labels are a combination of the following acronyms:

1. $\{C|SS|ES\}$, the generic function as a coordinator (C), the left boundary of a subordinate constituent (SS), or the right boundary of a subordinate constituent (ES).

2. $\{P|L|I|M|E\}$, the syntactic projection level of the constituent(s): prefix (P), lexical (L), intermediate (I), maximal (M), or extended/-clausal (E).

3. $\{A|Adv|N|P|Q|V\}$, the grammatical category of the constituent(s): adjectival (A), adverbial (Adv), nominal (N), prepositional (P), quantificational (Q), and verbal (V).

4. $\{1|2\}$, used to further differentiate subclasses on the basis of some other label-specific criterion.

The scheme uses a total of 42 labels to distinguish between different syntactic functions of the bounded constituents. Although signs are marked by a small set of tokens (words and punctuation), the high number of labels and their skewed distribution make signs highly ambiguous. In addition, each sign is only assigned exactly one label, i.e. that of the dominant constituent in the case of nesting, further increasing ambiguity. These characteristics make automatic classification of signs challenging.

The automatic classification of signs of syntactic complexity is achieved using a machine learning approach described in more detail in Dornescu et al. (2013). After experimenting with several methods of representing the training data and with several classifiers, the best results were obtained by using the BIO model to train a CRF tagger. The features used were the signs' surrounding context (a window of 10 tokens and their POS tags) together with information about the distance to other signs signs in the same sentence and their types. The method achieved an overall accuracy of 82.50% (using 10 fold cross-validation) on the manually annotated corpus.

3.2.2 Rule-based approach to simplification of compound sentences and complex sentences

The simplification method exploits two iterative processes that are applied in sequence to input text that has been tokenised with respect to sentences, words, punctuation, and signs of syntactic complexity. The word tokens in the input text

[2] http://clg.wlv.ac.uk/resources/SignsOfSyntacticComplexity/

Rule ID	CEV-12
Sentence type	Compound (coordination)
Match pattern	A *that* [B] $sign_{CEV}$ [C] .
Transform pattern	A *that* [B]. A *that* [C].
Ex: input	[Investigations showed]$_A$ **that** [the glass came from a car's side window]$_B$ **and**$_{CEV}$ [thousands of batches had been tampered with on five separate weekends]$_C$.
Ex: output	[Investigations showed]$_A$ **that** [the glass came from a car's side window]$_B$. [Investigations showed]$_A$ **that** [thousands of batches had been tampered with on five separate weekends]$_C$.
Rule ID	CEV-26
Sentence type	Compound (coordination)
Match pattern	A v_{CC} B: "[C] $sign_{CEV}$ [D]".
Transform pattern	A v B: "[C]". A v B: "[D]".
Ex: input	[He]$_A$ **added**[]$_B$: "[If I were with Devon and Cornwall police I'd be very interested in the result of this case]$_C$ **and**$_{CEV}$ [I certainly expect them to renew their interest]$_D$."
Ex: output	[He]$_A$ **added**[]$_B$: "[If I were with Devon and Cornwall police I'd be very interested in the result of this case]$_C$." [He]$_A$ **added**[]$_B$: "[I certainly expect them to renew their interest]$_D$."

Table 1: Patterns used to identify conjoined clauses.

have also been labelled with their parts of speech and the signs have been labelled with their grammatical linking and bounding functions. The patterns rely mainly on nine sign labels which delimit clauses (*EV)[3], noun phrases (*MN) and adjectival phrases (*MA). These sign labels can signal either coordinated conjoins (C*) or the start (SS*) or end (ES*) of a constituent.

The first iterative process exploits patterns intended to identify the conjoins of compound sentences. The elements common to these patterns are signs tagged as linking clauses in coordination (label CEV). The second process exploits patterns intended to identify relative clauses in complex sentences. The elements common to these patterns are signs tagged as being left boundaries of subordinate clauses (label SSEV).

The identification of conjoint clauses depends on accurate tagging of words with information about their parts of speech and signs with information about their general roles in indicating the left or right boundaries of subordinate constituents. The identification of subordinate clauses requires more detailed information. In addition to the information required to identify clause conjoins, information about the specific functions of signs is required. The simplification process is thus highly dependent on the performance of the automatic sign tagger.

Table 1 displays two patterns for identifying conjoined clauses and Table 2 displays two patterns for identifying subordinate clauses. In the tables, upper case letters denote contiguous sequences of text,[4] the underbar _ denotes signs of class CEV (in row *Compound*) and SSEV (in row *Complex*). Verbs with clause complements are denoted by v_{CC}, while words of part of speech X are denoted by w_X. The symbol s is used to denote additional signs of syntactic complexity while v denotes words with verbal POS tags. Words explicitly appearing in the input text are italicised. Elements of the patterns representing clause conjoins and subordinate clauses appear in square brackets.

Each pattern is associated with a sentence rewriting rule. A rule is applied on each iteration of the algorithm. Sentences containing signs which correspond to conjoint clauses are converted into two strings which are identical to the original save that, in one, the conjoint clause is replaced by a single conjoin identified in the conjoint while in the other, the identified conjoin is omitted. Sentences containing signs which indicate subordinate clauses are converted into two new strings. One is identical to the original save that the relative clause is deleted. The second is automatically generated, and consists of the NP in the matrix clause modified by the relative clause, a conjugated copula, and the predication of the relative clause. Tables 1 and 2 give examples of transformation rules for the given patterns. In total, 127 different rules were developed for the rewriting of complex sentences and 56 for the rewriting of compound sentences.

[3]In these example the * character is used to indicate any sequence of characters, representing the bounding or linking function of the sign.

[4]Note that these sequences of text may contain additional signs tagged CEV or SSEV.

Rule ID	SSEV-61
Sentence type	Complex (subordination)
Match pattern	A *s* B [$sign_{SSEV}$ C *v* D].
Transform pattern	A *s* B. *That* C *v* D.
Ex: input	[During the two-week trial, the jury heard how Thomas became a frequent visitor to Roberts's shop in the summer of 1997]$_A$, [after meeting him through a **friend**]$_B$ [**who** [lived near the shop,]$_C$ [described as a "child magnet" by one officer]$_D$.
Ex: output	[During the two-week trial, the jury heard how Thomas became a frequent visitor to Roberts's shop in the summer of 1997]$_A$, [after meeting him through a friend]$_B$. That **friend** [lived near the shop,]$_C$ [described as a "child magnet" by one officer]$_D$.
Rule ID	SSEV-72
Sentence type	Complex (subordination)
Match pattern	[A w_{IN} w_{DT}* n $\{n\|of\}$* $sign_{SSEV}$] w_{VBD} B {.|?|!}
Transform pattern	N/A
	Pattern SSEV-72 is used to prevent rewriting of complex sentences when the subordinate clause is the argument of a clause complement verb. The result of this rule is to strip the tag from the triggering sign of syntactic complexity
Ex: input	[Eamon Reidy, 32,]$_A$ fled [across fields in Windsor Great Park after the crash[**,** the court heard.]

Table 2: Patterns used to identify subordinate clauses.

4 Evaluation

The detection and classification of signs of syntactic complexity can be evaluated via standard methods in LT based on comparing classifications made by the system with classifications made by linguistic experts. This evaluation is reported in (Dornescu et al., 2013). Unfortunately, the evaluation of the actual simplification process is difficult, as there are no well established methods for measuring its accuracy. Potential methodologies for evaluation include comparison of system output with human simplification of a given text, analysis of the post-editing effort required to convert an automatically simplified text into a suitable form for end users, comparisons using experimental methods such as eye tracking and extrinsic evaluation via NLP applications such as information extraction, all of which have weaknesses in terms of adequacy and expense.

Due to the challenges posed by these previously established methods, we decided that before we employ them and evaluate the output of the system as a whole, we focus first on the evaluation of the accuracy of the two rule sets employed by the syntactic processor. The evaluation method is based on comparing sets of simplified sentences derived from an original sentence by linguistic experts with sets derived by the method described in Section 3.

4.1 The gold standard

Two gold standards were developed to support evaluation of the two rule sets. Texts from the genres of health, literature, and news were processed by different versions of the syntactic simplifier. In one case, the only rules activated in the syntactic simplifier were those concerned with rewriting compound sentences. In the second case, the only rules activated were those concerned with rewriting complex sentences. The output of the two versions was corrected by a linguistic expert to ensure that each generated sentence was grammatically well-formed and consistent in meaning with the original sentence. Sentences for which even manual rewriting led to the generation of grammatically well-formed sentences that were not consistent in meaning with the originals were removed from the test data. After filtering, the test data contained nearly 1,500 sentences for use in evaluating rules to simplify of compound sentences, and nearly 1,100 sentences in the set used in evaluating rules to simplify complex sentences. The break down per genre/domain is given in Tables 3a and 3b.

The subset of sentences included in the gold standard contained manually annotated information about the signs of syntactic complexity. This was done to enable reporting of the evaluation results in two modes: one in which the system consults an oracle for classification of signs of syntactic complexity and one in which the system consults the output of the automatic sign tagger.

4.2 Evaluation results

Evaluation results are reported in terms of accuracy of the simplification process and the change in readability of the generated sentences. Computation of accuracy is based on the mean Leven-

		Text category		
		News	Health	Literature
#Compound sentences		698	325	418
Accuracy	Oracle	0.758	0.612	0.246
	Classifier	0.314	0.443	0.115
ΔFlesch	Oracle	11.1	8.2	15.3
	Classifier	9.9	10.2	13.6
ΔAvg.	Oracle	-12.58	-9.86	-16.69
Sent. Len.	Classifier	-13.08	-12.30	-16.79

(a) Evaluation of simplification of compound sentences

		Text category		
		News	Health	Literature
#Complex sentences		369	335	379
Accuracy	Oracle	0.452	0.292	0.475
	Classifier	0.433	0.227	0.259
ΔFlesch	Oracle	2.5	0.8	2.3
	Classifier	2.3	0.9	2.3
ΔAvg.	Oracle	-2.96	-0.90	-2.80
Sent. Len.	Classifier	-2.80	-0.99	-2.11

(b) Evaluation of simplification of complex sentences

Table 3: Evaluation results for the two syntactic phenomena on three text genres

shtein similarity[5] between the sentences generated by the system and the most similar simplified sentences verified by the linguistic expert. Once the most similar sentence in the key has been found, that element is no longer considered for the rest of the simplified sentences in the system's response to the original. In this evaluation, sentences are considered to be converted correctly if their LS > 0.95. The reason for setting such a high threshold for the Levenshtein ratio is because the evaluation method should only reward system responses that match the gold standard almost perfectly save for a few characters which could be caused by typos or variations in the use of punctuation and spaces. A sentence is considered successfully simplified, and implicitly all the rules used in the process are considered correctly applied, when all the sentences produced by the system are converted correctly according to the gold standard. This evaluation approach may be considered too inflexible as it does not take into consideration the fact that a sentence can be simplified in several ways. However, the purpose here is to evaluate the way in which sentences are simplified using specific rules.

In order to calculate the readability of the generated sentences we initially used the Flesch score (Flesch, 1949). However, our system changes the text only by rewriting sentences into sequences of simpler sentences and does not make any changes at the lexical level. For this reason, any changes observed in the Flesch score are due to changes in the average sentence length. Therefore, for our experiments we report both ΔFlesch score and Δaverage sentence length.

The evaluation results are reported separately for the three domains. In addition, the results are calculated when the classes of the signs are derived from the manually annotated data (*Oracle*) and from use of the automatic classifier (*Classifier*).

Table 3a presents the accuracy of the rules implemented to convert compound sentences into a more accessible form. The row *#Compound sentences* displays the number of sentences in the test data that contain signs of conjoint clauses (signs of class CEV). The results obtained are not unexpected. In all cases the accuracy of the simplification rules is higher when the labels of signs are assigned by the oracle. With the exception of the health domain, the same pattern is observed when ΔFlesch is considered. The highest accuracy is obtained on the news texts, then the health domain, and finally the literature domain. However, despite significantly lower accuracy on the literature domain, the readability of the sentences from the literature domain benefits most from the automatic simplification. This can be noticed both in the improved Flesch scores and reduced sentence length.

Table 3b presents the accuracy of the rules which simplify complex sentences. In this table, *#Complex sentences* denotes the number of sentences in the test data that contain relative clauses. The rest of the measures are calculated in the same way as in Table 3a. Inspection of the table shows that, for the news and health domains, the accuracy of these simplification rules is significantly lower than the simplification rules used for compound sentences. Surprisingly, the rules work better for the literature domain than for the others. The improvement in the readability of texts from the health domain is negligible, which can be explained by the poor performance of the simplification rules on this domain.

[5]Defined as 1 minus the ratio of Levenshtein distance between the two sentences to the length in characters of the longest of the two sentences being compared.

4.3 Error analysis

In order to have a better understanding of the performance of the system, the performance of the individual rules was also recorded. Tables 4 and 5 contain the most error prone trigger patterns for conjoined and subordinate clauses respectively. The statistics were derived from rules applied to texts of all three categories of texts and the signs of syntactic complexity were classified using an oracle, in order to isolate the influence of the rules in the system output. In this context, the accuracy with which the syntactic processor converts sentences containing conjoint clauses into a more accessible form is 0.577. The accuracy of this task with regard to subordinate clauses is 0.411.

The most error-prone trigger patterns for conjoined clauses are listed in Table 4, together with information on the conjoin that they are intended to detect (left or right), their error rate, and the number of number of errors made. The same information is presented for the rules converting sentences containing subordinate clauses in Table 5, but in this case the patterns capture the subordination relations. In the patterns, words with particular parts of speech are denoted by the symbol w with the relevant Penn Treebank tag appended as a subscript. Verbs with clause complements are denoted v_{CC}. Signs of syntactic complexity are denoted by the symbol s with the abbreviation of the functional class appended as a subscript. Specific words are printed in italics. In the patterns, the clause coordinator is denoted '_' and upper case letters are used to denote stretches of contiguous text.

Rules CEV-25a and SSEV-78a are applied when the input sentence triggers none of the other implemented patterns. Errors of this type quantify the number of sentences containing conjoint or subordinate clauses that cannot be converted into a more accessible form by rules included in the structural complexity processor. Both rules have quite high error rates, but these errors can only be addressed via the addition of new rules or the adjustment of already implemented rules.

SSEV-36a is a pattern used to prevent processing of sentences that contain verbs with clause complements. This pattern was introduced because using the sentence rewriting algorithm proposed here to process sentences containing these subordinate clauses would generate ungrammatical output.

Table 5 contains only 4 items because for the rest of the patterns the number of errors was less than 3. A large number of these rules had an error rate of 1 which motivated their deactivation. Unfortunately this did not lead to improved accuracy of the overall conversion process.

5 Conclusions and future work

Error analysis revealed that fully automatic conversion compound and complex sentences into a more accessible form is quite unreliable, particularly for texts of the literature category. It was noted that conversion of complex sentences into a more accessible form is more difficult than conversion of compound sentences. However, subordinate clauses are significantly more prevalent than conjoint clauses in the training and testing data collected so far.

The evaluation of the rule sets used in the conversion of compound and complex sentences into a more accessible form motivates further specific development of the rule sets. This process includes deletion of rules that do not meet particular thresholds for accuracy and the development of new rules to address cases where input sentences fail to trigger any conversion rules (signalled by activation of redundant rules CEV-25a and SSEV-78a).

The results are disappointing given that the syntactic simplification module presented in this paper is expected to be integrated in a system that makes texts more accessible for people with autism. However, this simplification module will be included in a post-editing environment for people with ASD. In this setting, it may still prove useful, despite its low accuracy.

Acknowledgments

The research described in this paper was partially funded by the European Commission under the Seventh (FP7-2007-2013) Framework Programme for Research and Technological Development (FP7- ICT-2011.5.5 FIRST 287607). We gratefully acknowledge the contributions of all the members of the FIRST consortium for their feedback and comments during the development of the methods, and to Laura Hasler for her help with the evaluation.

ID	Conjoin	Trigger pattern	Error rate	#Errors
CEV-24b	B	A _ B	0.131	59
CEV-24a	A	A _ B	0.119	54
CEV-12b	A that C	A *that* B _ C	0.595	25
CEV-25a	NA	NA	0.956	22
CEV-26a	A v_{CCV} B : "C"	A v_{CC} B : "C _ D"	0.213	16
CEV-26b	A v_{CCV} B : "D"	A v_{CC} B : "C _ D"	0.203	14

Table 4: Error rates for rules converting sentences with conjoint clauses

ID	Matrix clause / subordinate clause	Trigger pattern	Error rate	#Errors
SSEV-78a	NA	NA	0.517	45
SSEV-72a	A , _ C $w_{\{verb\}}$ D	A s B _ C $w_{\{verb\}}$ D	0.333	4
SSEV-36a	NA	A told $w_{\{noun\vert PRP\vert DT\vert IN\}}$ * _ B	0.117	4
SSEV-13b	w_{VBN} w_{IN} ($w_{\{DT\vert PRP\$\vert noun\vert CD\}}$ |-|,)* $w_{\{noun\}}$ B	A w_{VBN} w_{IN} {$w_{\{DT\vert PRP\$\vert noun\vert CD\}}$ |-|,}* $w_{\{noun\}}$ _ B	1	3

Table 5: Error rates for rules converting sentences with subordinate clauses

References

Rajeev Agarwal and Lois Boggess. 1992. A simple but useful approach to conjunct identification. In *Proceedings of the 30th annual meeting for Computational Linguistics*, pages 15–21, Newark, Delaware. Association for Computational Linguistics.

D. J. Arya, Elfrieda H. Hiebert, and P. D. Pearson. 2011. The effects of syntactic and lexical complexity on the comprehension of elementary science texts. *International Electronic Journal of Elementary Education*, 4 (1):107–125.

Y. Canning. 2002. *Syntactic Simplification of Text.* Ph.d. thesis, University of Sunderland.

R Chandrasekar and B Srinivas. 1997. Automatic induction of rules for text simplification. *Knowledge-Based Systems*, 10:183–190.

T. Cohn and M. Lapata. 2009. Sentence Compression as Tree Transduction. *Journal of Artificial Intelligence Research*, 20(34):637–74.

W. Coster and D. Kauchak. 2011. Simple english wikipedia: A new text simplification task. In *Proceedings of the 49th Annual Meeting of the Association for Computational Linguistics (ACL-2011)*, pages 665–669, Portland, Oregon, June. Association of Computational Linguistics.

Iustin Dornescu, Richard Evans, and Constantin Orăsan. 2013. A Tagging Approach to Identify Complex Constituents for Text Simplification. In *Proceedings of Recent Advances in Natural Language Processing*, pages 221 – 229, Hissar, Bulgaria.

Richard Evans and Constantin Orasan. 2013. Annotating signs of syntactic complexity to support sentence simplification. In I. Habernal and V. Matousek, editors, *Text, Speech and Dialogue. Proceedings of the 16th International Conference TSD 2013*, pages 92–104. Springer, Plzen, Czech Republic.

R. Evans. 2011. Comparing methods for the syntactic simplification of sentences in information extraction. *Literary and Linguistic Computing*, 26 (4):371–388.

R. Flesch. 1949. *The art of readable writing*. Harper, New York.

Laurie Gerber and Eduard H. Hovy. 1998. Improving translation quality by manipulating sentence length. In David Farwell, Laurie Gerber, and Eduard H. Hovy, editors, *AMTA*, volume 1529 of *Lecture Notes in Computer Science*, pages 448–460. Springer.

M. A. Just, P. A. Carpenter, and K. R. Thulborn. 1996. Brain activation modulated by sentence comprehension. *Science*, 274:114–116.

S. T. Kover, E. Haebig, A. Oakes, A. McDuffie, R. J. Hagerman, and L. Abbeduto. 2012. Syntactic comprehension in boys with autism spectrum disorders: Evidence from specific constructions. In *Proceedings of the 2012 International Meeting for Autism Research*, Athens, Greece. International Society for Autism Research.

J. Levy, E. Hoover, G. Waters, S. Kiran, D. Caplan, A. Berardino, and C. Sandberg. 2012. Effects of syntactic complexity, semantic reversibility, and explicitness on discourse comprehension in persons with aphasia and in healthy controls. *American Journal of Speech–Language Pathology*, 21(2):154 – 165.

Wolfgang Maier, Sandra Kübler, Erhard Hinrichs, and Julia Kriwanek. 2012. Annotating coordination in the penn treebank. In *Proceedings of the Sixth Linguistic Annotation Workshop*, pages 166–174, Jeju, Republic of Korea, July. Association for Computational Linguistics.

Juan Martos, Sandra Freire, Ana Gonzlez, David Gil, Richard Evans, Vesna Jordanova, Arlinda Cerga, Antoneta Shishkova, and Constantin Orasan. 2013. User preferences: Updated report. Technical report,

The FIRST Consortium, Available at http://first-asd.eu/D2.2.

A. Max. 2000. *Syntactic simplification - an application to text for aphasic readers.* Mphil in computer speech and language processing, University of Cambridge, Wolfson College.

Ryan T. McDonald and Joakim Nivre. 2011. Analyzing and integrating dependency parsers. *Computational Linguistics*, 37(1):197–230.

Geoffrey Nunberg, Ted Briscoe, and Rodney Huddleston. 2002. Punctuation. chapter 20 In Huddleston, Rodney and Geoffrey K. Pullum (eds) *The Cambridge Grammar of the English Language*, pages 1724–1764. Cambridge University Press.

I. M. O'Connor and P. D. Klein. 2004. Exploration of strategies for facilitating the reading comprehension of high-functioning students with autism spectrum disorders. *Journal of Autism and Developmental Disorders*, 34:2:115–127.

C. K. Ogden. 1932. *Basic English: a general introduction with rules and grammar.* K. Paul, Trench, Trubner & Co., Ltd., London.

Thomas C. Rindflesch, Jayant V. Rajan, and Lawrence Hunter. 2000. Extracting molecular binding relationships from biomedical text. In *Proceedings of the sixth conference on Applied natural language processing*, pages 188–195, Seattle, Washington. Association of Computational Linguistics.

A. Siddharthan. 2006. Syntactic simplification and text cohesion. *Research on Language and Computation*, 4:1:77–109.

Helen Tager-Flusberg. 1981. Sentence comprehension in autistic children. *Applied Psycholinguistics*, 2:1:5–24.

Masaru Tomita. 1985. *Efficient Parsing for Natural Language: A Fast Algorithm for Practical Systems.* Kluwer Academic Publishers, Norwell, MA, USA.

Sebastian van Delden and Fernando Gomez. 2002. Combining finite state automata and a greedy learning algorithm to determine the syntactic roles of commas. In *Proceedings of the 14th IEEE International Conference on Tools with Artificial Intelligence*, ICTAI '02, pages 293–, Washington, DC, USA. IEEE Computer Society.

F.R. Volkmar and L. Wiesner. 2009. *A Practical Guide to Autism.* Wiley, Hoboken, NJ.

M. Yatskar, B. Pang, C. Danescu-Niculescu-Mizil, and L. Lee. 2010. For the sake of simplicity: Unsupervised extraction of lexical simplifications from wikipedia. In *Proceedings of Human Language Technologies: The 2010 Annual Conference of the North American Chapter of the ACL*, pages 365–368, Los Angeles, California, June. Association of Computational Linguistics.

Author Index